"Oftentimes Christians feel at a decided disadvantage in academic cultures that elevate pluralism and tolerance but have precious little tolerance for Christian faith. Bayard Taylor's spirited treatment of worldviews levels the playing field so Christians can confidently engage this marketplace of ideas. I urge every college student to absorb Bayard's timely counsel asap."

—Don Richardson, missionary, author of *Peace Child*

"When I read Bayard Taylor's book, words like *relevant, scholarly, well-researched, timely,* and *practical* come to mind. But one word exceeds all the others for me ... the word *needed.* Every Christian teenager needs this book. Every youth worker needs to study *Blah, Blah, Blah* if they are truly interested in their youth group participants becoming lifelong disciples of Jesus."

—Roger Cross, President Emeritus, Youth for Christ USA

"Taylor offers a readable, humorous, and entertaining interpretation of the current global debate over religion. It shows why Christian belief is rational conviction rather than blind faith. Parents with high school or twenty-something children should buy it, read it, give it to their children, borrow it back, read it again, and discuss it."

—Michael J. McClymond, Clarence Louis and
Helen Irene Steber Professor, Saint Louis University

"The plan is simple: Hand out copies of the book to my high school and college-age children, their friends, and their parents. When we gather to discuss the chapters, stand back and watch the fireworks! What a great way to teach this vital subject to our children."

—A. Randy Bozarth, Association of Christian Home
Educators of Ventura County (ACHEV)

"There is a huge need for what you're presenting here! ... I love the underlying position of the book—to make readers more confident, effective public representations of their faith. ... Content throughout is exemplary. Just solid down to the core."

—Marcus Brotherton, author, *The Reflector* journalist,
and former youth pastor.

BAYARD TAYLOR holds an M.Div. with an emphasis in cross-cultural studies from Trinity Evangelical Divinity School. He spent four years working with Campus Crusade for Christ and currently serves as Biblical and Theological editor at a major Christian publishing house. Bayard has also edited such bestselling books as *So What's the Difference?* by Fritz Ridenour and *Fasting for Spiritual Breakthrough* by Elmer Towns. Bayard and his family live in Southern California.

Learn more about the author and *Blah, Blah, Blah* at *www.blahblahbook.com*.

BAYARD TAYLOR

FOREWORD BY
CHARLIE LOWELL
OF JARS OF CLAY

BETHANY HOUSE
MINNEAPOLIS, MINNESOTA

Published by Bethany House Publishers
11400 Hampshire Avenue South
Bloomington, Minnesota 55438

Bethany House Publishers is a division of
Baker Publishing Group, Grand Rapids, Michigan.

Printed in the United States of America

ISBN-13:   978-0-7642-0187-5
ISBN-10:   0-7642-0187-5

Library of Congress Cataloging-in-Publication Data

Taylor, Bayard.
      Blah, blah, blah : making sense of the world's spiritual chatter / Bayard Taylor.
            p.   cm.
      Summary: "This book compares and contrasts Christianity with other worldviews to better equip young people for the questions they will face in college and beyond"—Provided by publisher.
            ISBN 0-7642-0187-5 (pbk.)
      1. Apologetics. 2. Christianity and other religions. 3. Christianity—Philosophy. I. Title.
      BT1103.T38   2006
      261.2—dc22

                                                                                    2005032603

ACKNOWLEDGMENTS

To write (and finish) a book you have to be at least a little bit obsessed. This has certainly been true of me, as my family knows well. A few months ago as we were sitting around the table at an evening meal, I asked for ideas on what to name this book. My sixteen-year-old son, Jeremiah, no doubt having heard quite enough about worldviews, said, "Why don't you just call it *Blah, Blah, Blah?*" And so it was.

I'd also like to thank the brave NFK group of high school students from Community Presbyterian Church (Jordan Frye, Amiee Vaughan, Kyle Shimubuku, Caitlin Adair, Eric Holmstrom, Kyle Duff, Lindsey Chandler, Theresa Waldron, Teressa Coenen, Jeremy Dugan, Anna Taylor, Mark Tapia, and my daughter, Karis)—who willingly became guinea pigs, and their fearless youth leader, Brian Hays—who let me conduct my worldview experiments on them.

I'd like to thank my readers (Marcus Brotherton, Sheri Blackmon, Tom Stephen, Tom Gengler, Charlie Lowell, Don Richardson, Jim Tonkowich, Hans Christofferson, Josh Unseth, Richard Kew, Mike McClymond, Joy Downing-Riley, Jennifer Cullis, Ryan Axtell, and my wife, June), who slogged through my rough draft.

I'd like to thank Charlie Lowell and the band Jars of Clay, who disproved my seventeen-year-old daughter's theory that I was unworthy to contact them.

I'd like to thank Kyle Duncan and the beautiful people at Bethany House (Christopher Soderstrom, Jeff Braun, Natasha Sperling, Dan Olson, Linda White, Brett Benson, Amanda Hall, and Tim Peterson) for giving this book a shot to reach more people than I could have on my own.

I'd like to thank Brent Nims, Webmeister extraordinaire, whose work on *www.blahblahbook.com* advanced me from "approaching somewhat legitimate" to "virtual legitimacy."

I'd like to thank my long-suffering wife, June, who just might not have to listen to quite so much worldview chatter now that this book has finally been written.

And I'd like to thank you, my reader, for taking your valuable time to read this book. If you're a Christian, this will be a window into your own faith as well as others' ways of thinking. If you're a non-Christian, or someone who's not so sure about your faith, you'll quickly see that this is a book written by someone who's just trying to follow Jesus, for others who want to do the same. Wherever you are in your faith experience, welcome to the Great Conversation.

Bayard Taylor
Ventura, California

FOREWORD

If you're anything like me, life feels a little awkward. It's strange to live in this world, knowing that this is not our true home, that we were created for something more. Yet we live among suffering and frustration, from corruption and disease to our own more personal struggles. I have been told all my life that my true identity is not to be found here on earth, but I still care deeply about this world and its people. Does any of this resonate with you? Then let's just say it—life is messy and confusing, and it's pretty tough to navigate our way through the mess. And where is God to be found in the midst of all this?

For the twelve years I've been in the band Jars of Clay, this word *worldview* has chased us around and haunted us as we travel this intriguing world and meet all sorts of people—each with their own set of beliefs. I like the idea of a window through which we see things—it gives us a context and a purpose, and it helps us make a little more sense of the chaos. Our worldview helps us understand who God is and who we are because of God. And understanding other worldviews can give us a better idea of how to work, live, and exist in a culture with people that don't always agree with us!

I grew up going to church and reading my Bible, but I see now that I had a tendency to live two lives—the "Good-Christian-Boy-Charlie" at home and church, and the "Insecure-Awkward-Not-Sure-How-This-All-Fits-Together-Charlie" at school and in social settings. The more I live and learn and make mistakes, I see how my Christian worldview helps cut through the lies about both versions of me, and the gospel of Jesus begins to inform and define who I am. There is a connection between what I believe and how I respond to God's love for me.

The more I spend time with my faith and God, the more I understand that my heart *is* designed to be engaged with this world—to not just cut off my longings and live in a Christian bubble. Jesus' life was one of stepping into messy relationships and bringing love and light into the pain. He gives us our true identity and becomes our sustaining reason to interact with others, to get our hands a little dirty.

I'm so thankful for this handbook that Bayard has given to us. It gives us a place to start thinking more about that window through which we filter our life. In reading this book, some of the concepts may be very new to you and may challenge what you were taught growing up in a church. Or you may find yourself surprised at how much you resonate with some of the words and ideas and have already developed some sense of your worldview. My desire for you is that this book will help make more sense of who you are, who God is, and what your purpose and identity are. You will also learn a lot about what the people around you believe.

Let me offer you one verse that has helped me make sense of my beliefs and continues to be a great encouragement to me. I might call it a "companion verse" because it has become a sort of compass that reminds me what is always true. It resonates deeply in my heart, I suspect, because it comes from deep in God's heart, and I am created to care about the things that He cares about.

"He has told you, O man, what is good; and what does the Lord require of you but to do justice, to love kindness, and to walk humbly with your God?" (Micah 6:8 NASB).

Justice, mercy, and humility. These are tools with which we can, and should, interact with this world we live in. Seeking justice, extending mercy, walking in humility. These are action words. We don't just sit back and admire the Christian life—we are invited to respond to it! My prayer for you is that this book would help you make a deeper connection between what you say you believe and how you live your life from day to day. Enjoy the journey, my friend.

Charlie Lowell
of Jars of Clay
Franklin, Tennessee

TABLE OF CONTENTS

A FEW CLUES ON HOW TO USE THIS BOOK

Imagine a condor, motionless wings outstretched on updrafts of warm air, circling his object of interest from afar. He's not in a big hurry. Before descending, he wants to get some perspective.

Now imagine a hummingbird hovering in midair, wings beating so fast you can't even see them, beak nosed deep into a flower. He quickly withdraws and instantly darts to his next meal.

Most books on worldviews are like the hummingbird. They plunge your nose deep into this or that complex idea, and then before you have a chance to catch your breath, they've shoved your nose deep into another subject—all at a pace so fast it makes your head spin.

This book's plan is more like the condor. In chapters 1 through 5 we'll circle from a distance, scanning the whole scene. In chapters 6 through 9 we'll make a second pass, coming somewhat closer, but looking at things from a slightly different angle. In chapters 10 through 14 we'll come close enough to see in detail how the basic worldviews work. Then in chapters 15 through 21 we'll settle in and apply our new worldview insights to Christian faith and what it means to be a human being who doesn't have all the answers.

In short, the book will start really simple and gradually get more complex. Toward the end, we'll be taking on some pretty tricky things. Hopefully we'll have a lot of fun as we go.

This book has a unique feature: It has both footnotes and endnotes. The footnotes will reveal things that I thought might be helpful to a person new to the world of worldviews, plus my reasons for choosing certain words over others, and also debates I have had with myself over how to present this stuff to you. The endnotes will give you access to my sources of information.

This book is supported by the *Blah, Blah, Blah* Web site (*www.blahblahbook.com*), where you'll find a blog, thought questions for the book chapters (for private study or group discussion), and additional material. So be sure to check it out. I put almost as much work into the Web site as I did the book.

Here's to your magnificent Blah experience.

1 | SPIRITUAL MEAT GRINDER

I t's the first day of Philosophy 101 at the local community college. After mumbling a few words about the syllabus and how hard people will have to work for an A, the professor pauses and asks: "Before we begin, is anyone in this class a Christian?" A first-year student two-thirds of the way back in the vast lecture hall shifts uneasily. She glances around. Among the sea of students, hers is the only hand raised.[1]

A twenty-three-year-old student has been sent to represent her church, Community Presbyterian Church, at its denomination's annual national youth gathering. At a break-out session on homosexuality, the group moderator prefaces the discussion by saying, "Let's not bring a lot of preconceived notions to the table here. . . . We shouldn't think of the Bible as a moral authority for all time but as a really good self-help book."[2]

An atheist in Swarthmore College's senior class laments that there's hardly any dialogue between believing Christians and non-Christians

because of the suffocating "discourse of tolerance that is such an impor-
tant part of liberal campus life." His observation? "Nonbelief is
assumed" and "religion is silent."[3]

———————

About one out of three teenagers is likely to actually attend a Christian
church after they leave home.[4]

———————

I'd like to come right out and ask you a question. It might seem impudent or harsh. It's a question about which there is almost a conspiracy of silence. Nobody seems to want to talk about it. But it's a very real issue.

Why do so many Christians apparently lose their faith after high school? What is it about life after youth group that overwhelms so many Christians?

I'm not trying to scare you. I'm just trying to get you to think about it.

I don't have a complete answer to my question, and I'm not going to speculate on all the reasons. For many, no doubt beer (the party atmosphere), peers (the desire to fit in), and fear (of being known as a Christian) all play a part.

But I think one of the big reasons—one that doesn't get enough attention at all—is "the bubble."

LIFE IN THE BUBBLE

Now, it's natural and good for parents and guardians to want to protect you from harm when you're little. They want to create a protective bubble around all areas of your life: physical, emotional, spiritual, and mental. It's a normal, healthy, honorable, God-given instinct.

The whole idea is that one day, when you're ready, you'll come out of the bubble and be able to deal with the outside world on its own terms.

Unfortunately, too many of us stay in the bubble too long. We know a few Sunday school stories, but we don't know the big picture of the

Bible. We know our own church but little of other churches. We had some really fun times in youth group, but we're completely stumped by relatively easy questions. We know precious little about the worldwide church and almost nothing about non-Christian traditions. As a result, we're unprepared for dialogue—that animated back-and-forth conversational jostling and wrestling necessary to strengthen and deepen our faith.

Meanwhile, the wide world of big ideas presses in on our fragile, childlike bubble. Everything seems sharp! For some, all it takes is a pinprick or a little puff of wind—and *poof!* No more bubble.

Here the road divides. Some take the path of least resistance and flow with the mindset of the dominant culture. They chuck the Christian thing and never darken the doors of a church again.

Others opt for the flat earth syndrome. They keep believing but shut their minds to new insights or better ways of understanding their faith. If anything appears to disagree with their set views, they reject it out of hand to keep from being challenged or frustrated.

> **Secret agent Christians are intimidated into silence.**

Others become secret agent Christians. Intimidated into silence, they try to keep their heads low and make their faith an intensely private affair between just them and God.

There's got to be a better way.

A LITTLE PERSONAL HISTORY

I'm writing this book to share some things I wish I'd known in my last two years of high school and after. Knowing these things would have made me more aware, would have helped me better understand my professors and fellow students, could very well have helped me get better grades, and might even have made me more popular with girls!

I became a Christian in the middle of my junior year in high school through Youth for Christ (YFC). I'd heard some Bible stories in the past, but I had never really heard the gospel—that God loved me and had sent His Son for me personally! Hearing the gospel for the first time was amazing. Finding other Christians and growing in faith with them was even better!

YFC stressed that in order to grow as a whole person, you needed to develop socially, physically, spiritually, and mentally. You weren't to neglect any area of your life.

Being social was not my strong suit. But I had a chance to grow socially through rubbing shoulders with people at school, in YFC, at church, and through a little bit of dating.

I took care of the physical growth by participating in team sports (football and tennis, if you must know).

Spiritually I grew through YFC Bible studies and events, through linking up with believers on my campus, and by getting involved in a Bible-believing church. I also started reading my *Reach Out: Living New Testament* and trying to spend time with God, if not each day, at least several times each week.

However, it seemed that YFC and the church expected that the mental part would take care of itself. You were supposed to simply put your nose to the grindstone and try to be a halfway decent student, and everything would turn out okay.

The only problem: It wasn't that simple then, and it isn't any simpler now. It used to be that being a committed follower of Jesus meant swimming against the cultural stream. Now you have to swim against the fire hose. And unfortunately, most young Christians simply aren't prepared *mentally* for the entirely predictable challenges that college and the wider culture will present.

The Deal About College

I went from a medium-sized public high school to a small liberal arts college. Large or small, prestigious or not, community college or university, the college environment will work you in many ways. It'll be a time of firsts: your first time away from home; (perhaps) your first serious dating relationship; your first time to be required to read three or four thousand pages—per class!

There is also time pressure, financial pressure, roommate pressure, grade pressure, and the pressure of choosing a field of concentration.

Duh, you may say. Okay. I'll move on.

In college I met quite a few people who had walked away from Christian faith. It seemed to me that more people lost their faith than held on to it. The spiritual meat grinder was churning away, but I was too busy trying to survive academically and spiritually myself to figure out what was happening.

One-on-one I was okay with people, but in public I was shy. I just didn't want to deal with the mocking and ridicule I knew would come if I really stood out as a Christian. I tried to fortify myself spiritually by getting involved with the Christian fellowship on campus, doing evangelism, and having dorm Bible studies.* There was one Christian professor who was really encouraging. And by doing some extra reading I was able to overcome that lonely feeling you get as a Christian in an unfriendly spiritual environment by enjoying the company of great Christian minds such as J. R. R. Tolkien, C. S. Lewis, and Frances Schaeffer.

WHOLE LOTTA SHAKIN' GOIN' ON

In today's college environment, on top of all the old biases and arguments against Christian faith, there are some unique new challenges.

Diversity and Multiculturalism

Many campuses are pursuing ethnic and social diversity (a good thing) by means of multiculturalism (a questionable proposition). *Multiculturalism* is the doctrine that no culture ought to ever be seen as better than any other and that no culture ought to ever be judged on terms other than its own.

What gets left behind in all this is exposure to a diversity of opinions. A "diversity agenda" ought to mean encountering a wide range of cultures and opinions so students can become well-read and well-rounded. Unfortunately, the diversity agenda often ends up promoting a

---

*Here's my big plug for finding vital Christian fellowship after high school: Yes, develop your own personal walk with Christ, but realize that the Christian life is not meant to be a Lone Ranger experience. Get plugged in. Give of yourself somewhere.

narrow band of approved opinion that is highly allergic to dissent.[5] On some campuses the pursuit of the diversity agenda can lead directly to racial and religious discrimination. A professor at Cornell Law School recounts:

> I sat in admissions committee meetings at Cornell in which African-American students who expressed conservative points of view were disfavored because "they had not taken ownership of their racial identity." An evangelical student was almost rejected before I pointed out that the reviewer's statement that "they did not want Bible-thumping or God-squading on campus" was illegal and immoral.[6]

At Tufts University, a Christian group was denied student funding because it would not allow an openly gay student to assume leadership. The group had to fight against much opposition to have its funding reinstated.[7] *

Anti-diversity can be amazingly strong in certain academic departments. For example, on some campuses, whole departments of Middle East studies have become hotbeds of virulent anti-American, anti-Israel, and anti-Jew sentiments, with professors not even trying for a semblance of balance in the classroom.[8]

Speech Codes, Thought Police, and Christophobia

Recently at Dartmouth University, the president of the Dartmouth Student Assembly addressed the freshman class in an opening-week convocation speech. He quoted Martin Luther King Jr., Shakespeare, and Bono. The Bono quote mentioned Jesus, and then the student president did: "Character has a lot to do with sacrifice, laying our personal interest down for something bigger. The best example of this is Jesus.... He knew the right thing to do. He knew the cost would be agonizing torture and death. He did it anyway. That's character."

The vice-president resigned in protest. The campus newspaper erupted in great indignation. The speech was denounced as "reprehen-

---

*The Foundation for Individual Rights in Education (FIRE) Web site, a nationwide networking tool, documents cases of discrimination and infringement of protected speech on campuses across the nation.

sible and an abuse of power" and "appalling." The student president had "embarrassed" the college and himself. He had chosen an "inappropriate forum" to exercise free speech. In short, he had broken the taboo of speaking on a topic that was considered off-limits. He had violated "polite society" at Dartmouth by being a public Christian.[9]

In the 1980s and 1990s, some three hundred American universities enacted (semi-legal) speech codes designed to limit "offensive" speech.[10] Allegedly for the purpose of encouraging civility and tolerance, along with appreciating differences,* speech codes often evolved into attempts to police thought through restricting speech.† On some campuses free speech could only be tolerated in designated "free speech zones," in effect making free speech off-limits everywhere else.

Strict speech codes have been used as weapons against individuals and groups. Enforcement can get ugly. One Cal Poly student was hanging up posters in a lobby advertising a black author coming to speak about how African-Americans need to take responsibility for their own destiny and work to get up in the world. One woman became very offended. The student's remarks were labeled "hate speech"; he was hauled before a student court and forced to undergo lengthy tribunals (during finals week), ordered to undergo psychological testing, and required to take "sensitivity" and "diversity" training. He was branded uncooperative when he refused, pressured to sign a "confession" that would have been entered into his permanent academic record, and threatened with academic probation and being thrown off campus! Only a lawsuit prevented Cal Poly from expelling the boy. The very clear message: Don't mess with tolerance![11]

Complicating the picture is Christophobia: an irrational, prejudiced, and judgmental reaction against Christ, Christians, and Christianity ("traditional" or "organized" religion).[12] If you "come out" as a Chris-

---

*Understood properly, all three of these values can be defended on biblical grounds. Jesus showed respect for all people based upon their common human dignity. He loved all people and persuaded them with His example rather than forcing His opinions on them. His love was universal, a love that goes far beyond tolerance, although tolerance is a good start for most of us. Also, "all things were created by him and for him" (Colossians 1:16), so of all people, He would be in the greatest position to appreciate the diversity in creation and cultures.

†I am thinking of George Orwell's great novel *1984* here. In *1984*, the powers that be used the technique of *doublespeak* (the changing and reversing of the meanings of words in order to confuse opponents and deny them the vocabulary to contradict their doctrines) to enforce *groupthink* (conformity of thinking). Read Orwell's essay at the end of the novel.

tian, you could very well be stereotyped as an intolerant, bigoted, funda-
mentalist, sexist, narrow-minded, judg-
mental, ignorant, hateful, homophobic,
holier-than-thou, hypocritical, sexually
repressed, redneck, racist, genocidal,
demagogic, warmongering, Fascist,
Nazi, running-dog capitalist, and/or
neocolonialist pig. You'd be better off if
you were Attila the Hun.

> **Christophobia: An irrational, prejudiced, and judgmental reaction against Christ.**

Taking the Log Out of Our Eye

Before we go any further, some self-examination is in order. Every
religion has its dark side, and Christianity is no exception. If we're honest about history, we have to admit that Christians (good intentions or
not) have committed atrocities in the name of God. Some Christians
have used the Bible to support white racial superiority. Eurocentric
Christians have sometimes confused the kingdom of God with Western
culture. The West has a legacy of slavery, witch burning, the Inquisition,
anti-Jewish pogroms, religious wars, and the colonialist oppression of
indigenous and aboriginal peoples. And let's not forget how the Lutheran
church in Germany allowed itself to be co-opted by Nazism; German
soldiers actually had *Gott mit uns* ("God with us") emblazoned on their
belt buckles.

It doesn't help when some Christians project an "us versus them"
image in which "we" are pure and moral while "they" are the opposite.
This perilous path denies two huge biblical truths: (1) that *all* are sinners and (2) that our righteousness/purity *only* comes from Christ. We
Christians need to have the humility and forthrightness to confess our
sins and the sins of our ancestors honestly and fully. We and our ancestors have missed the mark. We lose our credibility if we don't own up to
this fact.

NO MAGIC BULLET

The Christian bubble doesn't just affect college students; it affects all
Christians moving out on their own. There's a church-wide lack in pre-

paring young people to actually engage our culture. A simple-minded faith, a positive high school youth group experience, and a pat on the head are not enough.

Worse, the church has often painted Christian grade school and high school students into a tiny intellectual corner, feeding them a lot of either/or thinking. At the slightest hint that something might sound different from what they learned in Sunday school, kids are trained to stop listening and to offer conversation-stopping responses that amount to "I'm right and you're wrong" or "I'm going to heaven and you're not." There's a fearfulness and a brittleness of thinking that many churches unwittingly encourage, causing Christian kids to wither or withdraw from the culture rather than to engage it.

These attitudes not only lack compassion; they also lack Christian vision.

Now, if you are a youth pastor or youth volunteer, please do not take offense. I thank and praise God for you. I don't want to take anything away from what you are doing. Your ministry is immeasurably important. Teaching kids to walk with God, to love God's Word, and to resist the siren call of the world is sorely needed. All I am saying is this: The church also needs to prepare young people for the coming *intellectual* onslaught against the core of their faith.

You Can't Always Get What You Want

Some Christian parents, sensing that secular colleges and universities are minefields their kids shouldn't have to walk through, hope that putting their kids in an insulated and "safe" Christian college environment is the answer.

Like it or not, our society is now pluralistic—with many cultures, religions, philosophies, and lifestyles living side-by-side, jostling each other, influencing each other, and to a certain extent, trying to convert each other to their version of what's good and true. As good as a Christian college might be, there is no guarantee that at the end of four years a graduate will be any better prepared to function as an effective, confident public representative of Christian faith than a graduate of a secular university would be. The graduate of the Christian college may merely have obtained four more years of putting off the inevitable confrontation with non-Christian thought.

Another issue is that many kids who go to Christian colleges never had a living faith before they got there; others lose their faith at the very Christian schools that were designed to keep them in the fold.

Then there's the Harvard effect: Even colleges founded on Christian vision and principles can lose focus and gradually become, for all intents and purposes, secular. Many of the Ivy League schools, founded to promote Christian character and virtue, lost their Christian distinctiveness long ago. To compete for what they considered the best teachers, they loosened their doctrinal commitments. To appear to adhere to "academic freedom," they invited professors to come and to teach directly against Christian faith.[13]

I'm not against striving for excellence. But striving for excellence at a Christian college must *at least* mean exploring the unique and wildly attractive Christian worldview while covering the same knowledge base taught in secular universities. It's obviously not good to be taken over by non-Christian worldviews; but it's also not good to totally insulate students in Christian colleges from anti-Christian influences. A good Christian university that's preparing graduates to interact in a pluralistic world shouldn't want to do that anyway.

Bottom line: You need to prepare yourself spiritually *and mentally* for striking out into the big world. Without some idea of the rocks and shoals you're getting into, you can shipwreck your faith. It can happen to anyone at any time, inside or outside the college environment.

Just thought you might like to know.

2 | THE BIG "SO WHAT?"

This book is not just about surviving as a Christian in high school, college, and beyond. That goal is much too defeatist and limited, like saying, "Okay, we know you're going to get beat up, so here are the bandages. Just try not to get yourself killed."

This book is also not about avoiding the "party hearty" crowd or about resisting sexual temptation. Rather, the focus here is to look at Christian faith in a whole new way—as it contrasts with the other major worldviews out there. The aim is to give you a start at developing the *worldview* awareness you will need to hang tough with Jesus for the rest of your life.

In short, learn what's in this book and you'll become a more confident and effective public representative of Christian faith in the marketplace of ideas.

Let's expand a little on those key words.

Become more confident.

Paul had confidence when he wrote to the Corinthians, "Such confidence as this is ours through Christ before God. Not that we are competent in ourselves to claim anything for ourselves, but our competence comes from God" (2 Corinthians 3:4–5). He was saying, "Hey, we're not relying on our own shots—but on God's power working through us."

Yet confidence is not automatic. It's something you have to keep depending on God for, even when your emotions are telling you that you can't compete. Confidence comes through learning to trust God bit by bit, pursuing Christ through thick and thin, maturing spiritually over time, and developing your relationship with God (which includes prayer, Bible study, confession, fellowship, dependence on the Holy Spirit, and following Christ in obedience—a teensy weensy bit of knowledge about worldviews won't hurt, either). Gaining confidence doesn't *usually* come overnight. (God can break the pattern and give you extraordinary confidence in special circumstances.) And it's not dependent on your being the smartest or cleverest or most dynamic person in the room. It comes from being able to rely on God, on the truth God has revealed, and having a track record with God coming through in your life.

Become more confident and effective.

We want to be *effective* communicators. Paul said, "I have become all things to all men so that by all possible means I might save some" (I Corinthians 9:22). Paul wanted his efforts *to count* for the gospel and the kingdom of God.

Communications theory says that the message sent is not always the message received. Kind of like this: If I'm all bright and cheery in the morning, and my friend just isn't a morning person, my bright and cheery morning greeting might be taken as a deliberate annoyance.

We want to do our part to make sure—as far as it's up to us—that the message we send and what people receive is the authentic gospel. If people are going to be turned off to the gospel, we don't want it to be because of misunderstandings. Sometimes to get the true message across, we'll need to think of new ways of presenting the timeless gospel.

Become a more confident and effective public representative of Christian faith.

It is not enough to be a private, secret agent Christian, where no one ever knows that you are a follower of Christ. Jesus said, "Whoever acknowledges me before men, I will also acknowledge him before my Father in heaven. But whoever disowns me before men, I will disown him before my Father in heaven" (Matthew 10:32–33). Christian faith is intended to be public. We are to join in public debate, oppose injustice in the public square, rock the boat and make waves when our culture ignores God. Not every Christian is called to the same level of public exposure, but all Christians are called to live their Christian life out in the open. We can learn courage from brothers and sisters in Christ in other countries who do not have the luxury of living with laws of tolerance and religious freedom. Many martyrs have paid the ultimate price—yet Jesus says they are not missing out on anything now. They are in the presence of fullness of joy.

> **Christian faith is intended to be public.**

Consciously or unconsciously, everybody is a walking billboard for his or her worldview. We're constantly advertising what's most important to us. So what are *you* advertising? Jesus said in the Sermon on the Mount, "Let your light shine before men, that they may see your good deeds and praise your Father in heaven" (Matthew 5:16).

Too may Christians have the idea that witnessing is primarily verbal—either preaching the gospel or defending the faith against skeptics. But representing Christ in our culture means much more. We need to develop character and integrity. We need to do acts of goodness and kindness that point to Christ. We need to have ongoing conversations with people on all sorts of topics, not just "religious" ones. We need to strive for excellence and professionalism to make following Christ desirable. Christians need to establish institutions and projects that are not afraid to be known as Christian.

Paul, again to the Corinthians, said, "For I resolved to know nothing while I was with you except Jesus Christ and him crucified" (1 Corinthians 2:2). We are not called to defend the church or Christian history. What has happened under the name of Christianity and Christians can be faulted in many ways. Rather, we are to focus on Jesus and on following Him.

We are also not called to uphold our local church's version of Christianity as the only true church. All who put their trust in the Trinity— God the Father, God the Son, and God the Holy Spirit—have much more in common with each other than with other religions and philosophies. Therefore, regardless of backgrounds, *we as believers need to quit treating each other as unbelievers or second-class believers and recognize the unity we have in Christ* so that we can be a more credible witness to the world.

Become a more confident and effective representative of Christian faith in the marketplace of ideas.

A pluralistic culture ought to be a marketplace of ideas. This is not a bad thing for Christian faith! Christianity got its start in an intensely multicultural and pluralistic culture. When God brings together people from different backgrounds to worship Jesus, it's very exciting! It's a lot like the early church, when God looked at the pluralistic culture of the time and formed a motley crew of people, "neither Jew nor Greek, slave nor free, male nor female," into one body of Christ (Galatians 3:28).

In America, even though Christian principles have helped form our national soul, we've never had a state church. Instead, each version of Christian faith (each denomination), each semi-Christian sect, each sub-Christian cult, and each non-Christian religion—in short, each religion and worldview—must vigorously compete. If we are accustomed to thinking and speaking of a single "Christian America" culture, this thought can be unsettling. But it need not be if we have confidence in the innate power, beauty, and persuasiveness of God's truth.

So we need to ask ourselves: Given an open marketplace of ideas, what can we do to best persuade ourselves (!) and others to follow Jesus?

> **We can no longer take for granted that the man on the street has heard of the gospel.**

We can no longer take for granted—as Westerners one or two hundred years ago could—that the man on the street has heard of the gospel, that he has the vocabulary and familiarity with the Bible to recognize biblical concepts, that he shares any allegiance to the Biblical worldview, or that he understands or accepts Christian morality and values. We can't even assume that churchgoers understand these things.[1] With many of our fellow Americans, we'll need to start from scratch, just as if we were missionaries to a foreign (and effectively non-Christian) culture.

AVOIDING COW PIES

If you've never worked on a dairy farm, I highly recommend it. You'll learn some character-building things about life you can't learn elsewhere.

When you go into the field to mend a fence or to bring in a cow that's close to birthing a calf or to chase cows out of the corn—if you don't watch out it's really easy to put your foot somewhere it doesn't want to be. This happens even to experienced workers.

The same can be said for conversations. If you know how to keep your wits about you, maybe you can be spared from stepping into the most obvious nasties. Even if you're really good at tiptoeing around, if you're in the field a lot, your boots aren't always going to stay clean.

Yet here's some good news: You don't have to be a genius to understand and use the concept of worldview. You just need a few basic facts under your belt, and then you're good to go. Use a little bit of your worldview knowledge in public and people might start to think that you're a genius!

Here's another thing: *In the marketplace of ideas, you have every bit as much right to present your understanding of truth as anyone else.* No one can take that away from you. No one has the right to silence you.

You don't have to be a know-it-all. But you can have confidence (despite unanswered questions that you might have) that the Biblical worldview stands up just as well as—if not better than—all the other competitors out there.

3 THE BIG QUESTIONS

I read somewhere a while back about a guy who grew up in New York as a "red diaper baby." This didn't mean he had a bad rash. It meant his parents were committed communists. Anyway, when he was growing up, his father would ask everyone he met, "What's your purpose in life?"

A good question. A fair question. A universal question.

In my freshman year, my college roommate asked me, "How can you say that you, who grew up in Southern California, who have lived only about eighteen years on this earth, who have not traveled the world or even seen that much of the United States—how can you say that you know 'the truth'?"

A good question. A fair question. A universal question.

These questions and ones like them bring us to the heart of what it means to be human. What is our purpose, if any? How can puny people like us get to the truth about anything? What can we know? How can we know it? What is real? True? Good? People throughout history in every station of life have yearned for the answers to these questions.

And whatever the answer to those questions, its contours are going to be fixed by a whole set of almost-subconscious, rock-bottom convictions about how things really are and couldn't possibly be any other way.

These convictions come into play far before we even start talking about philosophical or religious doctrines.

You can call this set of underlying assumptions controlling or fundamental beliefs, preconceived notions, presupposed ideas (or if you want to get fancy, presuppositions), subliminal thinking, preconscious thought, conceptual worlds, deep mental frameworks, or arch-whatevers. Immanuel Kant, the eminent eighteenth-century German philosopher, called it *Weltanschauung* (velt-an-SHOW-ung).

CROUCHING TIGER, HIDDEN WORLDVIEW

Weltanschauung combines two German words: *welt* (world) and *anschauung* (view). Your worldview is your frame of reference, the spectacles through which you see the world.

Worldview is the biggest determiner of human behavior. You might say you believe one way, but your real worldview is revealed by what you do.

LOST IN TRANSLATION

Just as words, phrases, and entire speeches can get lost in translation, the concept of worldview can get lost in culture. But worldview is not the same as culture.

Culture is the sum total of language, behaviors, social hierarchies, religion, customs, taboos, and punishments for acting outside of social norms. Culture includes material artifacts like buildings, art, clothing, decorations, tools, and implements for war. In traditional cultures, there is one controlling worldview that pretty much everyone accepts without question.

In contemporary cultures (say, Southern California suburbia), where people have many more lifestyle and belief options available, you can have neighbors living side by side who share a similar culture but who have completely different worldviews.

WORLDVIEW MOSH PIT

The term *worldview* can be a mosh pit: vibrant, rough-and-tumble, and confusing. It's applied in all kinds of different ways in all kinds of fields, from culture, politics, economics, and save-the-world causes to religion, philosophy, and art. Sometimes you'll find it divided into two words (world view), and sometimes you'll see it as just one (worldview).

In this book I'll spell it as one word, and I'll be limiting the entire worldview discussion to the big questions mentioned at the beginning of the chapter.

No worldview has a monopoly on "the smart people." Wherever your life takes you after high school, you're bound to meet people who seem almost Godlike in intelligence who may have worldviews entirely different from your own. At such times remind yourself that a person's sharp wit and IQ do not make his or her worldview true. Sharp wit and IQ just help that person cleverly portray it.

It's easy to feel insecure around people who are exceptionally intelligent. But you don't have to be a genius to hold to a solid and legitimate worldview. When you find yourself with someone who's sharp as a whip, thank God for that person's smarts, ask questions, and see what you can learn. Don't be fooled into thinking that intelligence is the main factor in discerning or knowing truth.

> **You don't have to be a genius to hold to a solid and legitimate worldview.**

THE GREATEST SHOW ON EARTH

[Cue: calliope music] *The carnival barker strides to the center of the ring. Under his breath: "Drum roll, please!" Then suddenly, "And now, ladies and gentlemen, prepare to be electrified by a performance un-excelled in the entire earth! I give you the previously unpronounceable! Unparalleled! Unprecedented! Worldview mantra! The five—yes! You heard it right!—Five amazing things that are true about each and every worldview! (Step aside, lad, you're in the way.) And now, please, ladies and gentlemen, we need silence. . . ."*

I. Not everybody has a religion, but *everybody* has a worldview.

Having a worldview is part of our common humanity; we just can't get away from it. Everybody has a worldview, whether or not it's realized, thought through, or verbalized. People usually just assume that the way they look at the world is the right way. They don't necessarily analyze their assumptions or articulate them well.

So the big controversy is not between people who "think scientifically" and those who "need religion and superstition." No matter whether people consider themselves religious or not, *all* people live *religiously* by their worldview.

2. A worldview begins with a set of assumptions that can only be taken "by faith."

No worldview is established by the sheer force of logic or unassailable proofs. All worldviews have "faith" starting points. For example, some people say confidently that there is no God or that God cannot be real. But how can they *know* that? To *know* there is no God, you'd have to know everything in the universe and be everywhere in the universe at once to know that God wasn't hiding somewhere. In other words, to claim there is no God is not provable—it is an article of faith.

An apparently less extreme position than denying God outright is to say that even if there were a God, we can't ever know it for sure. But again, how could anyone claim to *know for sure* that God can't be known? You'd have to assume that either there is no God or that if there is a God, He can't bust a move or do anything confirmable in human experience. In this perspective, if two lawyers were arguing for and against God, the judge would throw out possible evidences for God's existence at the start of the trial. If the attorney for God attempted to reintroduce the evidences, he'd be ruled in contempt of court.

Sometimes Christians fall into the trap of thinking that the truth of Christianity can be conclusively settled either by bombproof arguments or by miracles. It's true that providing people reasons to believe in God (the study of apologetics) can help. It's also true that when God does a miracle in front of your own eyes, it can be a big eye-opener. But somewhere in there faith has to happen, and faith is the decisive issue.

It's not just Christians or religious people who take things by faith—while others rely only on reason and logic. *Everybody* has a faith starting point, even if that starting point is an article of nonbelief.

3. Worldview assumptions are rarely acknowledged openly, questioned, or challenged by those who hold them.

Worldview is the intellectual and cultural furniture in the room. We use it all the time and don't think much about it. Worldview is unseen, like the air we breathe. It's under our noses, but we don't notice.

Worldview assumptions pass under our radar screens, yet they control so much of life and behavior. As we think, so we do. And we act on what we really believe (not necessarily what we say we believe).

For most people, worldview assumptions go so deep that they don't know how to respond when their assumptions are brought out in the open. There's a Zen story about two fish swimming in a fishbowl: One says to the other, "Say, what's it like to live in water?" The other fish was silenced, a Zen way of saying the question blew his mind. The fish's whole existence had been always and only in water. He had never considered there might be an alternative.

Here's another example: A high school kid insists that "what's right for you might not be right for me." But if you slash his backpack, he'll protest strongly. Why? Because his professed worldview (moral relativism) conflicts with his actual worldview (that it's wrong to mess with *his* stuff).

Some people will act as if it's mainly (or only) Christians who have unexamined assumptions or who are unwilling to question their assumptions. In fact, it is something that happens to just about everybody no matter what his or her worldview is.

4. No worldview is totally open-minded; every worldview forces some narrowing of the mind.

If it's total open-mindedness you're after, you've got a problem; no worldview is (or can be) completely open-minded. All worldviews make truth claims that exclude other worldviews. It's what makes a worldview a worldview!

> **No worldview is completely open-minded.**

Some worldviews try to sidestep this issue. They condemn narrow-mindedness and say there is no truth, only "truths." But even these worldviews force significant narrowing of the mind because their truth (relativism) overrides all other "truths." Their worldview assumption alone is seen as right; any viewpoints or worldviews that disagree with their main assumption are obviously and horribly stupid or wrong.

One of the surest indicators that you're in a worldview conflict is when someone hints or says, "But that's absurd!" When someone says this, pay close attention to how that person's unstated worldview assumptions are being revealed.

A hundred years ago in our culture, most people believed that you could be neutral or objective regarding worldview and simply use reason to get to the ultimate truth of things. That's a myth. Everyone is biased, whether that bias comes from the influence of our culture, how we're brought up, our friends, or the sin that harasses us and deceives us. Everyone has an angle, a bone to pick, an axe to grind, an agenda.

This principle definitely applies in college classrooms. Professors with vast knowledge in their chosen fields of expertise can easily project an aura of neutrality and objectivity on worldview issues, as if they were above bias and prejudice. But rest assured, professors have not escaped the human condition. They are committed to one worldview or another, whether they admit it publicly or not.

This principle also applies in all human relationships. Since nobody can be totally open-minded, the best any of us can do is try to be aware of our own worldview assumptions, to be honest with others about where we're coming from, and to respectfully listen to others' point of view. By doing so we can sharpen our own understanding and perhaps even learn something new.

In short, it's not just the Bible that demands allegiance to truth at the exclusion of other worldviews. All worldviews draw lines. All worldviews have a fundamental exclusion factor working.

5. Every worldview has strict and inflexible rules, or Absolutes, that must never be broken.

I'd like to clarify something about the word *Absolute*. Normally when Christians speak of Absolutes, they are speaking of moral Absolutes (like "Thou shalt not steal"). In this book I use the term differently. I almost always use Absolute to speak of the foundational assumptions and internal logic that govern a particular worldview. (If the term Absolute appears in a moral sense, it will be clear from the context.)

Absolutes, the strict, inflexible rules of each worldview, must be obeyed without fail. They are revealed in superstitions and daily rituals, in religious rulings or secular laws, in a general sense of moral propriety, in philosophical ideas, in discussions of what we can and can't "know," in definitions of important words, and in taboos or in mockery and ridicule. Absolutes are unmistakably present in *every* worldview.

So it's not just Christian, Muslim, or Hindu "fundamentalists"* who have strict, inflexible rules. No worldview is rule-free. All worldviews expect their rules to be followed, period. The rules may be moral or philosophical. But the rules definitely cannot be ignored.

SPIRITUAL CHATTER

You can accept your inherited worldview, you can rebel against it, or you can adopt another. But there are *so many* worldviews. So many voices. So many answers. So much spiritual chatter. Each and every worldview says something it considers profoundly true about the way things are. How on earth can we cut through all the verbiage and make sense of all these competing claims? What are you supposed to do, just throw a bunch of worldview cards up in the air and pick one as it falls to the ground? What's the best way to go about selecting one that makes the most sense, that makes you feel and act most fully and authentically human? That is the task of the rest of this book.

But even beginning this task presents problems. The idea of worldview and the worldviews themselves can be sliced and diced in many ways. There is no way to approach the subject of worldviews with perfect neutrality. Everyone—politicians, media commentators, sociologists, psychologists, playwrights, screenwriters, philosophers, practitioners of various religions, and music artists—*everyone* who tackles this subject is already committed, and that includes me.

So to be up front about it, here's where I'm coming from: In this book I'll be using the word *worldview* to speak of people's understanding of what is ultimately true and real about (1) the spiritual world, and (2) what it means to be human in this real world.

---

*I put quotations (what journalists call "scare marks") around *fundamentalists* because it's very misleading (not to mention culturally insensitive) to lump all religious conservatives from whatever religion into the same reactionary, intolerant, violent, dangerous, and politically coercive camp.

Let's bring it home. Read this blurb of an interview between the online music ezine *Dead Angel* and Michael Hopkins of Tinsel.

> Dead Angel: "[Your] lyrics are often sardonic, most Cohenesque. . . . I'm curious about your worldview and how it applies to your lyrics."
>
> Michael Hopkins: "My worldview is a hodge-podge of ideas, probably best framed by existentialism and surrealism. To explain a bit, lyrically I take the point of view partly of the 'small man in a large uncaring world'; and partly of the dream-like, absurd, and childlike. Perhaps some non-music related preferences might offer better understanding. Kundera, Cornell, Magritte, Kafka, Brothers Quay and Dostoevsky would be a few of my worldview influences."[1]

I don't understand everything Michael Hopkins is saying here, and I don't expect you to. But please notice two things: First, the interviewer was comfortable shooting the breeze about worldview; and second, Michael Hopkins had a ready worldview answer for the despair that is in him (his belief in meaninglessness and the absurdity of life). How much more should we as believers have a ready answer for the hope that is within us! "Always be prepared to give an answer to everyone who asks you to give the reason for the hope that you have" (I Peter 3:15).

I'd like to ask you something: If people in the *music* business are familiar with these kinds of issues and are consciously using worldview in their art to portray their perspective on life, shouldn't Christians also be able to speak the language of worldview?

It's not as hard as it might seem. Even though theoretically there are uncountable worldview possibilities and every clever person you meet might seem to have a totally new worldview, I'd like to suggest that, despite the amazing diversity, all the worldview variations from whatever country, philosophy, or religion can be boiled down to just a few basic choices.

Does that sound ridiculously simplistic? If so, please hang with me for just a bit longer. I admit, what I'm about to show you is just one way of looking at worldviews. It might not be the best way.

But knowing worldviews will level the playing field for you because you'll see that the Biblical worldview is a legitimate contender in the marketplace of ideas. Later, if you're so inclined, maybe you can improve on what you find here.

In the meantime, at least this is a start.

When you start talking about worldviews, you're immediately confronted with the problem of infinite complexity. Since no two people picture the world in exactly the same way, you could say there's a separate worldview for every person on the planet.

But come on! Six billion is too many. Let's simplify.

To start the process, I d like you to think back to when you were a little kid at the zoo. Remember being delighted by something big—a Kodiak bear! Or something small—an Amazonian frog!

Wherever you went, you began to notice similarities and differences. Birds had feathery characteristics that you didn't see in mammals; fish were distinct from insects. Later, when you were reading an encyclopedia, you found some head scratchers. But for the most part, it wasn't too hard to group things according to their kinds.

So without further ado, let's head out to the Worldview Zoo and meet the worldview animals!

NAMING THE ANIMALS

The key to grouping the worldview animals according to their kinds is really simple: If it walks like a duck and talks like a duck ... it's not a rhinoceros. No matter what worldview animal you come across, even if you don't know its technical name, if you recognize its walk and talk, you'll be able to tell its basic type.

And here's the beauty of this system: We're going to boil down all six billion worldviews into six categories. If you can master these six—and it's easy to do—you'll be able to go anywhere in the wild world outside the zoo and quickly know what kinds of worldview animals you're dealing with.

For example, for those of you who are present or future students, wouldn't getting inside your professor's head be an awesome skill? If you could interpret the telltale signs of your teacher's worldview popping out here and there, it would help you in just about every class you take. You'd listen better, write better papers, and (hopefully) make better grades. Learn this chapter well and you'll be able to smoke out the worldview assumptions of just about any professor. They won't be able to hide behind an impenetrable sphinx-like mask or Mona Lisa smile anymore.

And think about this: If you can learn the skills to get inside your professor's head, you should be able to get inside just about anybody's. Knowing worldviews is going to help you the rest of your life, whether in late-night bull sessions, in trying to figure out your boss, in conversations with friends and strangers, in trying to understand the bias behind this or that Web site, in picking a church to attend, and even in selecting your life mate.

NOT ALL TREASURE IS SILVER AND GOLD, MATE

If grades, conversation, and practical decision-making don't motivate you, think of identifying worldviews as a game. Your mission, should you decide to accept it, is to crack the worldview code. Think of yourself as Sherlock Holmes on a quest for clues or Sir Galahad hot on the trail of the Holy Grail. This book is your dingy, edges-burned map to the buried treasure.

The funny thing is, if you know how to look for them, worldviews are hidden in plain sight. Sure, sometimes you'll have to make a guess—

but having worldview knowledge at your fingertips will help you make *educated* guesses. To mix metaphors: Soon, without investing too much time or effort, you'll be able to guess the destinations of trains by knowing where their particular tracks finish. A train can't go just anywhere; it has to go in certain directions.

A couple of things about this chapter: (1) This is the longest chapter in the book, so get comfortable, and (2) I'm going to ask you to interact with some vocabulary here that might stretch you a little. So please don't freak out if in the next pages you come across words that end in "ism."

1. THE HAUNTED WORLDVIEW

We'll call the first worldview the Haunted worldview. It is the deep structure behind most ancient religions. It is the worldview that preceded the Bible and into which the Bible was written. The two basic ideas are (1) that all the things around us (rocks, hills, rivers, trees, animals, weather, sun, moon, etc.) are animated by spirit beings, and (2) that there are gods or spirits, some of whom have really major powers, who at any time might appear in the world.

Naming this worldview is tricky. It has been called heathenism in the past, but today that term has connotations that stereotype all non-Western and non-Christian cultures as uncivilized, barbarian, and savage—an unjustified put-down. Other terms are animism (from the idea that all natural things are inhabited, motivated, and animated by spirits), Polytheism (the belief in many spirits), and paganism or neopaganism (new offshoots of old paganism).*

---

*Webster's hints that *pagan* is a loaded term. The Latin root, *rustic* or *peasant,* implies that a pagan is an uncivilized rube. The definition itself suggests that a pagan is someone who is not a Christian, Muslim, or Jew; is a heathen; or is a person who has no religion.

The term has positive or negative associations, depending on your perspective. (1) If you are a self-described pagan, it is a term of honor. (2) If you are a monist (read ahead to the section on Omnipresent Supergalactic Oneness), it might be a term of honor for polytheists and people like yourself. (3) Some Christians might point their finger at a pagan and think, *Sinner, sinner, sinner.* (4) If you are a materialist, you might mimic the term ironically ("Oh yeah, those *pagans . . .*") to mock Christian belief in heaven and hell. (5) If you are a party animal, you might call yourself "a red-blooded American pagan." In this book, we're using *pagan* in the first and third senses provided by Webster—as a term to describe those who believe in many gods and/or spirits.

A Lose-Lose Proposition

You may remember studying Homer's *Iliad* and the Trojan War in high school. The story wasn't just about heroes and battles. A fascinating back story gives us a window into Homer's worldview.

The back story: Hermes, messenger of Zeus, brings three gorgeous goddesses—Aphrodite, Hera, and Athena—before Paris, the handsome prince of Troy, and tells him he must choose who is the most beautiful among the three. Paris immediately realizes that he's in a cosmic no-win situation. Whichever goddess he chooses, the other two will be his enemies forever. Yet choose he must. He picks Aphrodite. Hera and Athena immediately begin plotting their revenge.

Hera and Athena's plan rolls into motion when Paris falls in love with Helen (the most beautiful woman on earth). Helen dumps her Greek king-husband, Menalaeus, and runs off to Troy with Paris, leading directly to war between the Greeks and the Trojans. Throughout the rest of the story, the gods and goddesses pull strings and manipulate events for their own advantage. Ultimately, Paris's choice, forced upon him by the gods, results in the utter destruction of Troy. The lesson: If you're up against the gods, you can't win.

Saturated With the Supernatural

Please refer to the diagram of the Haunted worldview. Let's start with the stick figures in the center. The ancients were people just like you and me. They were intelligent observers of their environment. They asked questions, thought things through, and made their best guesses at why the world was as it was.

The physical, material world surrounding had portals or windows into the supernatural, gates into the spiritual realm (the gaps in the box). As best as the ancients could tell, the world was full of moody, capricious, unpredictable spirits. Religion, then, was the way most people coped with this treacherous life. Sometimes they worshiped and hoped for the best, while other times they sacrificed just to get the gods off their back.

THE HAUNTED WORLDVIEW

The figure lying down with Xes in its eyes represents the brute fact of death. We empathize with the ancients because we experience the same thing—the loss of loved ones and the knowledge that we, too, will die. Like us, the ancients wondered what goes on beyond the grave. They believed the dead went to a place in or under the earth, kind of like a cave, a prison-house where people were punished or kept in a semi-comatose state.

Expressions of the Haunted Worldview

The Haunted worldview can be found all over the world in both ancient and contemporary cultures. Some animated movies that express this worldview are *Mulan, Pocahontas,* and *Hercules.* The occult side of this worldview—that is, secret, hidden spells and other ways to get various spirits (whether considered good, bad, or "flexible") to do your bidding—can be seen in films like *The Craft* and television shows like *Sabrina, the Teenage Witch* and *Charmed.* Contacting the dead, a common feature of this worldview, can be seen in TV shows like *Crossing*

Over and movies like *The Sixth Sense* and *Ghost*. As one network executive said about the 18–34 demographic, "This group skews toward ghosts."

Here are some characteristic sayings or attitudes connected to the Haunted worldview:

- It doesn't matter what you believe or what spiritual path you take, as long as you experience something powerful that works for you.
- You can get valid spiritual guidance from astrologers, fortune-tellers, psychics, and mediums (those who seek to contact the departed dead).
- It is important to get in touch with the spirits in trees, rivers, hills, and sacred places.

2. THE BIBLICAL WORLDVIEW

In this book the term *Biblical worldview* has been carefully chosen. I have avoided the term *Christian worldview* in order to emphasize that the Biblical worldview *includes God's revelation to the Jews prior to Christianity.* I have also avoided using *monotheism* or the *Monotheistic worldview* in order to put off until later in the book the tricky question of Islam's relationship to the Biblical worldview. We'll take up different aspects of that issue in chapters eight, eighteen, and nineteen.

I am assuming in this book that there is a single Biblical worldview upon which a Core of authentic Christian faith can be based. In history Christians have had somewhat different interpretations around the margins of it, but the Core remains.

The Biblical worldview accepts some aspects of the Haunted worldview and radically modifies others. Both assume the realities of the physical and supernatural worlds. However, the Haunted worldview urges us to try to get in touch with spiritual powers, whoever they are, including the departed dead. The Biblical worldview says, No! There is only one true God, and He alone deserves worship. Do not trust in those other spirits.

The Irony and the Ecstasy

We might expect ancient Israel to be a wonderful repository of true worship of the one true God. But for much of its biblical history, Israel followed in the footsteps of the emotional, polytheistic religions surrounding it.

Josiah is one of only a few kings in Jewish history who "got it." In the brief passage below, allow yourself to be amazed at the extent and number of pagan gods and practices Josiah removed from the land *and from the temple that had been built to honor Yahweh!* (For extra credit, circle every instance.)

> The king [Josiah] ordered Hilkiah the high priest, the priests next in rank and the doorkeepers to remove from the temple of the Lord all the articles made for Baal and Asherah and all the starry hosts. . . . He did away with the pagan priests appointed by the kings of Judah to burn incense on the high places of the towns of Judah and on those around Jerusalem—those who burned incense to Baal, to the sun and moon, to the constellations and to all the starry hosts. . . . He also tore down the quarters of the male shrine prostitutes, which were in the temple of the Lord and where women did weaving for Asherah. . . . He desecrated Topheth, which was in the Valley of Ben Hinnom, so no one could use it to sacrifice his son or daughter in the fire to Molech. . . . The king also desecrated the high places that were east of Jerusalem on the south of the Hill of Corruption—the ones Solomon king of Israel had built for Ashtoreth the vile goddess of the Sidonians, for Chemosh the vile god of Moab, and for Molech the detestable god of the people of Ammon. (2 Kings 23:4–5, 7, 10, 13)

It's a Wonderful Life

Now let's turn to the Biblical worldview diagram. Like in the Haunted worldview diagram, we find two stick figures of people like you and me looking out and experiencing their world. The physical world is real, as indicated by the solid lines, yet open to the supernatural (like the Haunted). The nature spirits have faded from view, and the realm of the departed dead is off-limits. God and Satan are in conflict, but in no way, shape, or form is Satan a worthy or equal adversary. The emphasis is firmly on the one true Creator God, Maker and Sustainer of the universe; if He wants to, He can act freely in it (either on His own or through angels), hence the large arrow. Satan is a created spiritual being; he is limited and inferior to God, and his demise is certain (see Genesis 3:15, Isaiah 14:12–15, Luke 10:18, 1 John 3:8, and Revelation 12:9). Satan and the demons—who as created beings cannot exist unless God permits them to exist—have much less power, authority, and scope of activity than God, hence the small arrow.

THE BIBLICAL WORLDVIEW

God (Angels)

Satan (Demons)

Expressions of the Biblical Worldview

Where in history can the Biblical worldview be found? Obviously, it is taught in the Old and New Testaments. Imperfect (and sometimes badly flawed) expressions of it can be found in Church history. The Judeo-Christian aspect of Western civilization also reflects (again, imperfectly) the basic Biblical worldview.

In American culture, Hollywood has sometimes come through: *The Ten Commandments, Ben Hur*, the animated *Prince of Egypt*, and *The Passion of the Christ* all artistically convey the Biblical worldview. Elsewhere in Western culture, Shakespeare, *Les Miserables, The Count of Monte Cristo,* and many other literary writers and works are saturated with biblical themes and allusions.

Here are some characteristic sayings or attitudes connected to the Biblical worldview:

- "Have no other gods before me" (the first of the Ten Commandments: Exodus 20:3).
- "Love the Lord your God with all your heart and with all your soul and with all your mind.... Love your neighbor as yourself" (Matthew 22:37–39).
- God is good. He loves you.
- "He has showed you, O man, what is good. And what does the Lord require of you? To act justly and to love mercy and to walk humbly with your God" (Micah 6:8).

3. THE WYSIWYG WORLDVIEW

The WYSIWYG (What You See Is What You Get)* worldview says that the physical, material, natural world—what we experience with our five senses—is the only solid reality. According to this worldview, religious and spiritual explanations or doctrines are imaginary superstitions, illusions, or wishful thinking having nothing to do with what is real or knowable.

The WYSIWYG worldview has many formal names. Some of them are: naturalism (the idea that nature is all there is); materialism (not the consummerist "desire to acquire" or the "shop till you drop," but the belief that the physical, material world is all there is); and atheism (a term I generally avoid in describing this worldview because it only tells what atheists don't believe, rather than what they do believe). I also include agnosticism (the sit-on-the-fence idea that you just don't know or can't be sure that there is a God) in this category because in my experience, agnostics *make daily decisions as if the WYSIWYG worldview is true.*

---

*"What you see is what you get" originally referred to computer interfaces (in the 1970s). It's also been used in lyrics to songs by Meat Loaf, Britney Spears, Save Ferris, and Xzibit; in advertising and business to denote no hidden meanings; and in dating. We'll designate it with the acronym WYSIWYG, pronounced "whizzy-wig."

> The WYSIWYG worldview is dominant among elite opinion makers.

Believing the physical, material, natural world is all the reality that matters is just as much of a "faith" position as that held in other worldviews. For decades the WYSIWYG worldview has been dominant in colleges and universities and among elite opinion makers.

The Authoritative Text

I spent years searching far and wide for the perfect authoritative text and name for this worldview. I thought I had finally found pay dirt with Carl Sagan in his famous book *Cosmos* and with his tag line for his TV series of the same name:

> *The Cosmos is all that is,*
>   *or ever was*
>   *or ever will be.*[1]

Then I discovered that *five years earlier,* Stan and Jan Berenstain had published an almost identical statement in their children's book *The Bears' Nature Guide.* In that book we find Actual Factual Bear telling the story that all the familiar things around us are Nature: the earth and its features, the moon and sun, the planets, the stars. Papa Bear then chimes in that we are also Nature. At this point, Actual Factual Bear hits us with this kicker:

> *It's all that IS*
>   *or WAS*
>   *or EVER WILL BE!*[2]

Looks to me like the Berenstain Bears scooped the great scientist Carl Sagan. Or maybe Sagan got his idea from reading the Berenstain Bears to his kids! Anyway, in deference to the law of publishing first, ladies and gentlemen ... let's give it up for Actual Factual Bear!

Is That All There Is?

To say that nature (or the cosmos) is all there is is a profound statement. From the perspective of the Biblical worldview it is profoundly wrong. But for the sake of the argument, let's follow the idea through to its conclusion: If Actual Factual Bear is right, what are the implications?

To answer that question, please turn to the WYSIWYG worldview diagram. As before, the figures in the box represent people trying to make sense of their world. But this time the box representing the physical, material, and natural world is hemmed in by a solid line. In effect, the WYSIWYG worldview reduces *everything* to a closed system of physical causes and effects. *Nothing real* exists outside the box: neither gods, God, angels, demons, the souls of the departed dead, heaven, nor hell. This worldview is hermetically sealed against the supernatural. Even if God did a miracle in front of his eyes, Actual Factual Bear would have to explain it away in naturalistic terms according to the strict, inflexible rules of his worldview.

Notice what this worldview does to our humanity. We become mere cosmic accidents, here *only* as a result of time, chance, and matter. When we die, *kaput!* That's it. There's no lasting meaning, purpose, or ultimate value to life.

THE WYSIWYG WORLDVIEW

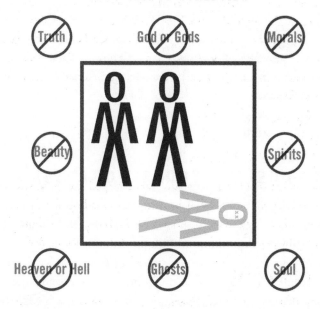

Furthermore, this worldview leads directly to extreme moral relativism. Since any one person's or culture's perspective is as good as any other's, there's no way to say with compelling authority that anything is *ever* right or wrong. You can't even say Hitler or Stalin or the Rwanda or Sudan genocides were wrong. You can never appeal to a higher authority (like God, since He's not supposed to exist). There are only opinions, man-made laws, social norms, prejudices, and personal tastes and whims—any sense of universal morals, virtue, truth, and beauty are terminated.

Expressions of the WYSIWYG Worldview

Some examples of this worldview are the movie *Life as a House* with Kevin Kline, Ingmar Bergman's existentialist films like *The Seventh Seal*, and the 1960 film *Inherit the Wind*. Quite a few films that do hatchet jobs on Christians have a materialistic or naturalistic agenda as their driving force. Books and movies sympathetic toward Communism and socialism are almost always cheerleading for the materialist worldview and gnashing their teeth against the Biblical.

Here are a few characteristic sayings or attitudes about the WYSIWYG worldview:

- There are *absolutely* no Absolutes. Everything is relative.
- You can only trust what can be seen, felt, heard, tasted, or smelled—in other words, only things that are physical.
- Science beats religion every time.
- There is no Truth. Only truths.

4. THE DUELING YODAS WORLDVIEW

In 1977, George Lucas brought to the silver screen the first of his *Star Wars* movies. One of the heroes in *Star Wars* is the diminutive Yoda, a yogi-like master who knows the ways of the Force better than anyone and who, by the way, wields a mean lightsaber. Since this worldview's nickname is in the plural, it might help you to imagine two Yodas—a Yoda and an anti-Yoda—spinning and parrying in mortal combat.

Lucas intended to create a modern mythology for our time, an epic morality play on the battle between good and evil, of the effects of courage and compromise. To achieve his vision, Lucas introduced us to the Force, a mysterious power or energy divided between a dark side and an unnamed good side. In the course of the story, these two sides of the Force weigh in, like a teeter-totter, swaying the fortunes of the protagonists.

The technically correct name for this worldview is Cosmic Dualism: *Cosmic* for gigantic, eternal principles; *Dualism* for two. In the ancient world, a few religions taught a full-blooded Cosmic Dualism, in which neither good nor evil were ever finally triumphant.

George Lucas took some artistic license with the idea of Cosmic Dualism—he didn't, or couldn't, go all the way with it. After all, he wanted to sell his movies (and toys) to American audiences who liked happy endings. Therefore, his good guys *had* to win. But credit Lucas for coming pretty close to the flavor of Cosmic Dualism.

THE DUELING YODAS WORLDVIEW

Again, our diagram shows a box representing the physical world, with figures inside. Unlike the WYSIWYG worldview (which rejects any transcultural moral Absolutes), the Dueling Yodas* worldview is a moral universe, a battlefield for the constant duel between good and evil. The good and evil principles may be conceived of as personal (such as a good

---

*Credit for this nickname goes to my brother, Eric Taylor, who in one evening came up with a great name, better than any I had thought up in months.

god versus an evil god) or impersonal (such as a good force versus an evil force). Each human being must choose which side to follow; to be moral, a person must master his or her passions to be able to make the right choices.

May the Force Be With You

A lot of people who have seen the *Star Wars* films have tried to interpret Lucas's Force in terms of the Judeo-Christian idea of God, as if "May the Force be with you" is interchangeable with "May the Lord be with you." However, the two worldviews just don't fit together.

For one thing, the God of the Bible is powerful, energetic, and *personal* (He has mind, emotions, and will; knowledge, desires, and intentions).* The Force, even though powerful, is no match for God and is merely an *impersonal* energy.

For another, through talent and vigorous training, a Jedi knight could hope to control the Force. However, the God of the Bible can never be harnessed, manipulated, or controlled in any way.

Also, the Force had a dark side. But the Bible teaches emphatically that "God is light; in him there is no darkness at all" (1 John 1:5).

Lastly, in the Dueling Yodas worldview, feelings are even more powerful than the dark side of the Force. As Obi Wan Kenobi reminds Luke Skywalker as he's hurtling through the Death Star's futuristic canyons on his near-impossible mission, "Trust your feelings, Luke!" In contrast, the Bible teaches us to trust God, who is always greater and more reliable than our human feelings or passions.

Expressions of the Dueling Yodas Worldview

Here are some sayings and attitudes of this worldview:

- Two dogs are fighting within me. The one that wins is the one I feed the most (possibly from Native American origin).
- Train yourself to be indifferent to pleasure or pain (Stoicism).
- Man is caught in a no-win situation (Cynicism).

---

*When we say God is a person, we are not saying God is human. We are saying that God is infinite, that God is Spirit, and that God has revealed himself as having mind, emotions, and will—aspects of personhood. We are also saying that God's person is perfect, unlike humans.

5. THE OMNIPRESENT SUPERGALACTIC ONENESS WORLDVIEW

The 1995 comedy *Ace Ventura: When Nature Calls* opens with Jim Carrey's character in an ashram somewhere in the Himalayas meditating with wild animals in blissful harmony. He's there hoping to achieve the pinnacle of enlightenment, but to the monks in the ashram he's a real pain. In an effort to get rid of him, the head monk tells Ace he just achieved his goal, "omnipresent supergalactic oneness," magnanimously awarding him a priceless medallion and freeing Ace to leave. Ace, in a gesture of great compassion for the other monks who must now go on without his presence, asks the head monk to "break it to them gently." Upon hearing the news, the monks raucously whoop it up with cheering, confetti, and somersaults.

Ace's ultimate goal is an apt nickname for this worldview. More technical and precise names for this worldview are pantheism (the belief that all is God or all is Spirit), holism (the belief that everything is connected because it is all part of the one), and monism (the belief that everything is one).

As an aside, I have found that many people confusedly think of monism and monotheism as the same thing. I think perhaps it's because they pronounce the "mon" in monism and monotheism the same way. However, monism teaches that all is one, that all distinctions between things are ultimately meaningless; monotheism teaches that distinctions (such as between God and His creation) are of the utmost importance. The basic monistic idea is that God and you are (Omnipresent Supergalactic) Oneness; the basic Biblical worldview is that there is one God and you're not it. Therefore, I urge you always to pronounce monism like "moan-ism" and the "mono" in monotheism as in "monorail."

Ultimate Reality Is "In Here," Not "Out There"

Refer to the diagram illustrating Omnipresent Supergalactic Oneness. In this diagram, the lines of the box are hash marks, not solid. This represents the idea that in this worldview, everything is spirit or mind—everything is one. In Omnipresent Supergalactic Oneness, the barrier between the physical and the spiritual (or anything having to do with the mind) is illusion. The physical world, the world we experience with our senses, only *seems* to be real. True reality is in the mind. Your mind is supposed to create its own reality, the only reality that matters.

The *I* between the stick figures represents the pantheistic idea that we are all divine, we are all God, or at the very least, we are all part of God; all you have to do is look within yourself to find God. Since according to Omnipresent Supergalactic Oneness *everything* is God, you are essentially no different from a blade of grass or that cockroach over there. All are equally God.

The swirl represents this worldview's belief about what happens when we die—that the soul is "born again" (recycled) in a new body, to live thousands or millions of lives on its way to eventual (and guaranteed) union with the one. Not every monist believes in *karma* and re-incarnation (we'll take these up in more detail in chapter 13), but on the whole this belief is very characteristic among monists and pantheists.

OMNIPRESENT SUPERGALACTIC ONENESS

The Impersonal Absolute

"I"

Karma & Reincarnation

Imagine No Religion; It's Easy If You Try

Omnipresent Supergalactic Oneness rejects the idea of a personal, theistic God (and any religion that supports that idea). Instead, the word

God means the sum total of everything. "God" is an indefinable, indescribable "Ultimate Reality," "Impersonal Absolute," or "Cosmic Vibration"—nothing like the Biblical worldview's understanding of God as a heavenly Father who created the heavens and the earth separate from himself. *The Lion King* presents an excellent example of Omnipresent Supergalactic Oneness:

> Mufasa: Everything you see exists together in a delicate balance. As king, you need to understand that balance and respect all the creatures, from the crawling ant to the leaping antelope.
> Young Simba: But dad, don't we eat the antelope?
> Mufasa: Yes, Simba, but let me explain. When we die, our bodies become the grass, and the antelope eat the grass. And so we are all connected in the great circle of life.[3]

Expressions of Omnipresent Supergalactic Oneness

Regarding the twin doctrines of karma and reincarnation, a lot of people think *karma* means "you reap what you sow" or "things happen for a reason"—you're mean to someone and then your car gets dinged in the parking lot, for example. However, karma goes much deeper. It teaches that the soul requires many thousands of lives of suffering to finally achieve perfection (guaranteed for every soul eventually, since all is one—mere drops emanating from the same ocean) and merge with the Infinite Absolute.

Here are some characteristic sayings and attitudes:

- You can do anything at all—if you just believe in yourself.
- The Christ is already within you; you just need to realize it.
- All spiritual paths lead to the same destination.
- What goes around comes around (referring to karma and reincarnation).

6. DESIGNER RELIGION

A lot of people today do not consider themselves part of any organized religion or thought-out philosophy. They like to pull from various traditions and come up with a religion of their own. It's known by various names: religious syncretism, the New Age movement, the Age of Aquarius, new religions, and a new religious consciousness. I'll call it Designer Religion.

DESIGNER RELIGION

The box here does not symbolize the physical/material world, like in the other box diagrams. Rather, it represents a gift box a person creates for him or herself. Designer Religionists cobble together different religions, philosophies, and whims into personally customized spiritualities. The result is full of religious, scientific, pseudoscientific, psychological, philosophical, and spiritual beliefs that may be disparate, contradictory, and incompatible with each other. It's like going to a cafeteria with an all-you-can-eat buffet and being offered dishes like sweet and sour kraut and egg foo schnitzel.

Designer Religion tries to neatly tie these concoctions with a bow. This worldview says that any way to God is cool—God being defined however the individual wants.

Same as It Ever Was—Sort Of

In one sense, Designer Religion is nothing new. For thousands of years, pagan and pantheistic religions have adapted and adopted aspects of various religious traditions. If you look closely, Designer Religion is strongly represented in the (badly compromised) Israelite religious practices found in the Old Testament. What's different today is the intense individuality factor. Designer Religion is loyal only to the individual. It is the opposite of traditional, inherited religions and worldviews.

One big attraction of Designer Religion, aside from the benefit of being able to think of yourself as creative, is that there is *no guilt!* Since you are customizing your own religion to suit yourself, there are no outside constraints—you can do whatever you want.

Due to travel, communications, and mass movements of peoples across borders, this mixing and matching of religions is likely to increase. Designer Religion will accelerate as our culture puts more and more emphasis on individualism.

Expressions of Designer Religion

Some examples of Designer Religion are Madonna's forays into Kabbalah, Dan Brown's *The DaVinci Code,* Scientology, and various other New Age spiritualities, which mix old and new religions along with pseudoscience and superstition.

Here are some characteristic sayings and attitudes of this pseudo-worldview:

- I'm not into "organized religion."
- "I'm spiritual, not religious."
- Whatever works for you.
- As long as it doesn't hurt anybody.

A SIX-PACK IS ALL YOU NEED

Imagine a six-pack of your favorite beverage. The six bottles or cans will represent the *only* worldviews you need to know! Can you remember them?

The great thing about knowing this six-pack of worldviews is that you can tote it anywhere. You don't have to spend years studying religion and philosophy to know where people are coming from. You don't need a bachelor's degree, master's degree, or PhD in this stuff. Now *you* can unlock the secrets of every philosophy, religion, or worldview perspective that comes down the pike. No matter what the situation, you'll be able to start breaking things down. In every new class you'll be thinking, *What is this teacher's worldview? What is the worldview behind this book?* When you go see a film you'll wonder, *What worldview is this movie promoting?* When you listen to music you'll ask yourself, *Which worldview is this musical group fronting for?* When you watch or read or listen to the media, your antennae will be out: *Which worldview?* And when you're talking to your friends or co-workers, you will have a much better idea of what they're talking about.

5 | STILL HAVEN'T FOUND

Now that you're getting the hang of the major worldviews, let's return to the big question of personal identity. Psalm 8 puts it this way:

> When I consider thy heavens, the work of thy fingers, the moon and the stars, which thou hast ordained; what is man, that thou art mindful of him? and the son of man, that thou visitest him? (vv. 3–4 KJV)

Who am I? How do I fit into this great big universe? What's my reason for existing? How can I make my life significant? And I'm going to die—what's that all about?

Who among us has not asked these questions? The way the worldviews answer gives valuable clues into how much (or how little) they value human beings. And to these deepest human questions and longings, the Biblical worldview's answers are amazingly powerful, unique, and, I think you will see, precious.

In the movie *Napoleon Dynamite,* Pedro intones in his campaign speech for student body president, "Vote for me and all your wildest dreams will come true."[1] I'm not going quite that far. But I will say, "Read the next few pages, and you'll better understand nine ways the Biblical worldview fulfills your deepest needs."

NOT THE STRONG, SILENT TYPE

The Biblical worldview insists that God is a passionate lover of His people. He is not silent! To affirm this takes nothing away from God's unutterable mystery and His unapproachable glory. The Biblical worldview is that God desires to be known by us, that God is able to speak to us, and that God has in fact spoken clearly to humanity through nature, through the history of Israel, through the prophets of the Old Testament, through Jesus Christ, and through the Holy Spirit speaking through the church. God is a person who is able and wants to love us and have friendship with us. We are not alone. God is not indifferent to us nor is He silent.

What do the rival worldviews say on this point? In none of them does it make any sense to say that God communicates to us clearly.

- The Haunted worldview: There is such a cacophony of voices from the many gods and goddesses that there is no way to know which ones are really trustworthy and true. They're all out for their own gain and they all use people for their own ends.
- What You See Is What You Get: There is no God, so it is moot to talk about God communicating.
- Dueling Yodas: Similar to the Haunted worldview, with spirits that compete against each other; or God as an impersonal Force, an energy (not a personality) that can be used for good or bad.
- Omnipresent Supergalactic Oneness: Because the infinite absolute is by definition vague, indefinable, and incomprehensible, this impersonal "God" simply cannot communicate truth in human language, because language, by definition, necessarily obscures and misleads regarding ultimate things. Language is inherently a barrier rather than a help to experiencing whatever "God" is.
- Designer Religion: It's up for grabs, depending on whatever worldview element is the leading idea at the moment.

OF MICE AND MEN

The very first chapter of the Bible states that for all time men and women are created in the image of God, so therefore all people have innate dignity and worth.

That we are created in God's image has immense implications. It means that our personalities somehow (poorly and imperfectly) reflect God's. It means that each individual person has innate, inalienable, inestimable dignity and value. It means that all the diverse clans, tribes, languages, and cultures on earth have great worth before God. It means that oppression, injustice, and a myriad of social ills are not God's intent.

Let's go further: The notion of people created in God's image provides the only really secure basis for a true humanism.* Three reasons are:

1. The Incarnation. Because we are so important to God, God's Son became a man, took on human flesh, and died to redeem us from our sin and foolishness. What more solid affirmation of human worth and dignity could there be?
2. The Value of the Individual. Before the Bible there were law codes, but essentially they were preferential to the rich. Punishments depended on one's social class. The lower on the totem pole, the worse the beating. The Bible introduces the idea of a moral law that applies equally to all, even kings.†
3. Human Dignity. The social justice laws of the Old Testament— like caring for widows and orphans, treating sojourners with respect and honesty, and providing for the poor by leaving some of the grain in the corners of fields unharvested—and especially the life and ministry of Jesus, show that God values each person: even the poor, the outcast, the marginalized, the infirm, the leprous, and the morally or socially degraded. This biblical commitment to human dignity forever rejects any political power system that treats "the people," "the masses," or unfavored groups as exploitable or expendable.

---

*Many Christians recoil at any mention of humanism. But humanism is just approaching things from a human perspective. You can be a Biblical/Jewish/Christian humanist, a secular humanist, a pagan humanist, or a New Age humanist.
†The Old Testament's legal system was not totally consistent on equality (different laws and punishments for men and women, slaves and free, Israelites and non-Israelites), and apparently Old Testament practice shifted with the times and was not uniformly carried out (David committed adultery and was not harmed, for example—see Leviticus 20:10; Deuteronomy 22:22–24; John 8:5). But in general, Old Testament law pointed in the direction of greater equality and justice than what had been experienced in society before.

So how do the other worldviews stack up regarding the innate dignity and worth of the individual?

- The Haunted worldview: You are at the mercy of the gods. The only beings that really have innate dignity and worth are those with the most power—in other words, the gods and demigods.
- What You See Is What You Get: You are nothing more than evolved primal slime. Whatever illusions you have about innate dignity and worth are futile and cruel hoaxes.
- Dueling Yodas: You are caught in a vice; you have no control over the forces that are squeezing you. You're nothing more than a pawn in their game. You can choose to act with nobility, but it doesn't really matter.
- Omnipresent Supergalactic Oneness: You are a single drop vanishing in a vast ocean. Everything is one; good and evil are one; insects and humans are one. You have no more value than a weed.
- Designer Religion: It's up for grabs, depending on whichever worldview element is the leading idea at the moment.

ARE YOU LONESOME TONIGHT?

The Bible states over and over again in hundreds of ways that God loves you. This is not the *Peanuts* cartoon variety of love that says, "I love humanity; it's people I can't stand." This is not an abstraction that has nothing to do with real life. Rather, it is a tender, compassionate, merciful, and abounding love for you personally.

Despite all your foolishness and sin, you are still lovable.

God's love for you is based upon the fact that you are created in His image, that God knows you intimately, and that He's invested himself heavily in redeeming you. Despite all your foolishness and sin, you are still lovable.

Here's the rub: *The Biblical worldview is totally unique and precious because it is the only worldview in which it makes any sense to say "God loves you."*

- The Haunted worldview: The gods, goddesses, and godlets that roam polytheism use people, sometimes extraordinarily cynically, for their own ends. Can we ever expect unconditional love from them? The gods don't love you. If they "love," it is with a self-serving agenda.

- What You See Is What You Get: The icy blackness of space doesn't care for you; a purely materialistic universe can't give a rip about you. If you're lucky, you might experience love here on earth, but it ends with death; no love is forever because there is nothing beyond the grave.

- Dueling Yodas: There is no love whatever in an impersonal "force" that can be turned toward good or evil. However, if the battle is between a good god and an evil god, a preserver versus a destroyer, what can be said? Only this: If good can never ultimately prevail over evil, what's the point? If there is love in this system, it is exactly balanced by despair.

- Omnipresent Supergalactic Oneness: A pantheistic or monistic universe absorbs your being until you cease to exist as an individual. That's not love. Love requires personalities in relationship with each other.*

- Designer Religion: It's up for grabs, depending on whichever worldview element is the leading idea at the moment.

FORGIVENESS IN A WORLD GONE WRONG

The ancients taught, "Know thyself." If we're honest, we'll admit that we don't measure up to the standards we measure others by. There's a built-in hypocrisy in almost all moralizing and judging. Meanwhile, we rarely stop to think that we might be guilty before God, stained by selfish motives, polluted by impurity, and enslaved by the power of sin.

Yet God became a man to rescue us from our predicament, to restore the image of God in us that is so badly corrupted. There really is forgiveness in the cross of Christ, where His blood buys our peace with God. Christ's arms were stretched out in love for us on the cross that we

---

*Jesus said to love your neighbor "as yourself." Monists say Jesus meant this to mean you should love yourself as a God.

might experience complete forgiveness for all the cruel, thoughtless things we have done.

What do the other worldviews say about forgiveness of sins?

- The Haunted worldview: Forgiveness just isn't the heart language of the Haunted worldview. You're supposed to do your duty, fear, bring your sacrifices to the gods, and don't ever do anything to offend them. You can never get out of their debt; you can never satisfy them.
- What You See Is What You Get: Since God does not exist, all religious guilt is false, and cosmic forgiveness doesn't exist.
- Dueling Yodas: Forgiveness is a foreign concept. You choose sides and pay the consequences. There's no free ride.
- Omnipresent Supergalactic Oneness: There is no forgiveness from God, since you are "God." There is also no guilt, since each soul makes its own path according to its own inclinations. In this scheme, there is only the iron law of karma. What you get in this life is exactly proportional to your actions in past lives. There is never the slightest bit of injustice at any time. You alone must bear the entire burden for your sins; you alone can save yourself from the cycle of karma and reincarnation.
- Designer Religion: It's up for grabs, depending on whichever worldview element is the leading idea at the moment.

TENDER MERCIES

> **Christians have a compelling basis to forgive others' wrongs.**

One of the most beautiful things the New Testament teaches is "as Christ has forgiven you, so forgive others." This is based upon the example of Christ himself, whose whole mission was to enact forgiveness. He prayed to the Father regarding his torturers, "Father, forgive them, for they know not what they do."

Because of Jesus' example, Christians have a compelling basis to forgive others' wrongs against them. For Christians, practicing forgiveness is not just a pragmatic thing to do because it's good for your health and psychological well-being. It's the only appropriate response to what Christ has done for us. "He who has been forgiven much, loves much," Jesus said. We enter into Christ's love when we forgive others, especially when it's hard.

What do the other worldviews say about forgiving others?

- The Haunted worldview: It might be a noble gesture. But you don't really see much forgiving among the gods. Their example is grudges, getting even, and doing one better. With them, it's not overcoming evil with good but doing whatever is necessary to save your face and your place.

- What You See Is What You Get: It might be a noble gesture; you might achieve some peace of mind if you forgive. But there's no moral law that says you need to or that you should. Maybe you should get some payback. It's your choice. Do whatever you want.

- Dueling Yodas: Forgiveness? Kind of stupid, don't you think? Why would you ever want to give evil a break? Okay, maybe to give a person a chance to change heart or switch sides. But freely? Not likely.

- Omnipresent Supergalactic Oneness: Extending forgiveness to someone who has wronged you might do you some good in the karma department. It might get you a little closer to enlightenment and oneness. And it'll make you feel good. You might discover some compassion along the way.

- Designer Religion: It's up for grabs, depending on whichever worldview element is the leading idea at the moment.

FULL OF SOUND AND FURY, SIGNIFYING NOTHING?

The Bible says that our life is about our relationship with God. We are created for Him. Our lives are not just about food, clothing, and shelter. Even if we attain these things, universally people feel there is more to life, even if lives are cut short, even if they are imperfectly lived, even if, even if.

There are many strong purpose statements in the Bible. "Love the Lord your God with all your heart and with all your soul and with all your strength." "Act justly and ... love mercy and ... walk humbly with your God." Bottom line: Our purpose in life and in death is to serve God, to live for Him, to enjoy Him, to seek His glory in what we do. We are promised and warned that what we do matters in the long term, not only in terms of immediate consequences but in terms of eternal rewards and regrets.

How do the other worldviews deal with meaning and purpose?

- The Haunted worldview: Your purpose is to serve the gods, but they don't really care for you. There is more meaning and purpose for them than for you.
- What You See Is What You Get: There is no ultimate or lasting meaning or purpose to life. When you die, you die, and that's the end of it. The best you can hope for is that people will remember you with fondness and respect once you're dead and gone.
- Dueling Yodas: Master your skills, master your knowledge, give your best. But ultimately your efforts will be nullified by the opposing principle. There is no final winner; there is no final arbiter of meaning.
- Omnipresent Supergalactic Oneness: The final meaning and purpose of everything is universal oneness, a blending of all consciousnesses and non-consciousnesses into a single, all-encompassing infinity. In that vastness, your individual identity and individual story become utterly insignificant.
- Designer Religion: It's up for grabs, depending on whichever worldview element is the leading idea at the moment.

LOVE ALTERS NOT WHEN IT ALTERATION FINDS

Truth in the Bible is not just thoughts that correspond with reality. It's not just a good argument backed up with logic and reason. It's not even having all the right answers.

Rather, in the Bible truth is faithfulness, steadfastness, acting with honor and integrity, not being two-faced, keeping one's word. A huge confirmation of truth is that God makes promises and keeps them. For a little glimpse of how this works, do a quick study on the word *fulfill*. (See Numbers 23:15; Psalm 138:8; Jeremiah 33:14.) Notice God making promises in the Hebrew Bible (the Old Testament) and how events in Jesus' life validate God's truthful character. (See Matthew 1:22; 2:15, 17, 23; 3:3, 15; 4:14; 5:18; 8:17; 12:17; 21:4; 26:54, 56; 27:9.)

Truth is also about living a life of virtue and integrity. It's not just knowing about good but doing good. It's not just knowing the wise thing to do, it's doing the wise thing. Jesus is the only one who has ever lived a perfectly virtuous life, but drawing on His life and power we can live in integrity and truth, too.

What do the other worldviews say about truth?

- The Haunted worldview: Truth? You can't handle the truth! Only the gods can, and they're not to be trusted unless you give them a little extra—if you know what I mean.
- What You See Is What You Get: Truth? What is truth? There's no truth, only opinions, superstitions, power plays, you name it. Take your ideas of truth to Sunday school; in the real world what speaks is will, steel, and blood.
- Dueling Yodas: There's never just one truth; there are always at least two. Hot, cold. Male, female. Cause, effect. Good, evil. You need to learn how to negotiate between them.
- Omnipresent Supergalactic Oneness: All is One. Therefore, the difference between good and evil is only apparent. If you raise your consciousness to the proper elevation, you'll see that good and evil are just two sides of the same coin.
- Designer Religion: It's up for grabs, depending on whichever worldview element is the leading idea at the moment.

WHERE THE STREETS HAVE NO NAME

In the Bible, eternal life is not just "pie in the sky when you die." It is both a here-and-now quality of life with God *and* the promise of being with God in heaven forever. Jesus promised that those who believed in Him "shall not perish but have eternal life."

There's an incredible amount of violent death in our world: disease and sickness, accidents, natural disasters, abortions, wars, terrorism, religious persecution, murder. Then there are slow deaths: poverty, lack of clean water, lack of access to basic food and medicine, horrible political leaders. And then there are plain old natural deaths. At any moment we can be taken out of this world to face the next. But the Bible says Christ is "the beginning and the firstborn from among the dead" (Colossians 1:18). Because of Christ's resurrection and ascension, we can have hope beyond the grave.

What are the other worldviews' answers to death?

- The Haunted worldview: You'll go to the land of shadows where the dead are in a kind of suspended animation: unable to move much, unable to care much about anything. The only people who make it to the Elysian fields (or equivalent) are the heroes and demigods. The rest basically bite the dust.
- What You See Is What You Get: The worms get your body. That's it.
- Dueling Yodas: Pretty much like the Haunted worldview.
- Omnipresent Supergalactic Oneness: The immaterial part of you recycles through thousands or billions of lives until you finally get absorbed into the Infinite Absolute. For all those lives you're stuck on the Wheel of Samsara, the great hamster wheel of suffering.
- Designer Religion: It's up for grabs, depending on whichever worldview element is the leading idea at the moment.

SOMEBODY UP THERE LIKES ME

Only in the Biblical worldview does it make any sense to say that we are not alone in the universe (that we belong), that we are greatly valued, that God loves us, that we can experience both forgiveness and forgiving others, that reconciliation between former enemies is a worthwhile goal, that life has meaning, that goodness will be rewarded, and that there is an amazing answer that overcomes death.

These are not idle talking points. They speak powerfully to our deepest needs as human beings. Small wonder that wherever in the world the gospel is preached, even when there is great persecution, people respond. Compared to the alternatives, the Biblical worldview doesn't look bad at all.

6 | COMMON GROUND

O ne of the main ideas of this book is to point out differences between the Biblical worldview and the other main contenders. But maintaining that the Biblical worldview is the best one for explaining our humanity and our place in the universe does not mean that everything about the other worldviews is wrong. In fact, there are some very significant areas of agreement between the Biblical and the other worldviews. Let's take a look at some of them. As we do, please refer to the diagram entitled "Worldview Overlaps."

(A quick reminder: Pagan refers to the Haunted worldview; Naturalist to What You See Is What You Get; Dualist to Dueling Yodas; Monist to Omnipresent Supergalactic Oneness. Designer Religion is not covered here as a separate worldview because it gets all its important ideas from the other worldviews anyway.)

PAGAN (HAUNTED WORLDVIEW) OVERLAPS

Western culture is rooted in Greek philosophy, history, and literature. Greek culture was thoroughly immersed in paganism. Most of the Greeks took the hierarchy of the gods of Olympus for granted, or at least as a point of departure. Some of them may have rejected the

WORLDVIEW OVERLAPS

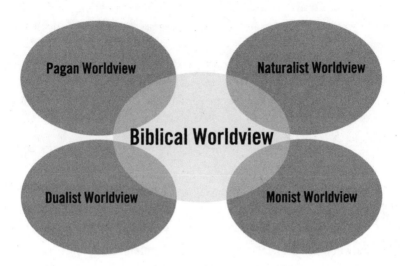

Pagan
- Humans are a complex bundle of contradictions
- Recognition of justice and the virtues
- Recognition of the supernatural world
- Recognition of the need for sacrifice to the gods

Dualist
- We live in a moral universe
- Good and evil are not arbitrary
- Courage and determination are high values

Naturalist
- The physical world is real and important
- Science and the scientific method
- Insatiable curiosity and desire for explanation

Monist
- The physical world is not all there is
- The physical world is sacred
- There is something of the Divine in all of us

supernatural stories, treating them as nothing but superstition. Others may have gravitated to the idea of one main or overarching God. Still others were willing to believe that gods and spirits were very much a part of everyday life.

The point is that the Greeks made many accurate observations about what it's like to be human living in a supernatural world. As a result, many Christians in the first centuries of the church treated some of the Greek thinkers almost as prophets of Christian truth. Plato's and Aristotle's ideas are especially reflected in certain spheres of Christian thought.

Without going into great detail, here are some pagan insights that are compatible with the Biblical worldview.

First, humans are a complex bundle of contradictions. Like the gods, they can be noble yet cruel; faithful yet vain; brave but foolhardy. This taint affects even the most godlike among men—each one has some fatal flaw of character, some great deed or aspect that eventually brings them down. Greek tragedy continually plays on the theme of various characters' pride or success as the very thing that brings their undoing. This realization is not unlike the biblical idea of sin catching up with us in the end or our prideful desire to imitate or challenge God and His wisdom.

> **Humans are a complex bundle of contradictions.**

A second pagan insight is the recognition of enduring values that cut across cultures. Chief among these is the idea of justice. The question that haunts each of us—What does it take to live a good life?—led directly to the development of the virtues, indeed a hierarchy of virtues. These kinds of thoughts were not far from Paul's when he said things like this: "Finally, brothers, whatever is true, whatever is noble, whatever is right, whatever is pure, whatever is lovely, whatever is admirable—if anything is excellent or praiseworthy—think about such things" (Philippians 4:8). Paul's exhortation here would have played very well among Greeks who gave thought to living a virtuous life.

A third pagan insight might seem too obvious to mention. It is the recognition that this present world can be influenced by spirit beings. The pagans could not only infer that God and/or gods had created the world, but that spiritual beings could bring banes and blessings. In this regard the pagan and the Biblical worldviews are similar: both acknowledge the existence of spiritual "principalities and powers" (the phrase comes from Romans 8:38 and Ephesians 6:12 in the King James Version) of hierarchies of spirit beings. The difference is that the pagans tended to look at these gods and spirits as mixtures of good and evil, like humans. They didn't really see the principalities and powers as locked in mortal combat for the souls and eternal destinies of humans, as we find in the Bible.

A fourth pagan insight is the recognition that the world is morally "out of joint." The way to bring things back into alignment is through sacrifice. This urge to sacrifice is seen in almost all pagan cultures. It can also be found in the Mosaic sacrificial system instituted by God himself, as well as in the whole significance of Christ's sacrifice on the cross.

NATURALISTIC (WYSIWYG) OVERLAPS

Since the Naturalist worldview denies the existence of a supernatural God, and since the Bible is admittedly concerned with the hereafter, at first it might appear that there isn't much in common between the Naturalist and the Biblical worldviews. However, even here there is common ground.

First, both agree that the tangible, measurable, physical world known through our five senses is real. The reasons for recognizing the reality and integrity of the physical world may be different (stuff has its own worth period versus stuff has worth because it is created by God and shows His glory), but the recognizing is the same. The world is not just something "in the mind of the beholder" or "in the mind of God." It has an existence and presence whether anyone sees it, feels it, hears it, tastes it, smells it, or measures it—or not! The Old Testament is especially strong on this. The world is real and has worth in and of itself. It therefore deserves respect as is. This respect for nature ought to lead directly to respect for the environment and the desire to maintain a healthy planet.

A second point of agreement is the validity of science and the scientific method. If the physical world has worth in and of itself, it stands to reason that studying the physical and natural world has value in and of itself. The reasons for doing so, again, might be different (say, pure curiosity or utility versus appreciating how God maintains and operates His world), but the activity of studying and applying the scientific method is the same.

A third point of agreement is the human desire to understand the natural world and an unwillingness to settle for superstition. This has not always been a strong point in Christian thinking, as the Galileo incident ought to have taught us,* but Christians entering scientific fields and following through in scientific endeavors can certainly be part of a comprehensive Biblical worldview.

Fourth, Christian faith and Naturalism agree—against Gnosticism (see chapter eight's subsection "Caveat Emptor" for more on Gnosticism)—that this present world is to be highly valued rather than denigrated as lowly matter. The attitude, "so heavenly minded they are no earthly good," doesn't describe Biblical worldview Christians. In fact, Christians go further than naturalists: Nature is important on its own terms, but what we do in the natural, physical world has impact in the spiritual realm and can have eternal consequences.

DUALISTIC (DUELING YODAS) OVERLAPS

A variation on the pagan theme of many gods and spirits is Cosmic Dualism—the idea that two mighty "spiritual" forces in the universe duke it out in an unending and unwinnable boxing match. Cosmic Dualism looks at these opposing principles either as named personal beings or as impersonal powers.

The chief historical example of Cosmic Dualism is Persian Zoroastrianism, in which the good god, Ahura Mazda (or Ohrmazd), fought against the evil god, Angra Maiynu (or Ahriman). Zoroastrianism was an ethical dualism because it focused on human choices. A different type of dualism is found in the Chinese religion of Taoism (also called Daoism),

---

*Roman Catholic teaching at the time of Galileo was that the Bible taught that the sun orbited around the stationary earth. Galileo's idea that the earth orbited the sun was considered heresy—persistent, deliberate opposition to what the church taught.

which supposed an eternal, dynamic tension between Yin and Yang (more on this in chapter 13). And in the first four centuries after Christ, the religion of Manichaeanism (also spelled Manicheanism and Manichaeism) tried to solve the problem of evil (how can an all-powerful and good God allow so much suffering in the world?) by blending Christian and Zoroastrian ideas. As a result, the Manichaeans rejected God's omnipotence and elevated Satan's status to that of an uncreated, self-existent entity equal in powers to God.

The choices we make have real consequences.

Despite these divergences from the Biblical worldview, one point full-strength Cosmic Dualism and the Biblical worldview have in common is that both say the world we live in is real. We live in a moral universe; the choices we make for good or evil are real. They have real consequences. Each of us must make a choice. The Bible puts it this way: "Choose ... this day whom you will serve" (Joshua 24:15); "Multitudes, multitudes in the valley of decision!" (Joel 3:14); "There will be tribulation and distress for every soul of man who does evil, of the Jew first and also of the Greek, but glory and honor and peace to everyone who does good, to the Jew first and also to the Greek" (Romans 2:9–10 NASB).

A second similarity is that both Cosmic Dualism and the Bible recognize that good and evil are not arbitrary. The good is really good. Evil is really evil. The Bible says: "God is light; in him there is no darkness at all" (1 John 1:5), but Satan is a liar and a murderer from the beginning (John 8:44). The big difference, of course, is that the Biblical worldview looks to the end of history and assures us that God will ultimately triumph over His foes.

Third, the virtues found in Cosmic Dualism (courage and determination to hold the course and behave honorably) are echoed in the Bible. The message of the book of Revelation may be boiled down to this: "Hold fast" to Christ and the gospel even though at times it looks a lot like God's cause is losing and the evil world system is winning.

MONIST (OMNIPRESENT SUPERGALACTIC ONENESS) OVERLAPS

While it might appear that there is no commonality of the Biblical and the Monist/Pantheistic worldviews, there actually are some fruitful convergences.

First, the Biblical and Monist worldviews both believe that the physical world is not all there is. "There's got to be more" is something that they both can say. As a matter of fact, on this point the Biblical, Monist, Dualist, and Pagan worldviews all agree (against the Materialist worldview). There's got to be more than just being born, living out your life, and dying. There's got to be some meaning to life.

Second, the monist sees world experiences as sacred. Since "everything is Spirit," everything is divine. To a certain extent, this comports with the Biblical worldview. But someone with a Biblical worldview would always have this significant difference with a monist: He or she might say, "Yes, I can accept that everything is sacred. You are half right. I believe that God is everywhere present, and therefore, everything is sacred. But I also believe that God is over and above what we experience and that God created everything out of nothing—therefore, God is not impersonal; He is not 'part of nature.' Neither is God 'the sum of the parts' of nature. God is infinite. God is personal. He has control over nature and He can intervene miraculously in it. God can listen to our prayers and answer them. And by the way, I'm not God."

A third way the Monist and Biblical worldviews are similar (not the same) is the idea of "the divine within." On this point we must tread carefully because language can be awfully tricky. Monists often rely on the phrase "the kingdom of God is within you" (Luke 17:21) to try to say that Jesus was really a closet monist teaching mystical pantheism.

However, there are two big problems with this. First, Jesus was a Jew who believed in one God, who taught people to worship the God revealed in the Jewish Scriptures, and who prayed to the God of the Jewish Scriptures. In the context of first-century Judaism, nothing He said or taught comes remotely close to monism or pantheism. Second, sorry, Jesus wasn't teaching a see-yourself-as-God self-esteem class.* The king-

---

*As would Tony Robbins, Deepak Chopra, Marianne Williamson, Andrew Cohen, and many, many others.

dom "within you" is a conversational relationship with God made possible by Jesus and made effective by the Holy Spirit.

To clarify further, the Bible clearly teaches that we are created "in the image of God" (Genesis 1:27). Therefore, there is something divine, spiritual, and special about who we are as created beings. We are not God; we are not gods; but we are imprinted with God's image. A monist—just like every human being, whatever his worldview—experiences this image of God in his person, in his soul, in his spirit; he then tries to explain his experience of being made in God's image according to his worldview (or her person, her soul, her spirit, her experience, and her worldview). As Christians, we can work with this common experience, but we explain it differently. We say, "God created us in His image. We sin and turn away from Him and His ways. This separates us from Him. But God has made a way for us to get back to Him. Would you like to know how much God loves you?" As Christians, we always want to go for the personal relationship angle. We do not believe that ultimate reality is impersonal. We believe ultimate reality is intensely personal, as God has proved by becoming one of us.

From the Biblical perspective, then, we can bank with confidence in the following truths:

1. There are at least some absolute truths, God himself being one.
2. We are not God.
3. No human (Jesus Christ is the only exception, since He is such a special case) can legitimately claim to have absolute knowledge about anything, especially God.
4. We must acknowledge our own limitations and exercise humility in our claims to knowing the truth. God can and has actively revealed himself to us through nature, Israel's history, the Bible, Christ, and the church. Therefore, even though there is absolute truth we cannot claim to know it absolutely.
5. We must acknowledge that our own church traditions and teachings—as good as they may be—are not exactly the same as absolute truth. They are limited by cultural shortsightedness, time restraints, and the simple fact that even human collective wisdom starting with God's truth is not total wisdom. God's self-revelation is absolute truth; church traditions and teachings are our best

interpretations of God's absolutely true self-revelation. No section of the church has a total lock on the complete or final truth. Only God does.

OUR COMMON HUMANITY

Despite all the differences in culture, language, history, ethnicity, and so on, we all share a common human experience. That common ground is rooted in the fact that each of us is created in God's image. That image produces a yearning for truth, goodness, justice, nobility, worth, belonging, and many other basic things. When we tap into the image of God in ourselves and in other people, when we can relate to them as one human being to another, God can work through us in amazing ways.

7 | QUICK ON THE UPTAKE

The flutter of a butterfly's wings in one corner of the world can cause a hurricane on the other side of the globe.

—an idea associated with the chaos theory

One of the most important skills I want you to take from this book is the ability to *rapidly* make educated guesses about which worldviews people are likely to believe based on casual remarks they make. This is not pigeonholing or stereotyping others—it is "reading" them. You can always revise or refine your guesses. But the sooner you have a handle on a person's basic worldview, the sooner you're going to understand what makes that person tick, the sooner you're going to have an idea what it's like to walk in that person's shoes, the sooner you're going to know better how to relate the gospel to his or her life.

So whenever you meet someone, watch TV, peruse a newspaper, read a textbook, enjoy a novel, or attend the theatre, you ought to be asking yourself, *What worldview is being promoted here?* Every person's worldview is some variation of one of the six basic worldviews we have addressed. If you don't know or can't figure it out super quickly, that's okay. You need some practice, and this chapter is about giving you some practice.

ANALYZE THIS!

Below I've assembled a few of the sayings you might typically hear in everyday conversations. Take a look at each saying and quickly make a guess as to which of the six worldviews you think it represents. A couple of hints: (1) Some of these sayings fit into more than one category. (2) Don't rely too heavily on Designer Religion, since it's possible to see almost every statement as coming from that worldview.

1. Nature is God.
2. We each find "God" in our own way.
3. Jesus was just a clever faith healer that Christians turned into a god.
4. The "Christ consciousness" or "divine light" within you is all the spiritual guidance you need.
5. God loves you and cares for you personally.
6. It doesn't really matter what you believe, so long as it works for you.
7. Psychic hot lines are a good source of information about love.
8. Angels lead us toward God; demons deceive us and lead us away from God.
9. Witches, magic, shamans, mediums, and channelers can put you in touch with dead relatives.
10. Good and evil, heaven and hell are within.
11. God answers prayer.
12. Faith is a crutch for the weak.
13. You can only trust what science can prove.
14. Everything is morally or situationally relative.
15. Beware the dark side of the Force!*

WORLDVIEW CHEAT SHEETS

Having practiced how to identify worldviews according to watch-words, slogans, and sayings—let's now turn our attention to expanding on the amazing variety of philosophies, religions, and practices that occur under each of the worldviews. Sooner or later you're going to come across many or most of these names.

Sometimes I call these expanded charts cheat sheets. Sometimes I call them depth charts. Whatever you call the charts doesn't matter. What matters is recognizing the characteristics and "the rules" of each philosophy, religion, and practice—not memorizing all the particular names.

---

*Answer key: Haunted (2, 7, 9, 14); Biblical (5, 8, 11); WYSIWYG (3, 6, 12, 13, 14); Dueling Yodas (9, 15); Omnipresent Supergalactic Oneness (1, 4, 10, 14); Designer Religion (2, 6, 14). Note: A more extensive list of sixty-five worldview sayings is available at *www.blahblahbook.com.*

THE HAUNTED WORLDVIEW

Gods & Goddesses

Spirits

Spirits

Spirits of the Departed Dead

Other Names and Practices, Old and New: Paganism; polytheism; Greek and Roman mythology; ancient Near Eastern religions; fertility religions; animism; spiritism; low Hinduism; Shintoism; goddess worship; astrology; worship of nature deities like the sun, the moon, and the storm; mystery religions; Mahayana Buddhism; Tantric Buddhism; shamanism; ancestor worship; esotericism; the occult arts; luck and fate; academic anthropology; tribal religions; wicca; witchcraft; magic (magick); channeling spirits of the dead; necromancy; mediums; voodoo (vudun); santeria; Satanism; henotheism; Bhakti devotionalism (a form of Hinduism); most pre-Christian religions; Christo-paganism; folk Islam; Freemasonry; Jungian archetypes (understood as actual spirits); Scientology and other science-fiction religions; aboriginal religions; the Burning Man festival; tarot cards; fortune-telling; palm reading; spell casting; liberal/revisionist "Christianity" (such as the "Re-Imagining God" movement).

The Rules: Eclectic. Syncretistic. Don't judge anybody. Get in contact with spiritual power, whichever spiritual power works for you.

THE BIBLICAL WORLDVIEW

God (Angels)

Satan (Demons)

Other Names: Judaism and Christianity; Judeo-Christian culture; Christendom; the "Western" worldview, "Western Civilization," or "Western culture." All major branches of Christianity (Roman Catholic, the Eastern Orthodox churches, and the Protestant churches) agree on the basic Biblical worldview. Judaism holds to the basic Biblical worldview except that it disagrees about Jesus being the Messiah.

Quasi-Biblical/Sub-Biblical Practices and Groups That Fatally Compromise the Biblical Worldview: syncretism (worshiping Yahweh alongside other gods; mixing Judaism with the religions of the surrounding peoples); Christian Gnosticism; Christo-paganism; Islam; deism; Mormonism; Unitarianism; Universalism; Jehovah's Witnesses; the kinds of revisionist Christianity that impose pagan religious forms into so-called "Christian" worship.

The Rules: Serve the one true God—the Creator of the Universe—alone. Since God loves you personally, love the Lord your God with all your heart, soul, mind, and strength, and love your neighbor as yourself. God's rules are good and are for our good.

THE WYSIWYG WORLDVIEW

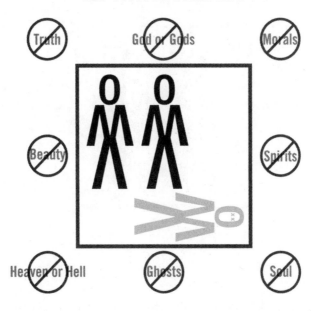

Other Names and Practices, Old and New: naturalism (Nature is all there is); materialism (matter is all there is); Epicureanism; Theravada Buddhism; scientific reductionism; atheism; empiricism; logical positivism; hard skepticism; agnosticism; non-theism; existentialism; nihilism; humanism; rationalism; romanticism; Marxism; dialectical materialism; communism; naturalistic evolutionism; social Darwinism; cosmic randomness; biocentrism; moral and ethical relativism; moral equivalence; American pragmatism; natural religion; comparative religions; Freudian psychology; solipsism; structuralism; post-structuralism; deconstructionism; consumerism; Nietzsche and Nietzschism; anarchism; meaninglessness.

The Rules: The physical world is the only reality. You can only know what is material. Any appeal to spiritual reality is outlawed from the start as mere superstition, hype, hokum, wishful thinking, or deception. All morals and ideas of good, evil, truth, and beauty are merely man-made.

THE DUELING YODAS WORLDVIEW

Other Names and Practices, Old and New: Dualism (can be seen as personal bi-theism or as non-personal "forces"); Zoroastrianism; Manichaeanism; Stoicism; Marxism.*

The Rules: Good and evil are in an eternal battle in a moral universe, but neither side ever wins. It is an eternal struggle.

---

*Marxism is a strange case. In one sense, Marxism is WYSIWYG materialism, pure and simple. It may be dressed up as "dialectical materialism," but the main thrust is material/economic leveling of wealth to achieve a utopia in this world.

In another sense, Marxism is a selective reading of the Biblical worldview. It receives ideas of social justice, the eventual triumph of good and the idea of everyone acting altruistically (as in heaven), but rejects belief in God as a mind-numbing and distracting opiate that keeps people from rising up against their oppressors.

And in another sense, Marxism is cosmic dualism, seeing a cosmic conflict between the revolutionary communists (the forces of good) and the capitalists (the forces of evil). Because the capitalists are seen as pure evil, the revolutionaries are justified in using any means to overthrow them and to establish themselves in power, including murder, mass enslavement, and mass starvation.

THE OMNIPRESENT SUPERGALACTIC ONENESS WORLDVIEW

Other Names and Practices, Old and New: monism ("all is one"); pantheism ("all is God"); panentheism ("all is 'in' God," the world/universe has a "soul"); "everything is connected"; "you are divine" or "you are God"; High Hinduism; Brahminism (the priestcraft of Hinduism); Yoga; Shaivism (a form of Hinduism); the Kama Sutra; chanting Aum or Om; I Ching; yin and yang; Taoism; Zen Buddhism; Neoplatonism; Gnosticism; emanationism; Western philosophical idealism; German romantic idealism; non-personal idealism; non-dualism; the Baha'i faith; Transcendentalism (Ralph Waldo Emerson); New Thought (nineteenth century); Unitarianism; Universalism; Science of Mind (Christian Science); Krishnamurti; theosophy; anthroposophy; "perennial philosophy"; mysticism; holism; Vedanta; Transcendental Meditation (Maharishi Yogi); Joseph ("follow your bliss") Campbell; Shirley MacLaine; martial arts; process theology; liberal/revisionist theology; much of Disney entertainment's "theology."

The Rules: Absorption of all things into pantheism or monism. Evil and good are only apparent opposites. There are no innocent sufferers, since suffering is exactly proportionate to one's karma. You create your own reality with your mind. According to the Omnipresent Supergalactic Oneness worldview, you are "God," but so is that cockroach scurrying across the floor.

DESIGNER RELIGION

A Description: It has been common in human history for people to have mixed and matched elements of various religions. In the twenty-first century, as the world has "gotten smaller" due to communications, travel, and mass movements of peoples across borders, human cultures have often become more pluralistic. This is particularly so in the United States with its emphasis on rugged individualism. Many postmodern people desire to move beyond "organized religions" and to create their own customized systems of belief. Some people even get rich creating and promoting their own new religions.

Designer religion may be non-sectarian and non-dogmatic—but may also be highly structured and cultlike. It very often seeks great distance from monotheistic religions like Christianity, Judaism, and Islam. Eclectic, it borrows from various religious traditions and isn't too worried about contradictions or inconsistencies. Common attitudes are "whatever works for you" and "as long as it doesn't hurt anybody." Often in designer religions, sexual morals are relaxed.

The Rules: It's okay to mix and match religions. Never judge anybody. Get in contact with a spiritual power that works for you.

An Observation: Designer Religions are unoriginal and totally derived from other worldview sources. They usually camp in one particular worldview and then borrow (or steal) elements from others.

8 | IF IT QUACKS LIKE A DUCK

T he other day I took my car into the shop for some repairs. Waiting its turn was this incredibly hot, totally buff, low-slung yellow Lamborghini. Ooh, that car looked sweet.

Only thing—the mechanics were laughing at it. It's a piece of junk, they said. I asked why, and they said the guy who built it put a Pontiac Fiero under the Lamborghini body. Later I did some research and found out that compared to a Fiero, a real Lamborghini has twice as many cylinders, 4.7 times as much engine capacity, three times as much horsepower, and can go 1.6 times as fast.

Now, the Fiero might be a reasonably sporty car on its own terms, but it's just not a Lamborghini. Lesson for the day: A car can look slick and spiffy on the outside, but you want to know what's under the hood before you buy it.

Religions and worldviews are like that. Religions are car bodies, but worldviews make cars go. And here we come back to one of the early points of the "Worldview Zoo" chapter: If it waddles and quacks like a duck, it doesn't matter what you call it—it's still a duck.

What I am saying now about religions is counterintuitive. Usually people talk and think about religions as if they are solid granite blocks of certain beliefs, practices, and behaviors. But when we apply the concept of worldview to religions, we find that all religions suddenly become more complex. There's not just one Hinduism or Judaism, for example, but several, each taking its cues from a different worldview.

What goes for other religions also goes for Christianity. Search the world over and you'll find not just one Christianity, but several, depending on which worldview is the driving force underneath all the trappings and forms.

In other words, *worldview is actually more important than the religious labels people give to themselves and their beliefs.* In the end, religious labels matter little; the worldviews behind the religious labels mean everything!

If a new friend tells me he is a Christian or a Buddhist or an atheist—I just nod my head and say something like, "That's interesting." I don't take what he says absolutely at face value; I take it with a grain of salt. I'm not calling him a liar; I'm just allowing my curiosity to be piqued. I might try to find out what he means. I start thinking, *What questions could I ask to help bring this person's real beliefs and assumptions (in other words, his worldview) out into the open? If I can figure out how to do that, I'll have a much better idea of where this person is coming from and how to share the gospel with him.*

MAKE WAY FOR DUCKLINGS

How can you figure out which worldview dominates a person's thinking? This is achievable if you're on the lookout for telltale signs of the six worldviews.

Let's apply some of our quacks-like-a-duck savvy to religions now. In each of the next sections, I'm going to cite several historical variations of that religion along with a worldview tag. I think you'll find some surprises. We'll put Designer Religion on the shelf for now, but later we'll devote an entire chapter to it in "Spirituals 'R' Us."

Let me also say that if you have minimal exposure to other religions or philosophies, this chapter could be hard to wade through. You might want to skip it and come back when you're more prepared.

Hinduism

Reaching back to its earliest stages perhaps four to five thousand years ago, Hinduism may have originated as a fertility religion, with a male fertility god (Shiva) and his many consorts. —Haunted

Most Hindus believe in many gods and perform many daily acts of worship and sacrifice to various gods and spirits. In India it is commonly said that there are thirty-three *lakhs* of gods (one lakh is one hundred thousand). —Haunted

A minority of Hindus are very philosophical and esoteric, promoting the idea that Brahma (or Brahman, both mean the same thing) is the ultimate uncreated and impersonal reality, and that everything is ultimately one with Brahma. —Omnipresent Supergalactic Oneness

Some Hindus choose one god among the many to whom to devote exclusive worship. This path is called Bhakti devotionalism. —A form of the Haunted worldview called henotheism

Buddhism

Siddhartha Gautama (about the sixth century B.C.) started out as an agnostic and a skeptic about the gods and goddesses of Hinduism. For the man who would become known as the Buddha, the question of whether God or the gods exist was irrelevant compared to the real issue of expanding the mind and consciousness. —WYSIWYG

Eventually, Siddhartha had an experience in meditation that he called enlightenment (*nippana* in Pali, *nirvana* in Sanskrit), in which he felt as if he was one with the universe and all distinctions erased. —Omnipresent Supergalactic Oneness

Siddhartha retained the bedrock assumptions of Hinduism: karma and reincarnation. —Omnipresent Supergalactic Oneness

Later, Buddhists held Siddhartha in such high regard that they elevated him to a godlike position and even worshiped him as a *Bodhisattva*. A *Bodhisattva* is someone who attains Nirvana but, instead of checking out of personal existence, stays available to aid meditators in their efforts. —Haunted

In some areas, Tantric Buddhism merges Buddhism with occult practices, seeking contact with spirits and gods of many types. —Haunted

Islam

The conventional wisdom about Islam is that it is in the same monotheistic stream as Judaism and Christianity. Some even think of Islam as
a kind of church denomination, like the Unitarian-Universalists. Actually,
it's more complicated than that. . . .

Islam did start off as a monotheistic movement in reaction against
rampant polytheism. —A movement away from the Haunted worldview

The monotheistic impulse can be attributed in part to the fact that
since we are created in God's image, the many selfish and competing
gods of polytheism fail to satisfy or correspond to our deepest spiritual
hunger. —Biblical (!)

There are significant connections to the Biblical worldview in Islam,
like belief in a high creator God, angels, demons, prophets, and Judgment Day. —Biblical (!)

However, Islam quickly veered away from the core messages of
Judaism and Christianity. The Koran accused Jews and Christians of cor-
rupting their scriptures. The god of Islam, Allah, displayed a different
character from the God of the Bible. Also, Islam promoted Muhammad
as "the seal of the prophets," thereby demoting Jesus and placing him
below Muhammad in stature. —Quasi-Biblical*

Islam explicitly denies that Jesus died on the cross for our sins (the
atonement), that He rose again from the dead (the resurrection), and
that He now sits at the right hand of the Father (the ascension)—events
that Christians consider the absolute Core of Christian faith.† —Quasi-
Biblical

Islam often is mixed with tribal and animistic cultures to produce
what anthropologists call "folk Islam." For example, in India, Muslims
and Hindus both visit the graves of Muslim and Hindu saints who have
died. At these graves mediums seek to contact the spirits of the departed

---

*Quasi-Biblical means intersecting with the Biblical worldview in some ways, but departing from it
substantially. Other religions and cults that try to appear as Biblical but are far removed from Biblical
faith are Mormonism, Jehovah's Witnesses, the Way, and the Children of God (also known as The
Family).

†The Muslim understanding is that we must pay for our own sins, therefore the cross is unnecessary.
Also, in Islam, God's prophets cannot be disgraced, so Judas was made to look like Jesus and was
crucified instead of Jesus (see the Koran 4.157). If Jesus didn't die on the cross, so the argument goes,
He couldn't have risen from the dead or been assigned a royal place at God's right hand, thus becoming "partners" with God (see Koran 10.66 and 42.21).

saints for healing and other favors. —Haunted

Some Muslim leaders (like the Baathists in Iraq and Syria) have adopted Marxism, Communism, and/or Fascism and interpret everything through those filters. Their culture is Islamic, but they cynically use the Islamic religion as a pretext to manipulate people politically. —WYSIWYG

Sufism, popular in India, Turkey, and the Balkans, is a pantheistic form of Islamic mysticism. —Omnipresent Supergalactic Oneness

Judaism

Judaism began as true revelation from God. —Biblical

> **Judaism began as true revelation from God.**

However, back in Bible days, the Jewish people had a very hard time coming to terms with God's basic message to them—to forsake all other gods and worship God alone, as stated clearly in the first commandment (Exodus 20:2–3) and the famous *Shema* ("Hear, O Israel: The Lord our God ... is one" Deuteronomy 6:4). The Bible and archaeology confirm that until the Babylonian exile (sixth century B.C.), the Israelites regularly reverted to pagan syncretism—worshiping God alongside of the other gods of the surrounding peoples. —Haunted

During the Hellenistic period in the Middle East after the death of Alexander the Great, a sizeable number of Jews adopted the ways, pagan religion, and culture of the Greeks. —Haunted

In the first century A.D., the Pharisees believed in the Bible, miracles, and the supernatural realm. —Biblical

Also in the first century A.D., the Sadducees rejected the supernatural beliefs of the Pharisees. —WYSIWYG

The person and message of Jesus created an entirely new group— Messianic Jews. —Biblical

Hundreds of years later in Jewish history, groups of Jews gravitated toward Kabbalah, a mystical interpretation of Judaism that accepted reincarnation and participated in occult practices. —Omnipresent Supergalactic Oneness

In the nineteenth and twentieth centuries, some nonreligious Jews adopted the materialism of Marx and Lenin. —WYSIWYG

Jews in Israel today are religiously divided. Some are secular (WYSIWYG); some are Orthodox (Biblical plus a lot of cultural stuff); some are Reformed (trying to adapt Judaism and the Biblical worldview to modern life); quite a few are attracted to mystical New Age religious movements,* including worship of "the goddess" (Omnipresent Supergalactic Oneness and Designer Religion). And a small but growing group are Messianic, having put their trust in Jesus as the promised Jewish Messiah and Savior of the world (Biblical).

Christianity

The church began as a sect of Judaism that believed Jesus to be the promised Jewish Messiah, the Savior of the world, and because of that belief reached out to non-Jews with the good news of the gospel. —Biblical

As Christianity spread to Europe and South America, the pre-Christian gods sometime found homes in the Catholic Church and were renamed as Catholic saints. —Haunted

Some forms of Christian mysticism have tended to drift off into pantheism. —Omnipresent Supergalactic Oneness

In the sixteenth century, the Protestant Reformation attempted to go back to the purity of the New Testament church. —Biblical

In the seventeenth and eighteenth centuries, many in the church elevated human reason to the position of highest authority, displacing the Bible and church tradition. —WYSIWYG

In the nineteenth century, German Protestantism mixed with idealism, a pantheistic worldview that believed God is equally in all religions. This produced radical criticism of the Bible and its miracles. —Omnipresent Supergalactic Oneness

In the twentieth century, some Christians blended Christianity with Marxism, Communism, Nazism, and Fascism, which resulted in mass

---

*See the *Watchman.org*'s profile on the New Age movement at *www.watchman.org/profile/nwagmpro.htm.*

slavery, mass murder, and two world wars. —WYSIWYG, Dueling Yodas, and Haunted

Also in the twentieth century, some Protestants and Catholics rejected monotheism and are openly promoting paganism in churches. —Haunted

Some Christians are much more concerned with making money and having a good time than in the advancing the gospel of the kingdom of God. —WYSIWYG

Paganism and High Paganism

Almost all peoples of the ancient world believed in many gods, known by many names. The gods, the spirits, and fate affected human life both with lows and highs. —Haunted

Even so, there was sometimes the recognition of the possibility of a singular high God behind all the other gods. He was seen as a "First Cause" of everything that exists, a static repository of ultimate values and truths. —Quasi-Biblical

By the time of Jesus, a type of high paganism (a name I use for paganism that gravitates toward monotheism) had evolved that was weary of low paganism and accepted the idea of one God. These high pagans took the old myths almost psychologically, as illustrations of the great potential and contradictory nature of humanity, not literally of the foibles of the gods. They wanted to be done with myths. —Quasi-Biblical

CAVEAT EMPTOR (LATIN FOR "LET THE BUYER BEWARE")

In our society, with tons of competing interpretations of what Christianity really is, and with the tolerance police telling us we should accept all religious expressions as valid, how do we avoid getting stung by religious con artists? Or by people who are sincere but sincerely wrong (from the perspective of the Biblical worldview, which we believe to be God's self-revelation)?

You have to develop some street smarts. Don't judge a book by its cover; don't judge a car by its body. A person might present his or her religious "credentials" for you, but those credentials don't mean squat compared to that person's controlling worldview! And remember that some forms of "Christianity" are fake and watered down, committed to worldviews that are actually alien and hostile to the gospel.

> **Remember that some forms of "Christianity" are fake and watered down.**

TAKING A TASTE TEST: GNOSTICISM

One of the first important challenges the early church faced was "Christian" Gnosticism. Gnosticism (from *gnosis*, "knowledge") was a form of Greek religious philosophy. When Gnostic thought encountered Christianity, it started using Christian terms and Scripture in Gnostic ways. The underlying worldview of Gnosticism didn't change; it just adapted its ideas to Christian terminology.

In the second and third centuries, the Christian-Gnostic blend was very popular, then went into decline. It never died out completely. Today Gnosticism is staging a comeback in those sectors of the church that don't have a good grip on the Biblical worldview.

Smells Fishy

There are many different kinds of Gnosticism, but a common theme is that spirit is good and matter is bad.

Let's follow the basic idea out. If spirit is good and matter is bad, then pure spirit is very good and the more physical something is the worse it is. This is the background for Gnostic misrepresentations of the God of the Bible. The Gnostics could not imagine pure, undefiled spirit-existence and light sullying itself in any way with material things. Horrors! Therefore, they reasoned, the God of the Bible was evil for having encumbered pure spirit-existence with corruptible matter. They labeled the Bible's God an inferior "Demiurge"—a foolish, prideful spirit several steps removed from pure spirit.

If Gnostics made the creator God of the Bible the bad guy, guess who became the good guy? (Puzzled? Just reverse the roles of Genesis 3 and you'll see what we're talking about.)

Since matter was bad, the Gnostics called the body the prison-house of the spirit. The practical application of teaching made the body and all its natural appetites evil. This led some Gnostics to forbid marriage and engage in extremely ascetic practices. The goal was to deny, denigrate, devalue, and punish the body in order to allow the spirit to be freed. Another Gnostic path was extreme indulgence in fleshly activities, ironically to purge the soul of its desire for physical things.

Notice: Here again we find the reversal of biblical values and a negation of what it means to live in God's image. The Bible teaches that creation is good and therefore the physical things that we want (hugs, food, sex, clothing) are not bad things in and of themselves but good things that need to be obtained in ways that bring about greater love between people and greater glory to God.

All Ashes to the Taste

In short, most (but not all) Gnostic systems are a form of Monism, which sees the physical world as illusion and inferior to the realm of pure spirit. Gnosticism denies core teachings of the Biblical worldview.

- Gnosticism denies that the physical, natural, created order was created by a good God and is itself good. (Genesis 1)
- Gnosticism denies that the physical world has value in and of itself and is never to be sneered at.
- Gnosticism denies that the physical world has been infected with and subjected to frustration, decay, and bondage by the moral choices humans make. (Genesis 3:17–19; Romans 8:19–21)
- Gnosticism overemphasizes the passages in the Bible about the physical world "passing away" (I Corinthians 7:21; I John 2:19); that it is like a garment that will be changed (Psalm 102:25–27; Hebrews 1:10–12); or that it will be destroyed by intense heat (2 Peter 3:10, 12).
- Gnosticism ignores or denies very strong biblical themes of our full redemption and our new bodies (I Corinthians 15:35–44; Romans

8:22–25) and glorious new heavens and a new earth (Isaiah 65:17, 66:22; 2 Peter 3:13) in which "there will be no more death or mourning or crying or pain, for the old order of things has passed away" (Revelation 21:4).

- Gnosticism misrepresents the Bible's balanced message: that the physical world is good, therefore our natural appetites are good—but they are not the *only* good. Our appetites must be subordinated to love.

- Almost all Gnostic systems have a ladder of secret initiations leading up to secret, mystical knowledge and powers; only a few get to become the elite "spirituals" who are vaunted as being better than merely human. The elite knowledge club idea goes directly against the open-to-all message of the gospel, the refusal of the New Testament to promote "other gospels" that detract from Christ, and the deep respect the Bible has for the common man and woman.

What is an adequate response to Gnosticism? Without going into a lot of detail, clearly the main thing is to stick to the Biblical worldview, especially the idea that the one true God is the Creator of heaven and earth.

Therefore, Christians should at the same time highly value the present world and yet not overvalue it. Jesus taught that we are to seek treasures in heaven, not things that can be stolen, rust, or fade (Matthew 6:19–21). But these heavenly treasures are made here and now through deeds of compassion and acts of wisdom in the real world as we know it.

Yes, the Biblical worldview puts a greater emphasis on what is eternal over what is temporary. But no, the Biblical worldview does not say that we are to somehow "check out" of the present world. We are to be fully engaged with it.

9 | THE POWER OF SAYING "I DON'T KNOW"

ait, hold on here. Is this a barbershop? Is this a barbershop? If we can't talk straight in a barbershop, then where
can we talk straight?

—Eddie in the movie *Barbershop* [1]

Some Christians think that representing Christian faith in the
barbershop (the marketplace of ideas) means you have to be a shining
star—an extroverted, magnetic personality who at the same time is a
quick-witted, sharp-tongued, rapid-fire debating machine. They have
this idea that you have to have your act totally together *and* know all
the answers to objections of Christian faith really well before you can
begin to speak out for Christ at all.

For a long time I bought into that mentality. I was shy and often
didn't know what to say about regular things, let alone spiritual ones. As
far as quick with the wit or tongue—I'd think of "quick" comebacks days
or weeks later.

As you can imagine, I was somewhat reluctant to be "out there"
with my faith.

But being a public representative of the Christian faith doesn't mean
it's up to you to be the star, or to make the other positions (or people)
look stupid. Our call is not to demonstrate how great we are or to prove

beyond the shadow of any intellectual doubt that Christianity is superior. It is simply to proclaim the truth in Christ as best as we can with who we are. We are to do it humbly, both with our lives and our words.

It's okay to say "I don't know."

Saint Francis said, "Proclaim the gospel at all times, and when necessary use words."[2] By this he was not saying words were unnecessary—he was saying our words have much more credibility if our lives back up our words. Pope John Paul II said this: "Proclaim the truth and let error destroy itself."[3] His point was that it is not necessary to know all the fine ins and outs of arguments—what is necessary is to allow God's truth to be heard by people. It's up to them what they do with it.

Along these lines, I'd like to release you right now from feeling you have to be able to instantly slay every dragon that rears its head against the gospel. There is tremendous freedom and power in admitting that you're not "all that," that knowledge doesn't begin and end with you. What's going to speak louder to most people is your joy in the Lord, your gratefulness for God's goodness in your life, your sense of destiny and purpose to glorify God in everything you do. In the Old Testament, God told Israel:

> A horse is a vain hope for deliverance; despite all its great strength it cannot save. (Psalm 33:17)

> The horse is made ready for the day of battle, but victory rests with the Lord. (Proverbs 21:31)

> Woe to those who go down to Egypt for help, who rely on horses.... (Isaiah 31:1)

Their "horses" were literal war-horses. Ours are intellectual arguments. We are not to rely on "horses" but on God and on His Holy Spirit, and on the inherent power of God's word to speak directly to our souls. Jesus said,

> No one can come to me unless the Father who sent me draws him.... (John 6:44)

> When [the Holy Spirit] comes, he will convict the world of guilt in regard to sin and righteousness and judgment. (John 16:8)

The fact is, we have no control over others. God can use us in bringing the good news to people; but God is the One who draws people; God's Holy Spirit is the One who convinces them that they are sinners, unrighteous, and in need of forgiveness.

Having all the right answers doesn't guarantee that anyone is going to be convinced the gospel is true. There's a whole spiritual dynamic going on—people are resisting God, looking for any excuse to keep God at arm's length. Sure there are some legitimate questions, but these questions are often just excuses to avoid dealing with God. As Mark Twain is reputed to have said, "It's not what I don't know about religion that bothers me; it's what I do know!"

> **People are resisting God, looking for any excuse to keep God at arm's length.**

And the fact is, there are always going to be tough questions that are really hard to answer, whether we are believers or not.

- What about those who have never heard the gospel?
- Is Gandhi (and by extension, every "good" person who dies without becoming a Christian) in hell?
- What about the guy who makes a profession of faith right before he dies? How can that be real?
- How could God condemn any human creature that He created in love?
- Why is there such terrible suffering in the world?

There are approaches to all of these questions. But there's no perfect, slam-dunk answer that will satisfy everyone. Very possibly, even in the afterlife, you're never going to have it "all figured out." The Bible says, "The secret things belong to the Lord our God" (Deuteronomy 29:29a). There are lots of imponderables. Faith says that all the greatest mysteries converge and are solved in God, not in our limited rational intellects. It's not about our intellectual prowess.

But the Bible also says that there are "things revealed" by God that we can take to the bank: "The things revealed belong to us and to our children forever" (Deuteronomy 29:29b). Everything doesn't have to be secret. He is trustworthy. He is faithful. He is good. He is not aloof. He has proven His love for us in Christ. We don't have to suffer alone.

Try to keep the emphasis on how the other worldviews limit God, as opposed to the Biblical worldview in which God is free to act. Try to point to the idea that only in the Biblical worldview does it make sense to say, "God loves you." You won't answer every question. You don't have to. Just come to the barbershop and be part of the conversation.

10 | GENESIS V. THE HAUNTED WORLD

Imagine yourself at a campfire somewhere in the Fertile Crescent some thirty-five hundred years ago. This boomerang-shaped area goes all the way from the eastern coast of the Mediterranean Sea to the Persian Gulf. A drama troupe from the temple in the big city nearby has come to your village. Everyone in your extended family, clan, and tribe, from oldest to youngest, has turned out. By torch and firelight, drum and flute, costumes and a few props, the players begin to speak and act out the cosmic story of creation. . . .

Before there was anything else, there was only the primal ocean of restless, churning, formless chaos. The beginnings of everything to come were contained in her.

After eons of time, the sun god, born from his own sheer will-power, emerged from the primeval sea. He looked around for a place to stand, but as far as he could see, in every direction there was only water. Taking some of the watery chaos in his hands, he squeezed and squeezed until he created a dry hill on which to stand. On this very spot a glorious temple would later be erected to honor . . . him!

Now, the sun god was lonely. He wanted to create more gods, but he had no partner. So he mated with his own shadow. He then gave birth to many gods by spitting or vomiting them out!

The actor playing the sun god really hams it up, and the entire village laughs. Now the story takes a more somber turn. ...

After a while, the sun god had become an insomniac. He was losing sleep because of all the noise of his children and grandchildren. It was chaos—a terrible racket. Nothing he could think of would quiet them down!

The sun god decided he'd take care of the problem once and for all—by killing all the younger gods! Finally he'd have some peace and quiet. He could almost taste his sleep.

But when Chaos, the younger gods' mother, heard of his plan, she opposed him. She mothered a brood of grim monsters to fight the sun god.

Meanwhile, one of the younger gods went on a quest. He learned magic and the secret occult arts, becoming a champion warrior with magnificent powers. In fact, he became far stronger than all the other gods. This warrior god then allied with his father the sun god against his mother, Chaos. A terrible war ensued. Marshaling all the forces of nature against Chaos, the warrior god defeated her in mortal combat. The victor split her body in two: one half became the sky, the other half became the earth. He smashed her skull, and out of her eyes flowed the great rivers.

Although the older viewers are familiar with the story, the audience is silenced by the intense violence. After a musical interlude, the players now strike a different emotional note.

After all the gore, the sun god's blood lust was slaked. He decided he wouldn't kill the younger gods after all. As a result, eventually there were hundreds of gods responsible for everything in the world—from mountains, trees, and rivers to crafts like beer brewing, pottery making, and iron smelting. And so, for a time, the gods were one big happy family.

Well, not perfectly happy ...

You see, the gods and goddesses actually had to work the land with their own hands to make a living. Farming the land to grow crops to eat was hot, dirty, and exhausting. Some gods and goddesses dug the fields and planted the crops. Others channeled water to the fields. Still others kept the ditches clear of weeds. They divided the labor, but it was still backbreaking.

And the gods and goddesses were not happy. They started fussing and fighting. They were grumpy most of the time. So after much discussion, the wisest and cleverest god among them suggested that they should make creatures who would work the land so they wouldn't have to. The gods and goddesses would finally be able to kick back and relax.

The other gods and goddesses thought this was a great idea. So the wise and clever god got some river clay and made some humans. He breathed into the clay models and they came alive! But he strictly limited how long they would live. Only the gods and goddesses would live forever.

Immediately the gods and goddesses forced the humans to work the land. Now it was humans who channeled water from the rivers to the fields, tilled the soil, planted the seeds, and harvested the crops. Every day humans slaved away for the gods, providing the gods with mounds of food and drink. For the time being, the gods and goddesses were happy.

Okay, we'll leave the storytellers and actors now. They'll go late into the night with this story and several others. I just wanted to have you think for a while how people thought of their place in the world five or six thousand years ago.

In the meantime I have to confess: This story is not in pure form. I have joined together bits and pieces of the earliest written creation myths from the Egyptian, Babylonian, Sumerian, and Ugaritic cultures. If you want to know the particular stories, you'll have to do some research on your own. And if you do, you'll see that while the personalities and details differ from culture to culture, there are also some common themes:

- Everything comes from chaos.
- Chaos is a constant threat to human life.
- The world as we know it is the result of an exceptionally violent cosmic struggle.
- The various gods and goddesses have agendas that, for their own interests and safety, humans need to take into account.

Before we move on, I'd like to insert this disclaimer: When I talk about the ancient gods "doing" this or that, please understand that there may be a difference, even a big difference, between these actions as actual events and these actions as ancient peoples' interpretations of the spiritual realm. All I am trying to do is tell the story *from within* the perspective of the Haunted worldview. Therefore, don't always expect me to insert qualifiers like "considered to be," "regarded as," "perceived," "allegedly," "supposedly," and other dodges.

A THREE-TIER UNIVERSE

The worldview of the ancient Near East—what we are calling the Haunted worldview—oozed with the supernatural. It was a mythological world, enchanted with all kinds of seen and unseen spiritual beings.

People in the ancient Near East experienced life as a three-tier universe. The top tier was the heavens, the realm of the major celestial gods and goddesses. The middle tier was earth, inhabited by lesser gods and spirits, people, plants, birds, insects, and animals. The lower tier was the underworld, populated by the ghostly spirits of the departed dead, demons, and monsters. In an age before MTV and the Internet, the stories of the gods, demons, ghosts, and monsters were as well-known as is the news about celebrities today. Let's break this down a little more.

Clash of the Titans

As we have said, the heavens were the domain of the gods and their consorts (the goddesses). If there was a high god, he was seen as utterly remote and unapproachable by humans; he was aloof, uncaring, unconcerned, uninvolved. Sometimes this aloof/remote idea was expressed as impersonal forces. People were puppets dangling on strings of inevitable destiny or jerked by the pulls and twists of the planets (astrology). At other times the aloof/remote idea was expressed through personalized "fates" and "furies" who could quickly and devastatingly turn people's lives upside down.

The heavens provided a stage for cosmic soap opera, drama, romance, farce, action, horror, and so on. Boy, those gods were messed up! They sure provided plenty of drama to life on earth. You couldn't ignore them. The barrier between the heavenly and earthly was very thin, like a permeable cell wall. The gods, although their homes were in the heavens, would suddenly appear like bulls in a china shop, ready to play around or to stir up trouble.

The top tier was reserved for the major celestial spirit personalities who guided the universe. Humans' lives hung in the balance, completely dependent on these gods who controlled the sun, moon, planets, eclipses, and stars as well as the seasons, rain, storms, floods, lightning, and winds. Mountains and temples, which "touched" the sky, were sacred places where people could make contact with these beings.

The sky gods were not all-powerful. They were fickle, dangerous, capricious, self-interested, and afflicted with the same petty jealousies and weaknesses that trouble humans. They competed with each other for supremacy, recognition, and power.

Earth and sky were sometimes seen as created from the bodies of gods defeated and killed in a primordial war. Perhaps their myths reflected the brutal wars of the time.

Every Rock and Tree and Creature . . . Has a Name

The middle tier was the world as humans experience it. This realm was also seen as chock-full of spirits. The ancients believed spirits were all around and very easy to offend. Instead of thinking of nature around them as purely impersonal (as we are likely to), the ancients believed that spirits animated hills, mountains, valleys, rocks, forests, trees, bodies of water, rivers, wild animals, domestic animals—even birds, fish, and insects. Spiritual power was personal and everywhere.

The societies of the ancient Near East were agrarian-based and depended on a fertile land for survival. Therefore, fertility religion was widely practiced. Fertility gods were thought to die (or be banished) from the earth during the dry fall and winter seasons and come back to life (or out of banishment) during the spring and summer. Every year humans helped rejuvenate the earth and sky through fertility rituals, where priests would perform acts on certain objects hoping to ensure the ongoing health and multiplying of flocks and herds, the abundance of vegetation and crops, and of course human procreation.[1]

Connected with fertility religion were grand temples of sacred prostitution and yearly festivals in which the king would have sex with a sacred prostitute, be symbolically killed, and then be brought back to life. Sometimes a male representing the king would actually be killed as an offering to the fertility gods.

The various gods were seen to have limited powers over certain localities, geographical jurisdictions, or tribes (for example, see Judges 11:24). These local, geographical, or tribal deities affected the fortunes of social groups. These gods or spirits could give favors, aid in war, or bring famine and blight. Also, minor spirits—like the trickster spirits, the "evil eye," sprites, fairies, djinni,* and daemons† found in cultures the world over—caused a lot of mischief. Furthermore, rulers and kings were often considered to be gods or demigods (part god, part man).

For good or ill, the rest of humanity was at the mercy of the whims of these competing spiritual forces. Men and women were stuck in a universe that—without rhyme or reason—frustrated their hopes for a decent and happy life.

Religion was a way to cope with the uncertainties and dangers of life. Public religion was very important. Each major city housed a temple that was the seat of a major god; the city's leaders had to keep their patron deity happy. Anger the wrong god or goddess and the entire pantheon of gods would be breathing down their necks. Woe to the city that did not properly satisfy its patron deities!

Shamans‡ navigated or "floated" between this world and the supernatural. They practiced magic, interpreted omens, and conducted rituals of divination (fortune-telling), sorcery (spell-casting), and witchcraft (seeking to get spirits to act in certain ways). The secret knowledge of the shamans and priests was highly valued because people felt as if the world were a hostile and unfriendly place, spiritually speaking. The more costly the rituals, the more influence the rituals were supposed to have with the spirits. Some rituals included the most costly sacrifice of all—human sacrifice.

---

*According to Islamic mythology, the djinni (jinni, jinns) are lesser spirits than angels who can appear as humans or animals and influence people for good or evil.

†According to Greek mythology, a daemon was a lesser god who might animate a place or be the "genius" of a person.

‡People considered adept at contacting the spirit world, whether those spirits are the departed dead or other kinds of spirits.

They're Creepy and They're Kooky

The spirits of the dead, monsters, and god-guards inhabited the third tier—the underworld. The departed dead were the "spirits under the earth" because their bodies had been buried or put into caves. Some of the departed dead did not go quietly; they would roam the earth causing mischief as ghosts. The rest were locked away in the prison-house of the dead and could never leave.

The underworld (Hades in Greek; Sheol in Hebrew) was a place of shadows, of dreamlike sleep, of relative immobility, of reduced emotion. It was a dismal place. There are many famous stories that have come down to us in mythology (such as the stories of Orpheus, Demeter, Isis) of the living going to the underworld to try to rescue loved ones from the grip of death. Their ventures were always poignantly unsuccessful.

Unlike a lot of people today who look at the dead as nonexistent, the ancients believed departed ancestors were an ongoing part of the social order. To not honor them would be to offend them; to offend them would be to risk their wrath. People also believed the ancestors had the power to impart blessings if properly honored.

> **The ancients believed departed ancestors were an ongoing part of the social order.**

Whether due to war, plague, pestilence, famine, disease, earthquakes, volcanic eruptions, floods, or just plain old age, everyone would eventually go to the underworld and join the totemic ancestors of clans and tribes: great hunters and warriors; wise men and women as well as fools; the rich and poor; the good, the bad, and the ugly. There was no escape.

TWILIGHT OF THE GODS

The Bible was not written in a vacuum. It was written *into* the Haunted world of the ancient Near East. The fabric and contours of this worldview were familiar to everyone. It supplied the context for the assumptions and questions people had about life. It was the furniture in the room.

What was the Bible's message for these people? The basic idea is that the gods are on their way out and Yahweh is asserting his rightful authority on the earth. Let's see how the first chapter of the Bible gives us a mother lode of insight as we pay attention to the author, the audience, and the clues left behind.

According to scholars, the Bible, Jesus, and Christian tradition, Moses was the lead author of the first five books of the Bible. Just as Lincoln was the Great Emancipator of the slaves during the American Civil War, Moses was the Great Liberator of the Israelites from slavery in Egypt. Moses wrote these books sometime after the Israelites' Great Escape from Egypt (the theme of the book of Exodus) and during the forty years of wilderness wandering (the theme of the book of Numbers) before they entered Canaan, the Promised Land.

Maybe you saw the movie *The Prince of Egypt,* which was loosely based on the book of Exodus. Moses, a Hebrew raised in the royal palace in Egypt by Pharaoh's daughter, was given the best education money could buy. He learned the wisdom, religion, and customs of the Egyptians. His training would certainly have included learning the wisdom, religions, and customs of the nations Egypt came in contact with. He grew up surrounded by the Haunted worldview.

The primary audience of Genesis was the Hebrew tribes that followed Moses out of Egypt along with the Egyptians who in faith had joined the Hebrews (the "mixed multitude" of Exodus 12:38 KJV), the same group that was completely out of control in an orgy of drunkenness and carousing when Moses returned from Mount Sinai with the Ten Commandments (Exodus 32:15–19).

The writing of Genesis was a way of chronicling the Hebrews' history and of setting forth in writing the key events in their national memory. It was a book of remembrance for later retelling and re-experiencing what God had done for them in actual living history. Genesis became the first book of the Torah.* The Torah (also known as "the Law") set forth the covenant relationship between God and Israel—that is, how Israel was to worship and how Israel was to be different from all the

---

*In Jewish tradition, *Torah* means (1) the first five books of the Bible, written by Moses; (2) the Mosaic law found in the first five books of the Bible; (3) the Hebrew Bible itself; and (4) the tradition that developed out of the Hebrew Bible and the experience of the Jewish people.

surrounding peoples. If all these events happened today, we might name the Torah *The Basics.*

Genesis is not just for Israel. We also are its audience. It is a book for all humanity and all time. It is intended to be the book that explains where the human family came from and to provide "the basics" for all who would come to believe in and follow the Biblical worldview. Even so, we need to at least try to hear the message as the ancient Hebrews would have heard it.

Genesis I gives us many clues to set the context of the whole Bible. In fact, Genesis I is the first salvo in an extended Bible-long argument against the pagan, polytheistic, and pluralistic set of beliefs of the peoples that surrounded Israel. As an opening assault, Moses doesn't beat around the bush; he comes straight to the point. There are many ways—both obvious and subtle—in which Moses crafted Genesis I to directly challenge the Haunted worldview of the ancients. Let's look at a few of the most enlightening.

1. You Gotta Serve Somebody

Moses knew the many myths and legends of gods who emerged out of nature, were born, or had at some time not existed. As we read earlier, there were even creation stories that told how the earth and sky were made out of the dead body of a defeated god. When Moses wrote, "In the beginning God created the heavens and the earth" (Genesis I:I), he was completely overturning conventional religious wisdom. He was saying that the one true God always existed; that before there was anything else, there was God; that God doesn't owe His existence to anything or anyone. God alone is the self-existent One. All the gods of the peoples were merely created, contingent, finite, contentious beings. On the contrary, the God of the Bible is totally unique and powerful.

Contrary to other stories about creation, Moses denied that the universe was eternal. God did not come from nature, nor did He exist with nature in the beginning. God preceded the universe and created it separate from himself.

2. Great Expectations

Moses knew that the surrounding people assumed that the high god, if there was one, was emotionally remote and relatively uninterested in affairs on earth. People had to make a big effort to get the high god's attention, if it was even possible.

Moses' repeated use of the literary pattern of "And God said" (ten times in chapter 1) shows an entirely different perspective. By speaking repeatedly into His creation, God gives notice to humanity for all time that (1) He is actively and intimately involved in his world, not just as Creator but as Sustainer; (2) He reserves the right as Creator of the universe to act in history and intervene in human affairs as He sees fit—whether through hidden ways, prophecy, miracles, or even misfortunes—whether we like it or not; (3) He is not powerless—God always has the ability and freedom to act, even if we don't understand what He's doing; and (4) God is verbal when He wants to be—He can speak clearly and with uncontested authority into His world.

To make a long story short: The Bible creates great expectations because God can do stuff.

3. That's So Random—Not

Moses knew that many people around him believed that watery chaos was the origin of all existence. But Moses wrote "In the beginning *God* created" and "the *Spirit of God hovered over* the face of the deep" ("the deep" very likely referring to chaos's primeval waters) and "'Let there be an expanse between the waters to separate water from water.' ... And it was so" (Genesis 1:6–7). In writing these words, Moses was throwing down the gauntlet to all worldviews—past, present, and future—that would suggest that ultimate reality is randomness, disorder, or chaos. In its place, Moses is telling us that the universe was created by a personal God, by a God of design and order and beauty, even if we might not necessarily discern that order with

An impersonal, chaotic universe cannot love you. Only a personal God can.

our minds. An impersonal, chaotic universe cannot love you. Only a personal God can.

4. A Need-to-Know Basis

Moses knew that people were very curious about the gods and had a story for every curious thought. We saw earlier the creation myth in which the high god was alone and lonely and had to create other gods by having sex with himself. When we compare this common story with the Bible, there are two outstanding differences: (1) There is no hint in the Genesis account that God was ever lonely or needy like the major gods, goddesses, and godlings of the surrounding peoples; and (2) It is startling how little Genesis 1 tells us about the "how" of creation. The point is, Genesis 1 tells about the "Who" of creation. We don't have to know everything. We don't have to have it all figured out. We don't have to make stuff up to fill in the gaps in our knowledge base. It ought to be enough simply to know the one true God.

5. Goodnight, Moon

Calling upon the names of gods and spirits in the spirit world is an act of great significance in occult magic. It was also of great significance in the ancient world. People everywhere assumed that behind the powers of nature were spirits with names, not just impersonal forces. Understandably, the sun and the moon were the principal sky gods in the ancient world. In Genesis 1:16a Moses could easily have called the sun and moon by their names, but he didn't. He called them the "two great lights—the greater light to govern the day and the lesser light to govern the night" (Genesis 1:16). He left the major gods of the sun and moon unnamed. In that simple act he demoted the celestial powers and over-turned the entire cosmology of the ancient world! He was telling his readers that whatever powers the greatest spirits in the spirit world may have had, they are nothing compared to the one true God, the Creator of everything. Therefore, we are to no longer call upon the names of any nature spirits. Rather, we are to worship and call upon the name of the Lord of Creation alone!

6. He Calls Them Each By Name*

Moses was well aware that the people of his time rarely made a significant decision in their lives without first consulting an astrologer. Ancient people believed that the stars and planets were gods who significantly influenced affairs on earth.

In the ancient world, with no light pollution from cities, on a clear, dark, moonless night, a sharp-eyed person could see maybe two thousand stars, plus the shimmering dusty streaks of the Milky Way. It would have been an awe-inspiring sight, but nothing compared to our views into deep space with the Hubble telescope. We now know there are billions of stars in our galaxy and billions of galaxies!

Notice what Moses says about the stars in the throwaway line, "He also made the stars" (Genesis 1:16b). By so casually mentioning the stars, Moses shows that God alone should get all the glory; He won't be sharing it with any two-bit space interlopers.

7. The Image Is Everything

In a world where the only humans that had a guaranteed dignity or worth were royalty and those favored by them, the Bible lifts up the common man and woman. The Bible says to warriors, merchants, farmers, artisans, slaves—rich and poor alike—that you have innate dignity and worth because you are created in God's image. This amazing passage strikes an irreversible blow against tyranny and injustice, against women being treated as second-class citizens, against racism, slavery, and a host of other social ills.

By contrast, in the Haunted worldview people are the mere slaves of the gods. The gods alone have dignity, and they don't have much of that if you look at their squabbles and how they disgracefully acted.

The "image of God" passage also says to each of us that individually we are important and valuable to God. It says that we never again have to see ourselves as alone in a hostile, uncaring world. This is a revolutionary, life-affirming, liberating idea that has untold ramifications. It is a message that makes sense in any culture.

---

*Psalm 147:4 declares, "He determines the number of the stars and calls them each by name."

Not only this, but in the Bible, men and women equally display God's image. Woman is not on some inferior level to man. This totally contradicts the Haunted worldview, almost all ancient cultures, and many cultures today that give women lower value than men.

And if we look closely at Genesis I, over and over it says, "And it was good." The things God creates are good! That includes you and me.

In short, in the Biblical worldview, no longer are humans at the mercy of unfriendly gods and spirits. Instead, we are created by a good God who has our best interests at heart. He loves us, invests us with dignity and value as human beings, and gives us freedom to follow Him. What a wonderful purpose!

Well, we could go on. I encourage you to use your imagination to compare the creation myth at the beginning of this chapter with Genesis I. See what insights you can come up with.

LET THE BIBLE SPEAK FOR ITSELF!

One of the most important rules for Bible study is context, context, context! The point is to let the text speak for itself! Don't try to impose meanings that the text doesn't support. In most cases, the better you understand the human author's intent, the closer you will be to the Divine Author's intent.

Clearly, the intent of Genesis I is to focus our attention like a laser beam on God the Creator. Now notice, as a twenty-first-century reader, what Genesis I doesn't do and what it does do very well.

Big Fish Stories

There are scholars and other readers who treat the Bible like fishermen's stories about "the one that got away." They lump the biblical stories together with ancient sky myths about gods throwing bears up into the sky, resulting in constellations. They assume that since ancient polytheism and the Bible came from the same cultural basin, they are primitive, backward, and dismissable.

But while the Biblical worldview accepts some Haunted worldview assumptions, it drastically modifies the Haunted worldview's three-tier model of the universe.

1. The supernatural realm is real, but there's only one true God who deserves worship.
2. Spirits both human and nonhuman are acknowledged, but rituals devoted to them, contacting them as independent beings, or otherwise striking deals with them is forbidden.
3. In Christian teaching, a future heaven and hell take the place of the underworld, thus radically modifying whatever goes on in the lower tier.

Angels in the Outfield

As we have seen, the Haunted worldview and the Biblical worldview share some beliefs. Both the Haunted worldview and the Bible accept that the natural and the supernatural realms are real and that the supernatural realm can burst into the natural.

This doesn't mean we have to believe every far-fetched story about angels that comes down the pike. But the Bible does recognize that there are various gods and spirits, principalities and powers apart from God (Romans 8:38; Ephesians 6:12 KJV). The Bible even adopts the metaphorical terminology of a three-tiered universe, using "high" and "the heavens" for the abode of God and the activity of angels (Isaiah 57:15; Psalm 89:6–7) and "under the earth" (Philippians 2:10) to speak of the realm of the dead. We don't need to take the "up" and "down" language absolutely literally to realize that the Haunted worldview and the Biblical worldview are each avowedly supernatural. The difference is in the nature of those spirits and who is to be worshiped.

Not a Science Textbook

Some people say science proves the Bible while others say science disproves it. What does the Bible actually say to science? This is a big question, and I can only make a few comments here.

First, since science had not yet been invented, the purpose of Genesis 1 was not to confirm or disconfirm any particular scientific theories. The burning issue of Moses' day was not whether the sun goes around the earth, nor to harmonize a six-day creation with modern geology, nor to refute Darwin's theory, nor to trash the Big Bang.

Second, focusing your attention on science in the Bible is like going to the circus and spending all your time watching the bearded lady or the two-headed taxidermic calf—morbidly fascinating, to be sure, but nothing compared to the skills and thrills under the big top. Let's try to make sure we don't get so absorbed in some sideshow that we miss the main event—what the original setting, author, audience, and intended message is about.

Third, let's focus on what the Bible focuses on. The Bible is more interested in giving us the Who than the how of creation; it wants much more to explain the meaning of our existence as relationship with God than to provide precise scientific explanations of Bible events. Genesis 1 shows us *a better way of thinking and feeling about God.* God is not chaos, nor does He owe His existence—nor do we owe ours—to chaos and randomness. The universe owes its existence to a personal God who has always been there since even before "the beginning." Whatever your personal theory about how to fit science and faith together, it was God who started it, God who brought it about, God who brought it to fruition, and God who sustains it—and God who gets the glory! He is the Infinite, Almighty, Personal, and Good God.

> Thine, O Lord, is the greatness, and the power, and the glory, and the victory, and the majesty: for all that is in the heaven and in the earth is thine; thine is the kingdom, O Lord, and thou art exalted as head above all. (1 Chronicles 29:11 KJV)

11 | 101 WAYS TO KILL GOD

Have you not heard of that madman who lit a lantern in the bright morning hours, ran to the market place, and cried incessantly: "I seek God! I seek God!"?—As many of those who did not believe in God were standing around just then, he provoked much laughter. Has he got lost? asked one. Did he lose his way like a child? asked another. Or is he hiding? Is he afraid of us? Has he gone on a voyage? emigrated?—Thus they yelled and laughed.

The madman jumped into their midst and pierced them with his eyes. "Whither is God?" he cried; "I will tell you. We have killed him—you and I. All of us are his murderers. But how did we do this? How could we drink up the sea? Who gave us the sponge to wipe away the entire horizon? What were we doing when we unchained this earth from its sun? Whither is it moving now? Whither are we moving? Away from all suns? Are we not plunging continually? Backward, sideward, forward, in all directions? Is there still any up or down? Are we not straying, as through an infinite nothing? Do we not feel the breath of empty space? Has it not become colder? Is not night continually closing in on us? Do we not need to light lanterns in the morning? Do we hear nothing as yet of the noise of the gravediggers who are burying God? Do we smell nothing as yet of the divine decomposition? Gods, too, decompose. God is dead. God remains dead. And we have killed him."

—"The Parable of the Madman," Friedrich Nietzsche[1]

Take a moment to let this parable written in the nineteenth century sink in. Read it again. Muse on the multiple ironies. Appreciate the power of the language.

Normally we think of prophets as people speaking for God or in the name of God. Nietzsche, on the other hand, was a prophet for atheism. He was the first one to see clearly where Europe was heading—to the culture's wholesale abandonment of God and the church. Nietzsche wasn't just saying that the idea of God in Western civilization was dead; he was saying God had never existed.

Nietzsche wasn't horsing around. He was deadly serious. And far from mourning this future turn of events, he reveled in them. For Nietzsche, God had come and gone, and as far as he was concerned, good riddance. In his thinking, now man could finally be free to live passionately to his fullest potential.

> **For Nietzsche, God had come and gone, and as far as he was concerned, good riddance.**

Nietzsche has cast a long shadow over many European and American intellectuals. If you want to understand the movers and shakers in Western culture, you just can't ignore this guy.

So what were Nietzsche's clues? What did he see that others missed? Why has Europe undergone the titanic cultural shift from Christendom—a thousand-plus-year culture in which Christianity and Christian thinking permeated all of life and all branches of knowledge—to a European Union whose proposed constitution refuses even to mention the role Christianity has played in its history?

A HITCHHIKER'S GUIDE TO ATHEISM

Wait a minute, you might say. What's the big gee whiz? There have always been people who have disbelieved in God (or the gods).

And if you said that, you'd be partly right. Historically, the world-views of naturalism, materialism, and atheism have appeared in:

- *Early Buddhism,* which shunned gods and priestcraft, focusing attention instead on human psychology and the development of the human mind.*
- *The Ionian Materialists,* early Greek thinkers who rejected mythology and religious explanations for things. These men believed the essential "stuff" of the universe to be physical and material.
- *Hedonism* (also called Epicureanism), which is about maximizing pleasure and minimizing pain as the highest good, since this physical world is all there is.
- *Stoicism,* which is about developing as the most noble course of action an attitude of indifference to pain or pleasure, since events in this physical world (the only known world) are unpredictable.
- *Plain old unbelief in God* (see Psalms 14 and 53).

But Nietzsche wasn't concerning himself with these beliefs so much as with two sets of utterly opposed understandings: the Medieval Synthesis, which had laid the foundations for Western civilization, and the Radical Enlightenment, which ferociously sought to tear down those foundations.

THE MEDIEVAL SYNTHESIS

From the early church fathers (Christian pastors and leaders from the second through the fourth centuries) to the beginning of modern science (the eighteenth century), Christian thinkers and artists were often comfortable borrowing from the mythology and philosophy of the Greeks and Romans and setting them side-by-side with the stories and

---

*You may recall reading Hermann Hesse's *Siddhartha,* required reading in many high school literature classes. It's a well-written story about the life and thinking of Siddhartha Gautama, later known as the Buddha ("great one").

teachings of the Bible. Gradually and carefully they worked out a way of looking at the world that covered all of life and knowledge.

The illustration titled "All Branches of Knowledge" indicates the breadth of this enterprise.* Language occupies the central position because all other fields of knowledge depend upon human language. Without words and grammar you can't have a knowledge base, you can't bring forth or disprove theories, and you can't even have a decent argument. (Mathematics occupies a similar position in the sciences.) Emanating from the center are the various branches of knowledge. In the Medieval Synthesis all branches of knowledge were governed by God, with the church (for better or worse) playing the role as mediator of truth.

ALL BRANCHES OF KNOWLEDGE

Here I want to make an important point: Many people equate the Medieval Synthesis with the Biblical worldview and with Christian faith.

---

*A caution: The breakdown here isn't the only or perhaps even the best way to divide up all areas of knowledge, but it adequately serves the purposes of this chapter.

This is a mistake. The Medieval Synthesis was not and is not the Biblical worldview, but rather it is *a rough approximation of the Biblical worldview based on the experience and knowledge of people at the time.* Looking back on it from the perspective of the twenty-first century, we can see both its pluses and minuses.

On the minus side, it was pre-scientific, believing the earth to be the center of the universe. It also overvalued class and hereditary bloodlines. It made too much room for slavery, trial by ordeal, anti-Semitism, the Inquisition, and wars of religious conquest. At times it fell in love with political power. Tolerance was not its long suit.

On the plus side, the Medieval Synthesis preserved some very important aspects of the Biblical worldview. God was creator of heaven and earth. The world was ordered, with God as the designer. God cared for people and listened to their prayers. The Medieval Synthesis respected the Bible, the church, and Christian tradition. It had serious problems, but it also got some major things right.

SCHOOLS THAT ROCKED

About three hundred years ago, an intellectual movement called the Enlightenment began chipping away at the foundations of the Medieval Synthesis. It started small, with some modest tweaking of accepted theories, but ended up really rocking "the Man" (the Roman Catholic Church).

The Enlightenment wanted to overthrow superstition, to unshackle human reason and apply it to all branches of knowledge. The goal was to arrive at certainty in knowledge—rather than just accepting things as true merely on the basis of speculation, tradition, or authority (whether the authorities were Aristotle and Plato or the church fathers).

But like the religions we studied three chapters back, the Enlightenment was not one huge block of granite (as is often taught), as if a single frame of mind motivated all participants. Analyzing it from the perspective of worldviews, there were actually two Enlightenments: the Glory-to-God Enlightenment and the Radical Enlightenment.

The Glory-to-God Enlightenment

[Cue: light classical music.] The Glory-to-God Enlightenment was led by scientists, many of them Christians, who sought to learn about nature's God by discovering nature's laws. The Glory-to-God Enlightenment reinforced the Medieval Synthesis, forged over the preceding thousand years, bringing together faith and reason, and recognizing God's order and design in all areas of life. However, the Glory-to-God scientists sometimes had pitched battles with the church. In one infamous example, the Inquisition accused Galileo of heresy (no light matter, considering that the Inquisitors could sanction the confiscation of one's property, enforce imprisonment, and commit torture or death) for claiming, against what the holy church taught, that the earth orbited the sun.* But the Glory-to-God Enlightenment operated within the framework of the Biblical worldview.

Eternal Sunshine of the Spotless Rational Mind

[Cue: dark, forboding music.] The Radical Enlightenment—the branch of the Enlightenment that Nietzsche celebrated—was led by thinkers who didn't just want to break reason out of jail. They wanted to make reason the sheriff of all knowledge. The Radical Enlightenment deputized each and every intellectual discipline as a posse ready to hunt down any vestiges of the Medieval Synthesis and to capture God, dead or alive.

I want you to get a feel for the immense, all-encompassing impact the Radical Enlightenment has had on our culture. It doesn't just surface in esoteric salons—it's everywhere in the arts, the sciences, and the humanities. Unless you have blinders on, you can't escape its reach or influence.

The Radical Enlightenment has had a long run as the dominant worldview in Western colleges and universities: a good couple hundred years in Europe, a little less than a hundred in America. The academy— meaning the college and university culture—feeds most future leaders into the culture and is generally a place of deep skepticism or downright

---

*A wrong-headed interpretation that foists Ptolemy's ancient earth-centered (geocentric) theory of the universe on the interpretation of certain biblical passages.

hostility toward the Biblical worldview. What happens in the academy is not just ivory-tower thumb-twiddling. People act on what they believe to be true. These things matter because they determine behavior. *Ideas have consequences.*

What does this mean for Christians? Whenever you enter an intellectual environment, it's not just your personal faith that's going to be challenged. It won't even be just one or two obvious areas of knowledge in which you might expect conflict with the Christian message, like world religions or philosophy. Unless you're concentrating on pure math, across the whole spectrum of every branch of human knowledge, in every class the underlying assumptions will be that that the Christian belief system is untenable, that it has little or nothing to contribute, that it has already been tried and found wanting. Get ready for this prevailing attitude.

Subjecting yourself to this kind of environment is not necessarily a bad thing. If you want stronger muscles, you need to train. If you want more patience, you need people in your life to test your patience. If you want a faith that stands up to intellectual challenges, you

If you want a faith that stands up to intellectual challenges, you need to wrestle with the ideas out there that go against Christian faith.

need to wrestle with the ideas out there that go against Christian faith. (Remember, Jesus said to love the Lord your God with *all your mind.*)

There's no doubt that taken together, the furnaces of the two Enlightenments have tried Christian faith. On the negative side, the Radical Enlightenment has caused some to lose their faith altogether. Others, embarrassed by what they see as the old-fashioned ideas of the Bible, have downgraded their idea of God from a supernatural, miracle-working God to one who is aloof, unconcerned, and uninvolved in His world.

But on the positive side, the challenge of the Radical Enlightenment has caused Christians to value what is essential to the Biblical worldview and to chuck nonessential add-ons. We really don't want to be burdened with some parts of the Medieval Synthesis. We can believe what God has revealed clearly in the Bible yet enjoy the advance of knowledge in various fields. We can pray for the sick, but we don't rely on quackery and superstition anymore—we gladly take advantage of advancements in medical science and public health. When it comes to civil and human rights, we have sharpened our understanding of the Bible's teaching on freedom and human dignity. Most Christians in leadership positions no longer try (as they did in the Middle Ages) to impose state punishments or threats of punishment for violations of church teaching or ethics.

ALL QUIET ON THE WESTERN FRONT?

The April 8, 1966, cover of *Time* magazine asked, "Is God Dead?" It's still a live question. Has Western culture killed off the idea of God? My answer is: I don't know. There are encouraging signs and discouraging ones.

In Europe, the answer is sobering indeed. The continent is awash in unbelief, a spiritual wasteland despite numerous cathedral spires that dot the landscape. There are pockets of vitality, and Christian faith is always hopeful. But to be honest, revival there will require a major, miraculous work of God.

Many commentators have observed that America is "more religious" than Europe. Perhaps part of that is our puritan/Protestant heritage, but there is no guarantee the current situation will last. Each generation must relay the gospel to the next. We haven't done the job if we have not at least tried to engage the culture's biggest questions. This doesn't mean we have to be knee-jerk defenders of the past. We ought always to stay teachable. In this way we can encourage Glory-to-God believers to move into their own Glory-to-God Enlightenments.

12 | RULES OF ENGAGEMENT

What do you do if you're a U.S. Marine taking hostile fire, and the enemy is using women, old men, and children as human shields?

What if you're a Los Angeles police officer and a driver has been cornered but now has freed his car and is aiming it at you?

Answer: In military conflicts or on big city streets, soldiers and officers are guided by rules of engagement. The rules of engagement are orders that tell them how to make split-second high-pressure decisions when life or death is at stake. They are rules about when it is and when it is not permissible to use deadly force. These rules are based on lots of experience, trends, and what's worked in the past and what hasn't. They are designed to be effective in the real world and to protect human lives, not to be useless, namby-pamby restrictions.

Rules of engagement are always more powerful if they are based upon good intelligence-gathering. The more you know about a person who's acting dangerously, the better you'll be trained in how to deal with him.

Same thing with worldview. If you know the basic playbook of the other worldviews, you'll have a much better idea of where the people with those views are likely to go, what they're likely to do, and the best way to respond. So for the rest of the chapter, we're going to be getting inside the playbook of naturalism.

YOU LIGHT UP MY SENSES

> **God created humans to be able to grasp the physical realm through the five senses; He created the spiritual and moral realms of life to be known through the spirit and soul.**

In the Biblical world-view and the Medieval Synthesis, it was understood that God created everything seen and unseen (Hebrews 11:3), the physical and the spiritual worlds. God upheld the moral order. God created humans to be able to grasp the physical realm through the five senses; He created the spiritual and moral realms of life to be known through the spirit and soul.

It was assumed that people could have true knowledge of physical, spiritual, and moral reality because God was the reality behind these realities; Christ was the Word behind all true words.

Nobody ever seriously suggested that we could know truth exhaustively as God knows it. As limited human beings, however, we could know physical realities truly and substantially. For example, a horse is not a turtle, and neither of them is a rock. True, we might mistake a turtle for a rock of a certain size and shape, but if we examined it more closely, we would soon realize the difference.

People could also have true knowledge of God himself and of moral truth truly and substantially—not exhaustively as God knew them. People could know God not because of their great intellects but because God in His grace had revealed himself through Christ.

A basic assumption of naturalism is that we can only know about the physical world, and then only through the five senses. Morals and spiritual meaning, therefore, are utterly unknowable. We can see how this idea has developed through Auguste Comte and Immanuel Kant.

A Comte Runs Through It

The Empiricism of the Radical Enlightenment changed all this. Empiricism says you can only "know" what comes through your five senses, a belief known as logical positivism. Auguste Comte spoke for this view when he wrote, "All good intellects have repeated, since Bacon's time, that there can be no real knowledge which is not based upon observed facts."[1]

Please notice what Comte is doing in this short sentence. First, he puts forth the great scientist Francis Bacon as an authority for his viewpoint. Bacon, who promoted experimentation over superstition, magic, and unsupported theory, is widely recognized as the father of the scientific method. But Bacon was also a believing Christian and never intended the scientific method to encompass all of knowledge. Second, Comte insults anyone who doesn't agree with him, saying, in essence, "If you disagree with Bacon, other smart people, and me, then you're just plain dim-witted!"

Third, Comte redefines the term *knowledge*. He says that real knowledge (what came to be called "positive" knowledge or "positivism") can only come through the observed facts of science (i.e., measurable scientific experiments). By this neat little trick, then, Comte claims any fields of knowledge not based on his definition are meaningless. He automatically dismisses the spiritual, religious, aesthetic, and moral wisdom of the ages as mere fables, old wives' tales, superstition, irrationality, prejudice, emotionalism, taste, cultural training, or wishful thinking. Whatever they are, positivism holds they are certainly not in the category of things that are knowable.

Comte's positivism was part of the Enlightenment's quest for invincible, logically unassailable certainty—to grasp with the mind physical things "as they are." Things were going swimmingly for Comte's view of the world—until Kant.

Kant, the Anti-Comte

Immanuel Kant was another of Europe's greatest thinkers. To reduce Kant's theories into one sentence: Categories or processes in our individual minds control how we perceive and experience the world. (If you know anything about Kant, don't get on my case that this is too simplistic—I'm trying to simplify!) Radical Enlightenment skeptics ran with Kant's ideas and concluded that since everyone's mind filters and alters his or her experience, no one ever experiences things "as they are"—we only experience what's "in our head." For radical skeptics, there is no longer any reason whatever to believe in objective reality (reality outside of your head).

Thus in European intellectual history, even though Comte came after Kant, Kant became the anti-Comte. Comte's theory sought invincible certainty; Kant's theory led to unassailable uncertainty.* (For an elaboration of this idea, please read the section "If a Man's Standing Alone in a Forest . . ." in chapter 16.)

EXCELLENT ADVENTURE AND BOGUS JOURNEY

In the Middle Ages faith and reason were inseparable. Theology was the queen of the sciences and reason was theology's handmaiden. Reason served God's revelation. God's revelation was clearly seen in nature, in the history of Israel, in the written words of the Bible, in Christ, and in the church, all as superintended by the Holy Spirit.

Naturalism turned reason into an excellent adventure and faith into a bogus journey. It fundamentally rejected the possibility of a true revelation from God, cutting reason off completely from faith. David Hume, an influential skeptic, wrote,

> A miracle is a violation of the laws of nature; and as a firm and unalterable experience has established these laws, the proof against a miracle, from the very nature of the fact, is as entire as any argument from experience can possibly be imagined.[2]

Notice Hume's tactics here: First he defines a miracle as a violation of nature's laws. Since nature's laws are, by his definition, impossible to break, all seeming violations of that rule (i.e., miracles) must be explained away by purely natural causes. Hume said he had never personally experienced a miracle, and since no one he knew had experienced a miracle, he thought the only reasonable conclusion was that miracles simply don't happen. Hume's worldview and mindset would not allow a supernatural God to intervene in his own world.

---

*Kant tried to posit his own theory of morals, but he had already pulled the rug out from under himself with his emphasis on the primacy of perception over anything objective "out there."

THROW MOMMA FROM THE TRAIN

The Biblical worldview teaches that we are created by God and are morally accountable to Him. Because we are created in God's image, we have a sense of what is right and wrong, compassionate and cruel, noble and shameful. These moral perceptions, which to a greater or lesser extent can be found in various cultures' norms and laws, imperfectly reflect God's moral law as revealed in Scripture.

Naturalism denies God and therefore denies God's moral authority. It argues that since there are so many conflicting versions of morals, no universal, cross-cultural, objective, or absolute morals exist.* Fyodor Dostoevsky expertly explored this theme in his great novels *The Brothers Karamazov* and *Crime and Punishment*. Dostoevsky understood that if people believe there is no God, "everything is permitted."† Good-bye right and wrong!

In the early twentieth century, Albert Einstein's Theory of Relativity led many to the conclusion that since there was relativity in physics, there must also be relativity in morals. Later anthropologists like Margaret Mead studied aboriginal tribes and promoted cultural relativism, the idea that no culture should claim superiority or morally judge any other culture in any way. Like a giant broom, Einstein's Relativity, Moral Relativism, and Cultural Relativism widely diminished our culture's belief in objective, universal morality. Many people came to believe that there were *absolutely* no absolutes.

FEAR AND LOATHING OF THE SUPERNATURAL

The Biblical worldview is that we can have a relationship with God, the ultimate personal spiritual reality who is really "there" (not just an

---

*Jesus condensed the entire Old Testament into two commandments: "Love the Lord your God with all your heart and with all your soul and with all your mind.... Love your neighbor as yourself" (Matthew 22:37, 39). These commandments are examples of universal (for all peoples), cross-cultural (for all cultures), objective (not based in subjective opinion), and absolute (authoritatively binding) morals.

†In Katharena Eiermann's essay "Existentialism and Dostoevsky," she wrote, "Jean-Paul Sartre has said that all of French Existentialism is to be found in Ivan Karamazov's contention that if there is no God, everything is permitted," quoted in *www.tassos-oak.com/extras/soundbite.html.*

idea in our heads). St. Cyprian, one of the ancient fathers of the church, said, "You cannot have God for your Father if you do not have the Church for your mother."[3] The spiritual reality of God working through the church was assumed.

Naturalism denies any supernatural, spiritual reality. For example, the Greek materialist thinker Epicurus asked:

> Is God willing to prevent evil, but not able? Then he is impotent.
> Is he able, but not willing? Then he is malevolent.
> Is he both able and willing? Whence then is evil?[4]

Epicurus didn't believe in God or theology. Yet he was not above using a theological argument against God. He asked, "How could a good God allow innocents to suffer and evildoers to go unpunished?" Epicurus's innate sense of justice—imprinted in him because he, like all of us, was created in God's image (Genesis 1:26)—shows the stamp of awareness of God's standards of good and evil on Epicurus's heart. Even though he denied God, he couldn't shake the idea of good and evil.

A modern example is novelist Richard Heinlein. His character Lazarus Long says,

> The most preposterous notion that H. sapiens has ever dreamed up is that the Lord God of Creation, Shaper and Ruler of all the Universes, wants the saccharine adoration of His creatures, can be swayed by their prayers, and becomes petulant if He does not receive this flattery. Yet this absurd fantasy, without a shred of evidence to bolster it, pays all the expenses of the oldest, largest, and least productive industry in all history.[5]

This idea that all religions are purely man-made is a popular sentiment among naturalists. Thomas Paine said, "I do not believe in the creed professed by the Jewish church, by the Roman church, by the Greek church, by the Turkish church, by the Protestant church, nor by any church that I know of. . . . Each of those churches accuse the other of unbelief; and for my own part, I disbelieve them all."[6] Napoleon Bonaparte said, "I would believe in a religion if it existed ever since the beginning of time, but when I consider Socrates, Plato, Mohamet [i.e., Muhammad], I no longer believe. All religions have been made by men."[7]

The naturalist attitude toward all religions is reflected in the way Harvard University professor William James, the founder of the academic field of the psychology of religion, narrowly focused his studies. Personally, James himself may have believed in some form of supernaturalism; he called himself "a piecemeal supernaturalist."[8] Yet for his academic study of religion, James narrowly defined religion as "the feelings, acts, and experiences of individual men in their solitude, so far as they apprehend themselves to stand in relation to whatever they may consider the divine."[9] James's definition of religion excludes the supernatural! It is entirely based in human this-world experience and perception. He's not looking at people's experience of God; rather, he has neatly limited his scope of inquiry to people's perception of what they consider to be God.

Ruling God out from the start of serious discussions happens a lot. In the future, please don't be shocked if you hear or read an expert in religions saying something like, "Let's avoid judgment and leave aside for the present whether a religion is true or false, real or speculative. Let us instead look at *varieties of religious experience* as an outworking of common human experience across time and cultures. What is important is how people's beliefs influence their behavior." These words are like the gestures of a magician who distracts you with one hand so you don't notice what he's doing with the other. In other words, the intense study of the human side of religion alone could (doesn't have to, but could) mask an agenda of ignoring or explaining away a supernatural worldview. (On the other hand, the professor could be saying provocative things to jump-start a legitimate discussion; he might honestly be trying to make everyone feel comfortable by not bringing up religion if it has led to unfruitful discussions in the past. Don't be too quick to jump to conclusions.)

Not all experts in religions will agree with the anti-supernatural mind-set. Some will have adopted the Haunted worldview of the cultures they have devoted their lives to studying. Others may be on Omnipresent Supergalactic Oneness. It'll be up to you to figure out which worldviews religious experts around you are following.

DECONSTRUCTING TOM, SALLY, SUE, DICK, AND HARRY

The Bible teaches, and the Biblical worldview has always affirmed, that we are body, soul, and spirit (or body and soul/spirit). This unity of body, soul, and spirit somehow extends to the afterlife, as Jesus said regarding the resurrection of all to judgment (John 5:25–29) and as Paul said about being clothes with a new "tent" (2 Corinthians 5:1–10).

Compare the biblical perspective to Margaret Jacob, a professor at UCLA: "Contemporary neuroscientific work has conflated spirit into matter, soul into body ... [and] emotions into the cerebral cortices, the amygdale, the hypothalamus and the viscera."[10] Jacob is saying that what we experience as emotions and soul-intuitions are nothing more than complex chemical reactions in the brain. In other words, she believes that there is no soul separate from or beyond the physical body. She places soul and spirit purely in the physical world. There is simply no room in her worldview for anything outside of the physical, natural world.

Peter Singer, ethics professor at Princeton University, goes further. "Surely there will be some nonhuman animals whose lives, *by any standards,* are more valuable than the lives of some humans."[11] It is clear that Singer is denying human dignity to some humans, since it is a very short distance from this argument to euthanasia for "undesirable humans." By using the phrase *"by any standards,"* Singer, a leader in the animal rights movement, is saying that you must agree with him because no other standards count. No standards other than his are allowed.

The view of man as a mere biological machine is bleak indeed. For example, Charles Darwin said in an early edition of his *Origin of the Species*: "At some future time, not very distant as measured by centuries, the civilized races of man will almost certainly exterminate and replace throughout the world the savage races."[12] Darwin looked at where his theories were leading and arrived at the obvious conclusion—*the extermination of inferior races.* (Given nineteenth-century racial theories and prejudices, which human races do you think he was talking about?) In fairness to Darwin, we do not know whether he would have supported heartless Social Darwinism, slavery, or genocide of inferior peoples. However, it is clear that some people in the twentieth century have justified their racist, mass-murdering ideologies on ideas like that expressed in Darwin's quote above.

There's a very poignant poem by Erich Fried on his understanding of what it means to be human. I couldn't get permission to quote the whole thing, but in effect he says that we die like dogs. Look up his name, "Definition" (the name of the poem), and 1964 (the year of the poem) on the Internet. Your effort will be worth it. Anyway, for Fried, there's nothing more after death. No dignity. No meaning. No justice. No afterlife. Just bone-chilling silence and worms. Finished.

I HAVE A NIGHTMARE

As contemporary Christians, because of our history with democracy and our experience with civil rights and human rights, we are likely to be very uncomfortable with the Medieval view of political and social order. With a good deal of hindsight, we might ask ourselves, *How could they have had a Biblical worldview and gotten so many things so wrong?* It's an important question, but unfortunately we don't have space to settle on any definitive answers here. I'll leave it to your further study to think through how to apply biblical principles to society and politics to promote the greatest common good. Likely you'll need a lot of humility, wisdom, prudence, and trial-and-error experience to come up with a workable solution.

For now, though, I'd like you to consider how naturalism cuts the legs out from under any ideas we might have about civil and human rights. Naturalism reduces humans to mere cogs in the social and political machine. Naturalism provides no rational reasons for upholding or preserving human dignity or from preventing exploitation of the weak by the strong.

For example, in the twentieth century, Karl Marx's economic theory was based upon the Materialistic worldview. In Russia, China, and just about everywhere else it has been applied to society, it has led to massive crimes against humanity. Raising the Communist state to the place of highest authority, anything the state does is justified, including stealing the property of peasants and giving their wealth to Communist party higher-ups; mass enslavement (if they are lucky) of those same peasants—and if they complain, systematic starvation; perversion of law; a police state; huge and secret prison systems; physical and mental torture of clergy; and repression of all dissent—all, ironically, to keep the vision of a *utopian* society alive.*

A SERIES OF UNSUPERVISED, IMPERSONAL EVENTS

The Biblical worldview says that history is moving toward a grand finale when all wrongs will be righted, every tear wiped away, and death abolished (Revelation 21:4). In that day there will be representatives of every tongue, tribe, and nation worshiping the Lamb (Revelation 5:9; 7:9); the martyrs will be vindicated (Revelation 12:10–11); the mission of the church to bring the gospel to the whole world will have been accomplished (Matthew 24:13); and the devil will get his due (Revelation 20:7–10).

Stephen Jay Gould, professor of evolutionary biology at Harvard University, had a different viewpoint:

> We are here because one odd group of fishes had a peculiar fin anatomy that could transform into legs for terrestrial creatures; because the earth never froze entirely during an ice age; because a small and tenuous species, arising in Africa a quarter of a million years ago, has managed, so far, to survive by hook and by crook. We may yearn for a higher answer—but none exists.[13]

Were you jolted by that last sentence? Gould is saying there is no higher answer; there is no purpose to life at all. It's all just time, chance, and matter. Nothing more. No God, no Spirit, no purpose for history. Nada. Of course, Gould had to say this because the strict, inflexible rules of his worldview did not permit any intervention or direction by a supernatural God. (Toward the end of his life, Gould seemed to modify his viewpoint somewhat, leaving some room, perhaps, for a supernatural God.)

---

*For an exhaustive documentation, see Stephane Courtios, *The Black Book of Communism: Crimes, Terror, Repression* (Harvard University Press, 1999).

Another example is the 1995 "Statement on the Teaching of Evolution," by the National Association of Biology Teachers:

> The diversity of life on earth is the outcome of evolution: an *unsupervised, impersonal,* unpredictable and natural process of temporal descent with genetic modification that is affected by natural selection, chance, historical contingencies and changing environments.[14]

Think for a moment: Why were the words *unsupervised* and *impersonal* used? Even if evolution happened as biological evolutionists say it did, does evolution therefore *prove* that there was *necessarily* no God to supervise things? Or that the universe is *necessarily* impersonal? Can you see the worldview agenda, the "faith" assumptions, and the unquestioned and unchallenged givens* of the people who wrote that statement? Do you see how the *strict, inflexible* rules of naturalism forbid God ever to do anything in His world?

DUST IN THE WIND

We could go on and on tracing the influence of naturalism on all areas of knowledge. But you get the picture.

Naturalism says you're nothing but dust in the wind. It creates a God-shaped vacuum, a gaping hole in your chest.† I am not saying that naturalists are incapable of recognizing justice, beauty, and morals or loving their kids or doing good in society because they don't believe the Bible. I am saying that, by definition, their worldview goes against the universally God-given ideas of justice, beauty, and morals that are part of what it means to be created in God's image (Genesis 1:26). Contrary to these innate truths that can be seen in every culture (although, admittedly, differently described and perceived), naturalism teaches explicitly that there is no real truth, no beauty, no morals, no meaning, no values, no purpose, and no significance beyond death. Furthermore, naturalism teaches that the universe doesn't give a rip about you.

---

*A leap of faith; an unprovable worldview assumption.
†See C. S. Lewis's great essay "Men Without Chests," at the end of his book *The Abolition of Man.*

And yet many naturalists yearn for God. Some of the most heart-rending complaints to God have been written by atheists. Why is that?

Here's what St. Augustine of Hippo wrote in his *Confessions:* "Thou hast made us for thyself and restless is our heart until it comes to rest in thee."[15] And Blaise Pascal, mathematician and inventor of the vacuum tube, is credited with this quote: "There is a God-shaped vacuum in every man which can only be filled by Jesus Christ."[16]

> **No matter what your worldview is, if you're not in relationship with Christ, your heart is trying like crazy to fill that void with something.**

No matter what your worldview is, if you're not in relationship with Christ, your heart is trying like crazy to fill that void with something. Something isn't right. You can get mad at God for not creating a perfectly just planet; you can try to run from God; you can deny the hole. In the end, only Jesus Christ can complete you and meet your deepest spiritual needs.

Colossians 2:8 says, "See to it that no one takes you captive through hollow and deceptive philosophy, which depends on human tradition and the basic principles of this world rather than on Christ." Paul's warning is still valid no matter where you are in your life, whether you're about to enter college, in college, never going to college, or glad to be out of college. No matter what, you need to recognize the naturalist duck when you see it, whether it's making its appearance in psychology, sociology, politics, religion, art, anthropology, education, music, entertainment, or anything else.

But if you do go to college, please take this sketchy picture into your own chosen field of study. Maybe Naturalism is not as dominant now as it was a generation ago. Possibly there will be other worldviews more vigorously competing in the marketplace of ideas. Either way, you'll need to stick close to Christ and be on your guard not to be taken captive by these other worldviews, these basic principles of the world, these siren voices of spiritual chatter.

13 | DREAMS OF SPACE DOGS

A while back I was driving across the country late at night. To keep awake I turned on the radio and came across a guy talking about "dreams of space dogs." That piqued my curiosity, so I listened for a while. The gist of the show was this: How do we know that our realities are not the dreams of space dogs? There's no way to prove it either way. . . .

As waves crash on the Malibu shoreline, John Heard, in the character of a spiritual mentor and guru, is teaching Shirley MacLaine the great truth that Jesus and all the other spiritual masters had taught but the church had covered up. He starts to suggest an exercise. She is to say out loud, "God is in me" or "I am divine." He changes his mind. "No, this is better. . . ." They both stand, arms outstretched, and Heard says, "Say, 'I am God.'" After some initial resistance, MacLaine complies. The scene ends as they slowly turn toward the sinking sun, in unison chanting, "I am God. I am God.'*

---

*Shirley MacLaine, *Out on a Limb,* produced by Stan Margulies, television miniseries, 1987. *Out on a Limb* is an autobiographical account of Shirley MacLaine's search for meaning. This television miniseries gave a significant impetus to the New Age movement in America.

In the last two chapters we saw how the Naturalist/Materialist worldview answered the big questions of life. Who am I? (Nothing but a cosmic accident—a blip of living tissue that winks on and off.) Where did I come from? (Time, chance, and matter, period.) Where am I going? (Death and nothingness.) Does the infinite and personal God of the Bible exist? (No! The universe doesn't give a rip about you.)

In this chapter, we're going to look at the worldview that says: *Anything* is possible. This is just one of *an infinite* number of realities. You've got *unlimited* potential. Reality, truth, and beauty are located *in you*. You can do and be *anything* you set your mind and your consciousness toward. Don't worry about death—with reincarnation you have plenty of time to figure things out. Eventually you are *guaranteed* to become one with everything. So, believe in *yourself!* You are God.

The big selling point of this worldview is that all spiritual paths are going up the same mountain. This makes the worldview seem like it is the most open-minded and tolerant of all worldviews.

Many Christian writers call this worldview the Eastern worldview, as opposed to the Western worldview. I think this is a mistake, because the East has never had a monopoly on this worldview, and it has in fact long been known in the West. In this book we call it Omnipresent Supergalactic Oneness.

The five main historical roots of this worldview are:

- High Hinduism, originating in India
- Taoism, which comes from China
- Zen Buddhism, a Japanese offshoot of Buddhism
- Certain forms of Native American religions
- Western Idealism,* which originated in ancient Greece and has long been a minority opinion in Western thinking.

*The common way people use the word *idealism* is as a synonym for "having high principles." Having ideals and principles is a good thing—people should never get so cynical that they lose them. However, I'm not using idealism in that sense in this book. Here, Idealism will always be capitalized; it is derived from the word *idea* (not *ideal*). It is the belief that, in contrast to materialism, the essential stuff of the universe is ideas/mind/consciousness. If it is unclear now, don't worry. I'll explain it more as we go.

HINDUISM, HIGH AND LOW

Fade in to the syncopated thumping of a tubla drum and the unfamiliar strains of the strings of a sitar. Incense permeates the air. A statue of an elephant-headed god stares impassively at you, while a monkey perched on a wall munches a piece of fruit that someone left as a sacrifice—for sacred monkeys! You've just entered a Hindu temple.

From your studies in geography, you probably already know some things about Hinduism. When you get down to it, though, Hinduism is difficult even for experts to describe because it is so amazingly diverse.

Scaria Thuruthiyil, a Roman Catholic scholar from India and dean of the Faculty of Philosophy at the Pontifical Salesian University in Rome, gives this apt description of Hinduism:

> Hinduism is not just a single religion, but a "mosaic of religions," within which we can find most elementary superstitions and mythologies, from the cult of inanimate objects, like stones, rivers, planets to animate objects, like trees, animals, heroes, dead ancestors and spirits. At the same time it presents itself as a fertile field for a most elevated mysticism, which seeks to reach not only the union of the soul with a personal God, the creator and governor of the universe, but even to overcome this dualistic attitude by "realizing" one's identity with the Absolute Spirit.[1] *

In the first sentence, Thuruthiyil describes "Low Hinduism," which you will recognize as the Haunted worldview. Thuruthiyil's second sentence describes "High Hinduism" (all is one, all is God). Hinduism, with such a

Hinduism, with such a wide array of beliefs, may seem "tolerant," but it actually tries to absorb every religion into itself.

---

*"Union of the soul with a personal god" perhaps sounds like the Biblical worldview, but it's not. It is actually henotheism, a type of polytheism in which you choose one god from the many to worship. "Realizing' one's identity with the Absolute Spirit" refers to the spiritual goal of monism/holism/ pantheism.

wide array of beliefs,may seem "tolerant," but it actually tries to absorb every religion into itself. Let's look into these main assumptions in a bit more detail.

The Supreme Self

From the perspective of High Hinduism, ultimate reality—the "Absolute Spirit" of Thuruthiyil's essay—is Brahman (or Brahma). Brahman is the supreme, impersonal, indescribable, unformed essence or spirit of the universe. Everything is connected to Brahman; Brahman is "in" everything. Everything—from an ant to a blade of grass to a human being to a god—*is* Brahman. Therefore, in Hinduism:

- All the thousands of gods in Low Hinduism are considered manifestations of Brahman and therefore are valid objects of worship. Idolatry is approved!*
- Nature is considered one with Brahman. No "dualism" or separation between "God" and nature is allowed. Nature is eternal; nature *is* God. God is nature. All is one.
- The supreme self, the higher self—the *atman*—is part of Brahman and therefore eternal, divine, and uncreated. The famous Hindu saying *Tat svam asi* ("That is what you are")[2] means that Brahman and atman are one.
- "The supreme Self is neither born nor dies. He cannot be burned, moved, pierced, cut, nor dried. Beyond all attributes, the supreme Self is the eternal witness, ever pure, indivisible, and uncompounded, far beyond the senses and the ego."[3]

Obviously, the idea of a supreme or higher self is incompatible with the Biblical worldview. The Bible says God alone is God, and you are *not* Him!

I'm Pickin' Up Good Vibrations

One way Hindus try to get their consciousness in tune with the "Brahman is atman" theme is to chant the sound Om (or Aum). In one

---

*Compare to "Have no other gods before Me. You shall not make for yourself an idol" (Exodus 20:3–4 NASB).

quotation from the Upanishads (Hindu holy books), Death says:

> I will tell you the word that all the Vedas glorify, all asceticism expresses, all sacred studies and holy life seek. That word is OM. That word is the everlasting Brahman: that word is the highest end. ... Concealed in the heart of all things is the Atman, the Spirit, the Self, smaller than the smallest atom, greater than the vast spaces.[4]

Chants of Om (and other sacred sounds) are found in Hinduism, Transcendental Meditation (a modern form of Hinduism), traditional Buddhism, and newer religions like the Sokka Gakkai cult. These chanting practices have also spread to the West.

Chanting Om is drastically different from Christian worship or prayer.* In chanting Om, you seek impersonal oneness with the vibrations or energy of the universe. In Christian prayer we humbly bring ourselves, our families, our friends, our peers, and even our enemies before the loving heavenly Father, asking His blessings and action on their behalf.

The Iron Law of Karma

Virtually all Hindus believe without question the doctrines of reincarnation and karma. Reincarnation is the belief that one's supreme self is recycled through many physical bodies on its way to perfection. Other terms for this belief are "rebirth" and "transmigration of the soul."†

Karma literally means "action," whether good or bad. Karma is described as "the iron law of cause and effect." Karma from past lives affects your present life and karma will determine your station in your next life. It takes thousands of lives on the great wheel of suffering (in Sanskrit, called *samsara*) to work off karma and achieve the Hindu

---

*Gregorian chant (also called Plainsong) in Catholic spirituality is nothing like Om-chanting. Never in Christian spirituality will the chanter think of him or herself as God or as merging with an impersonal absolute.

†Thuruthiyil says reincarnation "concerns the rebirth of the soul or self in a series of physical or preternatural embodiments, which are customarily human or animal in nature but are in some instances divine, angelic, demonic, vegetative, or astrological." From his essay "Reincarnation in Hinduism," quoted in *www.spiritual-wholeness.org/faqs/reincgen/hindrein.htm* (accessed April 19, 2005).

version of salvation, which is liberation* from the (nearly endless) wheel of suffering.

It is impossible to underestimate how different the Biblical world-view is from these Hindu absolutes. First, the Bible firmly rejects reincarnation: God has made it clear that "it is appointed for men to die once and after this comes judgment" (Hebrews 9:27 NASB).

Second, the Bible's idea of sin is nothing like karma. In the Bible, innocents can suffer horribly because of others' sin. With karma, each person on earth gets in this life *exactly* what he or she deserves. In the Bible, sin breaks our relationship with God but can be forgiven and the relationship restored through Christ. With karma there is only an iron, impersonal law that has nothing to do with a person's relationship with God.

Third, the Bible rejects self-salvation and salvation through your own works. Salvation is a work of God and a gift of God that we thank Him for giving us. With karma, if you manage to save yourself from the Wheel of Suffering and achieve liberation, you have no one to thank but yourself. No one can help you. No one needs to help you. You're on your own for your soul's very lonely journey.

TAOISM

Drive past any martial arts studio. Check out the ads for certain cigarette brands in newspapers or magazines. Look at the logos on skateboards and on skateboard attire. You might notice a common symbol—a circle divided by an S-shaped line. One field is black with a white dot; the other is white with a black dot. This is the main symbol of Taoism (also spelled Daoism).

Arising in China, Taoism takes a somewhat different track than high Hinduism. Taoism starts off similar to the cosmic dualism of the Dueling Yodas worldview. With Dueling Yodas, the dualism is between a good and an evil principle. In Taoism, there are many oppositions, or reciprocities, called yin and yang. Some examples: hot/cold; spicy/bland; daylight/nighttime; observer/observed; male/female; you/me; possibil-

---

*In Sanskrit, *moksha* means absorption into the infinite absolute—no more reincarnations!

ity/necessity; active/passive; odd/even. According to Taoism, neither the yin nor the yang is purely yin or yang; there's always some yin in yang and some yang in yin. Taoism goes further: It says that all the opposites or dualities that we regularly experience are interdependent, they support each other, and they consume/transform into each other. In short, they are only *apparently* opposite—they are really just part of a larger whole—the Tao.

This unity of all things in the Tao means there is *absolutely no moral black and white*—all moral concepts are relative.*

The Thing About the I Ching

Lao Tzu, who lived about five hundred years before Christ, authored the *I Ching* (the "Book of Changes"). He spoke of the all-is-one principle by saying that ultimate reality (the Tao) is both *being* and *emptiness:*

> The Great Tao flows everywhere. It may go left or right. All things depend on it for life.... Always without desires, it may be called the Small. All things come to it and it does not master them; it may be called The Great.[5]

Lao Tzu also believed the Tao to be utterly indifferent to human affairs:

> Heaven and earth are not humane.
> They regard all things as straw dogs.[6]

Lao Tzu had a hard time describing the Tao:

> The thing that is called Tao is eluding and vague.
> Vague and eluding, there is in it form
> Eluding and vague, in it are all things."[7]

Given the assumptions and strict, inflexible rules of Lao Tzu's worldview, the Tao *had to be* vague! It was impersonal, indifferent, and it couldn't communicate. Really smart philosophically minded people could

---

*Of course, this conflicts with the Biblical worldview where "God is light; in him there is no darkness at all." (See 1 John 1:5.)

barely understand it—a far cry from the Biblical worldview where the God who created us wants passionately to reveal himself to us and for us to know Him personally.

BUDDHISM

The spiritual goal of Buddhism and Buddhist meditative practice is Nirvana or enlightenment. Don't get Buddhist enlightenment and the European Enlightenment of the eighteenth century mixed up. The European Enlightenment was a quest for rational certainty based upon hard-nosed scientific research and strict adherence to a set of intellectual rules about what was and what was not allowed. Buddhist enlightenment is release from the suffering and pain of rebirth and the extinguishment of all desire; positively, it is a mystical realization or an intuitive consciousness-raising.

There are three great Buddhist traditions. Theravada, "the way of the elders," tries to get back to the original non-theistic Buddhist teaching of Siddhartha Gautama. Mahayana, "the great raft," a later development of Buddhism, turned the Buddha and others who have attained Nirvana into gods or saints in heaven who can aid Buddhists on their spiritual quest. Tantric Buddhism, the Buddhism of the Dalai Lama, borrows from Theravada and Mahayana and adds to them occult practices.*

Sometimes the Dalai Lama sounds like a Theravada or Mahayana Buddhist, such as in these quotes: "Ignorance is the source of hatred, and the way to get rid of ignorance is realization." "All religions are essentially the same in their goal of developing a good human heart so that we may become better human beings."[8]

In the next chapter you'll see examples that show the occult side of the Dalai Lama's Tibetan Buddhism.

What Is the Sound of One Hand Clapping?

DT Suzuki, a famous Zen teacher, once spoke at a packed-out auditorium at UCLA. He came to the podium, looked around, and said in

---

*How can you borrow from all three traditions, even though they seem to contradict each other? This is Designer Religion at work within Tibetan Buddhism.

halting English, "Zen Buddhism. Very hard understand." Then he left the stage. The crowd went nuts. The sponsors of the lecture at length persuaded Suzuki to stand for a question-and-answer session.

Zen Buddhism is a branch of Mahayana Buddhism that arose in Japan. It became popular in America after World War II with the beat generation of Alan Watts, Aldous Huxley, and Jack Kerouac.

Its ideas have continued to make headway in popular culture through characters like George Lucas's Zenlike master, Yoda, and his pupil, Luke Skywalker, who must cast off his rational mind and rely purely on his feelings. Zen *koans,* or riddles, like, "What is the sound of one hand clapping?" are techniques to move a person from rational to intuitional thinking.

Zen ideas can also be found in films like *Little Buddha, Bulletproof Monk, What Dreams May Come, Groundhog Day,* and *Crouching Tiger, Hidden Dragon.* It also appears in the novel *Siddhartha* by Hermann Hesse.

DT Suzuki was the first important promoter of Zen Buddhism in America and the West. He would say things like, "If I were asked then, what Zen teaches, I would answer, Zen teaches nothing." He also said, "Whatever teachings there are in Zen, they come out of one's own mind. We teach ourselves; Zen merely points the way."[9] Suzuki meant that we need to throw off rational constraints, get to a "no-mind" attitude, and rely solely on direct experience and intuition. Very much like in Hinduism, we need to realize our identity with—and our undivided connection to—the One.

NATIVE AMERICAN SPIRITUALITIES

There isn't just one Native American spirituality—there are many.*

Although it is dangerous to try to find historical truth in animated feature movies, the film *Pocahontas* had the natives practicing animism or nature worship (what we have called the Haunted worldview). Other

---

*There's a pretty good article about Native American spirituality at the Religious Tolerance Web site, *www.religioustolerance.org/nataspir.htm.* A word of caution about the Web site: It tries to be non-judgmental, but its worldview is either Naturalism or some form of Omnipresent Supergalactic Oneness.

Native American religions are nontheistic, more like pantheism. And some North American tribes believe in a Great Spirit who is creator of all, an idea quite close to monotheism.

Omnipresent Supergalactic Oneness and Designer Religion advocates often incorporate Native American spiritualities (or what they imagine Native American spiritualities to be) into their worldview systems. The environmental and radical environmental movements also appeal to Native American spiritual themes.

WESTERN IDEALISM

The basic idea of Omnipresent Supergalactic Oneness is the unity of all things. The vehicle for this realization is mind mysticism. Since all is believed to be one (monism) and all is God or all is spirit (pantheism), truth or reality is ultimately in your consciousness, in your mind. In Hinduism, you find Brahman by going within yourself and discovering your atman, your mind. In Taoism you reject apparent dualities and accept the oneness of all in the Tao through a mystical mind experience. In Buddhism you experience Enlightenment through a direct, intuitive expansion of consciousness through the mind.

Similarly, Western Idealism is pantheistic and monistic, relying on mind mysticism to capture the meaning of life. Since everything is one, the Impersonal Absolute (often called "God") is only discoverable through a person plumbing the depths of his or her mind.

Western Idealism has a long and strong pedigree. It began with the ancient Greeks. In Europe it was a minority opinion until it started gaining ground in the early Enlightenment period with Baruch Spinoza. It really caught on in eighteenth- and nineteenth-century Germany and in nineteenth-century America. And in the latter half of the twentieth century and beginning of the twenty-first century, it has grown explosively with the New Age movement.

Who were America's first New Agers?*

---

*In this book, the New Age movement (a form of Designer Religion) can have elements of the Haunted worldview (pagan polytheism), Dueling Yodas (dualism), and/or Omnipresent Supergalactic Oneness (pantheism/monism).

The First Euro-American New Agers

Imagine it's the mid-nineteenth century and there is no network TV, no cable, no dish, no multiplex movie theatres. Ahhh—but there are magnificent lecturers and storytellers. You hear that the famous Ralph Waldo Emerson is going to appear at the Masonic Temple. Excitedly, you arrive an hour early and it's already standing-room only. Just slightly deflated, you wait as the buzz in the room increases to a near fever pitch. Finally, the speaker is announced and the famous man with the tousled hair and chiseled face emerges. He takes command of the podium, and after a dramatic pause brings the audience to a far-away place, reading from the Bhagavad-Gita, a Hindu story about Lord Krishna and a huge battle—a story, he says, that holds the most sublime truths imaginable.

Normally, we think of the New Age movement as having begun sometime in the 1960s or 1970s. It actually got started in America with the New England Transcendentalists over 150 years ago.

When my high school literature class studied Ralph Waldo Emerson and Henry David Thoreau, I had *no idea* what Transcendentalism was.* It sounded like a very cool word, but when I looked up the definition, the explanations made *no sense.* The problem was, I had no training in worldviews. I had never heard of pantheism, monism, or idealism. I lacked context, so I was *clueless.* I didn't figure any of this out until years later.

Don't Know Much 'Bout Transcendentalism

Ralph Waldo Emerson, the leading Transcendentalist of his time, tells us *exactly* what he meant by the term in his essay "The Transcendentalist":

> The first thing we have to say respecting what are called the *new views* here in New England, at the present time, is, that they are not new, but the very oldest of thoughts cast into the mould of these new times.

---

*Transcendentalism is usually a fancy word for pantheism. It means there's something beyond the physical world that's totally spirit, or something like spirit. What it is, exactly, can't be known rationally. It can only be experienced.

What is popularly called Transcendentalism among us, is Idealism; Idealism as it appears in 1842. . . .[10]

We see from these excerpts that Emerson knew Transcendentalism to be very old, indeed—as old as Pantheistic Hinduism. He also understood that Transcendentalism was a form of Idealism. Later in the essay Emerson shows how Transcendentalism rejects materialism in favor of *ideas in the human mind that create our subjective experience of reality.* Emerson's Idealism, essentially, was pantheistic mind mysticism. According to Emerson, the creator God does not determine what's true. We do—with our minds.

Generations of students have been compelled to read Emerson's "Self Reliance."[11] As you look at some quotes from that famous essay, imagine Emerson energetically preaching, persuading, and proselytizing for his worldview!

> To believe in your own thought, to believe that what is true for you in your private heart is true for all men—that is genius.

> Trust thyself; every heart vibrates to that iron string.

> Prayer as a means to affect a private end is meanness and theft. It supposes a dualism and not unity in nature and consciousness. As soon as the man is one with God, he will not beg.

> Nothing can bring you peace but yourself.

Now that you know Emerson's worldview, can you see why he said you can only trust yourself? That you need to be "self-reliant" instead of "God-reliant"? Can you see why he ridiculed and denigrated asking God for things in prayer? Do you see why he said that you are the only one who can bring yourself peace?

Look around you, at your friends, teachers, co-workers, and what you see on TV or read in the paper or books: Can you identify any examples of how these ideas have "settled in" and made their home here in our culture?

One Flew Over the Spider's Nest

Let me first say about Henry David Thoreau that I really enjoy reading him. His eye for intricate detail, such as how a spider might spin a web, is wonderful. Having read his stuff, I have all the more enjoyed my backpacking ventures. But there's more to Thoreau than just learning to enjoy the great outdoors.

Thoreau is America's "patron saint" of nature mysticism. Consider this quote from his famous "I wanted to suck the marrow out of life" passage that a lot of eleventh graders read in American Lit:

> For most men, it appears to me, are in a strange uncertainty about it [here Thoreau is speaking about Life, or Nature], whether it is of the devil or of God, and have *somewhat hastily* concluded that it is the chief end of man here to "glorify God and enjoy him forever."[12]

Notice three things. First, Thoreau directly quotes from the Westminster Shorter Catechism* that our main purpose is to "glorify God and enjoy him forever." He assumes his readers have familiarity with the phrase and will catch the allusion.

Second, Thoreau assumes that "most men" are Christians who "hastily"—that is, unthinkingly—believe glorifying God is their main purpose in life.

Third, Thoreau says these Christians aren't sure if nature is a good thing or a bad thing ("whether it is of the devil or of God"), and so have rejected nature—turning from real life (the woods) to the city, from nature on earth to the supernatural and nonearthly.

So what was he driving at? He was saying that the meaning to life *is not found in glorifying God, but rather in a first-hand, mystical experience with nature.* Why? Thoreau's worldview is to experience nature mystically, and you have all the experience of "God" you need.

The New England transcendentalism of Emerson and Thoreau is the background for the film *Little Women.* In one scene Winona Ryder tells Gabriel Byrne about her family's transcendentalist beliefs. Byrne's character lights up with recognition: "But this is German Romantic philosophy, where we throw off all our constraints and rely instead on sheer intuition."[13] Bingo! Do you see? Transcendentalism, pantheism, monism,

---

*The Westminster Shorter Catechism has been used for centuries to teach Christian faith to children, especially among Presbyterians and other Reformed denominations. Most (if not all) of Thoreau's readers would have instantly recognized the "chief end" phrase.

mind mysticism, nature mysticism, German romantic philosophy—many different names all coming from the same basic worldview.

HEARTS OF SPACE

Omnipresent Supergalactic Oneness has penetrated American pop culture in many ways, softening us up to space dogs' dreams, hearts in space, space music, and general all-around spacey-ness.

A Beautiful Mind

Preachers often bring forth Albert Einstein's quote, "God does not play at dice with the universe," hoping to support the idea of an orderly and designed universe—not a random one. What kind of God did Einstein really believe in? Listen closely to these words:

> It was, of course, a lie what you read about my religious convictions, a lie which is being systematically repeated. I do not believe in a personal God and I have never denied this but have expressed it clearly. If something is in me which can be called religious then it is the unbounded admiration for the structure of the world so far as our science can reveal it.[14]

> It seems to me that the idea of a personal God is an anthropological concept which I cannot take seriously. I also cannot imagine some will or goal outside the human sphere.[15]

> I believe in Spinoza's God who reveals himself in the orderly harmony of what exists, not in a God who concerns himself with the fates and actions of human beings.[16]

In the first quote, Einstein makes it plain that he believes only in an impersonal god, not the personal God of the Biblical worldview. In the second he can conceive of no personal will outside of human will. And in the third he says he believes in Spinoza's God, and as we have seen, Spinoza's God was pantheistic. Einstein explicitly spells it out to us that he, too, believes that nature is God.

I Am the Walrus

In 1967 the Beatles came out with a blockbuster album called *The Beatles—Magical Mystery Tour*. This album celebrated the Beatles' recent explorations into Indian and Hindu spirituality and experiences with mind-altering drugs. This album had a tremendous cultural impact in America. A lot of people thought the Beatles were just fooling around or on acid when they wrote the song "I Am the Walrus" for their *Magical Mystery Tour*. However, the lyrics are unabashedly all-is-one monistic. According to this song, there is no essential difference between you, me, he, she, the eggman, the eggmen, or the walrus—"goo goo g'joob!"

Follow Your Bliss

In the Public Broadcasting System (PBS) archives there is a fascinating series of interviews that Bill Moyers taped with mythologist Joseph Campbell toward the end of Campbell's life. The series is entitled "Joseph Campbell and the Power of Myth," and PBS affiliates have aired it many times.

Campbell had written in his famous book *The Hero With a Thousand Faces*: "Myth is the secret opening through which the inexhaustible energies of the cosmos pour into human manifestation."[17] In the interviews with Moyers, Campbell said:

> Each of us is an incarnation of God.
>
> We are all manifestation of the Buddha consciousness or Christ consciousness, only we don't know it.
>
> Follow your bliss.

Campbell's all-is-God pantheism is plain as day. There's nothing unique about Jesus; it doesn't matter if your consciousness is that of Christ or Buddha, since all religions are basically the same. Campbell says in effect, Don't worry about sin or external rules. Rather, Follow your bliss. Why? Because you are God! You can do whatever you want!

The Matrix

There's an entrancing scene in *The Matrix* when Neo (Keanu Reeves) is first introduced to Morpheus (Laurence Fishburne). Morpheus asks Neo, "What is reality? What is truth?" The screenwriters then play with the contradictory ideas that (1) truth is all in the mind; and (2) what Neo takes for granted is really a dreamlike state force-fed to him by the Machines. The rest of the movie is a rapid-fire back and forth between one "reality" and the next. The total effect is to reinforce the idea that the mind creates its own reality.

The Terrible, Horrible, No Good, Very Bad Catholic Church

Dan Brown's novel *The Da Vinci Code* has sold twenty million copies. As I write this, a movie based on the novel is set to hit theaters in May 2006 and is expected to make a big splash at the box office. What's all the fuss about?

Here's Brown's worldview agenda: Brown believes the Christian God is a power-hungry, macho, and evil god that must be replaced with the Divine Feminine that existed before Christianity. Brown's matriarchal paganism is a form of ancient Gnosticism (the Haunted worldview), in which the Goddess, representing all of nature, was to cast the God of the Bible into hell.[18]

Running With Scissors

Well, I could carry on with multiple examples. Like the PETA (People for the Ethical Treatment of Animals) ad campaign that posted large blow-up posters of Nazi concentration camps alongside turkey slaughterhouses—implying that humans should have no more dignity or rights than animals, and that you should practice vegetarianism (*ahisma*, non-violence) and not mess up your karma by killing other living things.

Or Anthony Robbins, the guru of "unlimited potential." Or Krishnamurti. Or Madame Blavatsky of theosophy. Or the practice of anthroposophy. Or the Christian Science of Mary Baker Eddy. Or worship of the great pantheistic mother goddess. Or the celestine prophecy. Or the gaia hypothesis of a world soul. Or the idea that all spiritual paths lead up the same mountain. Or Christian Gnosticism.

The fact is that Omnipresent Supergalactic Oneness worldview is quite appealing to sinful human beings. There are no binding *external* morals (after all, if you are God, who has the right to tell you what to do?); no guilt (why should you feel guilty if you're just following your bliss?); unlimited power (you have unlimited potential in yourself!); and no fear of God (why fear God when you *are* God?).

There's a very old lie at the heart of Omnipresent Supergalactic Oneness. It's right there in Genesis 3, where the serpent told the woman to take the fruit. He told her she wouldn't die—on the contrary, she'd *be like God.*

Sounds good. But should we trust the old serpent?

14 | SPIRITUALS 'R' US

Spiritual Psychic:

Reader and advisor can predict past, present and future. Can give never failing advice on love, marriage, money and career. With her psychic healing powers, she can help recover your passion and destiny, and can help restore your own energy and reduce stress and worry. Open your spiritual mind and discover your chakra centers to release your emotional and physical blocks with a psychic and tarot card reading.

- *Past Life Readings*
- *New Age Insights*
- *Guardian Angel Readings*
- *Tarot Cards*
- *Channeling*
- *Palmistry*

Clara [phone number withheld]

- *Appointments*
- *Reading by Phone*

Small print: Clara is 98% accurate on all readings. MasterCard and Visa accepted.[1]

Gemini (May 21–June 20)

You're in a phase of your yearly cycle when fate will conspire to expand your perspective, get you naturally high, and turn you into an explorer. To align yourself with these cosmic tendencies, you might want to charter a supersonic MiG-25 Foxbat plane to ferry you to the upper edge of the atmosphere, where you can see the curvature of the Earth. Other good ideas: Sail over Tanzania's Serengeti Plains in a hot-air balloon; paraglide off the sea cliffs at Oahu's Makupuu Point; or take a class in shamanism at a local yoga center.[2]

From a believer's point of view I do have some special relationship with some higher beings. But in my own mind I am still an ordinary Buddhist monk. . . .[3]

> **Seems like everybody wants to be "spiritual." Nobody wants to be "religious." Why?**

Psychics. Horoscopes. The Dalai Lama. Wicca. Witches. Crystal therapy. Calling up departed loved ones from the dead. Worshiping the moon goddess. Past life regression. Contacting higher beings. White magic* and black. Spell-casting. Feng shui.† Finding your soul mate.‡ Catch the vibe? Feel the energy? Seems like everybody wants to be "spiritual." Nobody wants to be "religious." Why? Let me bottom-line it for you:

I CAN'T GET NO ... SATISFACTION!

We are created hungry for God. Created in the image of God, we're hard-wired for a spiritually dynamic relationship with Him. Our souls cry out for Him, our spirits pant for Him every day (Psalm 42:1–2). If we're out of relationship with God, *something* has to fill that painful ache inside.

When spiritual seekers perceive church people as hypocritical, holier-

---

*Magic such as card tricks and pulling rabbits out of the hat is harmless and fun. In this chapter, magic has to do with contacting and using spiritual powers to achieve results.

†Feng shui's original purpose was spiritual: to not offend visiting spirits as they might flow through a house or other building.

‡According to the eighteenth-century philosopher and spiritualist Emanuel Swedenborg, if you find your soul mate, you should leave your current mate, because only your soul mate can "complete" you spiritually.

than-thou, spiritually sluggish, mentally musty, and fat and happy with their station in life—and the church as a bureaucratic institution unresponsive to people's needs, cramping creativity, and mired in the Middle Ages, rather than a place to meet *the ultimate thing in life*—they start looking anywhere but to traditional organized religion.

Where to go?

Many people turn to the New Age movement. In an earlier chapter I called it Designer Religion. As you can see from the illustration (on the next page), the New Age Movement can give you lots of different looks. Those looks derive from three worldviews that have some interesting common features:

1. They pick and choose from different religions and practices;
2. They easily shift from one worldview or set of gods to another;
3. They are like Jell-O when trying to nail down any definitive doctrines;
4. They gravitate away from absolute morals toward more relative morals;
5. They all seem comfortable with mind- and consciousness-expanding activities, occult magic, mystical knowledge, rituals, and ladders of initiation;
6. They emphasize the vast untapped potential in humans, such as the idea that we use only 10 percent of our brains; and
7. They tend to break down the distance or barrier between God in heaven and humans on earth.

THE GLITZ AND GLAMOUR OF POWER RELIGION

Whichever manifestation of the New Age Movement you're talking about, the driving force is getting connected to supernatural power. The source of power is much less important than what it can *do*. Whoever* or whatever† it is, it must be *powerful*.

---

*Personal spiritual entities include lower beings (ghosts, nature spirits, angels, demons, jinn, sprites) and higher (ascended masters, angels, demons, gods and goddesses), or one's own "higher self."
†Impersonal sources of power include ideas like "the Force," mana, chi, chakras, yin and yang, harnessing natural powers or other energies light or dark. The important thing here is not knowing about all the names, but realizing that they are perceived as impersonal and manipulatable.

MAINSTREAMS AND TRIBUTARIES OF THE NEW AGE MOVEMENT

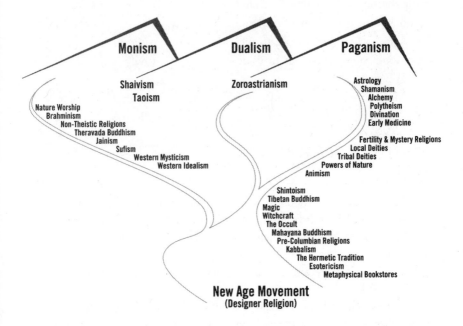

Oh, there's often more than a dash of sex appeal. This is especially true of fertility religions, which once sought to ensure crop cycles through sex-oriented rituals.

Once power is attained, it is hoped that power can be used to bring about certain desired effects.

The ironic thing is, New Age practitioners *and many Christians* look at Christianity as having very little to say about all this spooky spiritual stuff. The assumption seems to be either (1) the Bible is fairly silent about these things; or (2) the Bible used to speak this way, but Christianity is beyond all that now; science and the Enlightenment have pretty much disenchanted and demystified how we look at the world. As a result, both groups miss or downplay the fact that the Bible is very familiar with this territory. But what's going on now in the New Age Movement and what was going on in the Bible are amazingly similar. And knowing about worldviews will help you see these connections more clearly.

THE YEARS OF LIVING DANGEROUSLY

[Cue: John Williams' space opera music.] *A long time ago in a place far away, two closely related but estranged rebel kingdoms were being threatened by powerful empires. Their only chance was to turn to God and reaffirm their covenant with Him. Would they return?*

To a large extent, the Old Testament is a chronicle of Israel's many years of living dangerously: refusing to love, cherish, and worship God; enamored by the gods of the surrounding peoples; ignoring the handwriting on the wall about what would happen to them if they continued to rebel. I'll go out on a limb and say that the two most important passages for understanding the big story of the Old Testament are in 2 Kings, chapters 17 and 23. With 20/20 hindsight and prophetic insight, the author of Kings explains why the northern Israelite and southern Israelite kingdoms *had to fall* to foreign invaders.*

Dances With Wolves

Chapter 17, verse 7, of 2 Kings sounds like a legal brief: "All this took place because the Israelites had sinned against the Lord their God, who had brought them up out of Egypt from under the power of Pharaoh king of Egypt."

1. They worshiped other gods, breaking the first commandment.
2. They practiced fertility religion rituals in places they considered to be sacred and spiritually powerful, "on every high hill, and under every green tree" (1 Kings 14:23 KJV), violating the first, second, and third commandments.
3. They prayed to other gods.
4. They did "wicked things" (fertility cults often involved sex in their rituals) and otherwise did not live ethically, which is a pillar of biblical faith.
5. Just like their ancestors, they were stubborn and stiff-necked, refusing to trust God.
6. They rejected God's covenant with them over and over; therefore, just as He had warned them would happen in Deuteronomy 28

---

*The northern kingdom fell in 722 B.C. to the Assyrians. The southern kingdom fell to successive waves of Babylonian invasions in 605, 596, and 587 B.C.

and Leviticus 26, God brought destroyers upon them and let them reap what they had sown.

7. Instead of being a light to the nations surrounding them and setting the example for what it meant to trust God, they imitated the nations around them.

8. They repeated the idolatry that the people in the wilderness during Moses' time performed when he went up on the mountain to receive the Ten Commandments.

9. They were heavily involved in astrology.

10. They gave their children in human sacrifices to bloodthirsty pagan gods.

11. They practiced divination and sorcery and sold themselves to do evil, provoking God to anger (directly disobeying Deuteronomy 13 and 18).

Bottom line: "They worshiped the Lord, *but they also served their own gods* in accordance with the customs of the nations from which they had been brought" (2 Kings 17:33, italics added). "Even while these people were worshiping the Lord, they were serving their idols" (2 Kings 17:41).

O Brother, Where Art Thou?

Chapter 23 of 2 Kings seems like an upbeat story of how Josiah the boy-king turned the southern kingdom (Judah) back to the Lord. But read between the lines and you'll see what Josiah was up against. It was exactly the same stuff as in the northern kingdom, and it was just as deeply entrenched. We find later in the story that Josiah's reforms were short-lived. After Josiah, Judah quickly reverted to the same old, same old.

Obviously, as a whole, neither kingdom had learned the basics of the Biblical worldview. Rather, they opted for the glamour and power of fertility religions. The rest of the Old Testament tells how the Jews, looking back on what God had said would happen to them and what did happen, finally got it. After the debacle of the Babylonian exile, the Jewish people have been (more than less) monotheistic.

COSMIC SMACKDOWNS

So the big story running through the whole Bible is Yahweh's* war against the false gods. The God of the Bible is not a spirit or a force to be controlled or manipulated. Any spirit or force that opposes Him is asking for it.

Genesis I set the stage for a historic series of cosmic smackdowns. Starting with Exodus, one by one Yahweh takes the pretender gods, spirits, and demons out.

This is a message that people in our culture are likely to miss. We generally don't think the old pagan gods had any validity or reality, so we discount a major theme in the biblical story. I have begun a list of pagan gods and supernaturalistic practices that are mentioned in the Bible, often in passing. So far I have 184 of them, but I know my list is incomplete. If you'd like to see more or contribute to my growing list, please visit *www.blahblahbook.com.*

GETTING FREE FROM UNCLEAN SPIRITS

This chapter is partly a serious warning. When you mess with unclean spirits, for whatever reason, you are playing with fire and could get severely burned. They are using you for their ends; they will take advantage of you; they will enslave you until you think there is no way out.

When you mess with unclean spirits, you are playing with fire and could get severely burned. They are using you for their ends; they will take advantage of you; they will enslave you until you think there is no way out.

The Bible isn't kidding around when it talks about spiritual warfare. The Biblical worldview doesn't allow for Satan to be thought of merely as a symbol for evil.

---

*In Exodus 3:14, God revealed His personal name to Moses as "I am that I am." From the Hebrew, we derive the name Yahweh. (Earlier generations translated the name as Jehovah.) In Jewish tradition, it was forbidden to pronounce God's name for fear of taking God's name in vain (Exodus 20:7).

If you have ever dabbled in the evil spiritual beliefs or practices listed in this chapter, you need to do the following things:

1. Stop doing them immediately.
2. Renounce the devil and all his works. Renounce the seductive offer of spiritual power apart from the Lord Jesus Christ.
3. Trust God that His power is always greater than any evil spirit's.
4. Remember that Christ's blood can cleanse you from every sin, even though evil spirits will try to convince you that you have committed sins that are unforgivable.
5. Ask God to apply Christ's blood on the cross to you personally.
6. Ask God to wash you clean, forgive you completely, and fill you with the Holy Spirit.
7. Do not rest until you have found a solid group of believing Christians who have a Biblical worldview, who exhibit love, and who can provide an environment for your falling totally in love with Jesus.

15 | ASKING CREATIVE QUESTIONS

I'd like to bring you back to the list of sayings and slogans in chapter 7 ("Quick on the Uptake"). Of course, that list is merely suggestive of a million ways to express worldview viewpoints. I was just trying to give a sample of common sayings to get you thinking.

But sometimes hearing people's remarks isn't enough to figure out where they're coming from. When this happens, it's good to have some creative questions handy. As Christians, we want to engage those around us, not blow them off when they disagree with us. Creative questions are conversation-continuers, not conversation-stoppers. They invite people into dialogue, better understanding, and possible friendship.

Unfortunately, too often Christians are taught not to ask questions at all but rather to declare to people, before they may be receptive, "Verily I say unto you, thus saith the Word of God!" This approach can be very off-putting to those who do not share the Christians' view of the authority of Scripture.

Also unfortunately, too often Christians ask questions that stifle dialogue, generate confusion about the Biblical worldview, and derail friendships with people who don't think like them. At the risk of going out on a limb, here's an example of something I consider to be counterproductive and negative. This is what *not* to do. Disagree with me if you want, but please hear me out first.

A COUNTERPRODUCTIVE QUESTION

A scientifically minded person (MB) is having a discussion with a Christian (KH):

MB: Dinosaurs were not on Noah's ark. Dinosaurs and man have both walked the earth, but sixty-five million years apart.

KH: How do you know? Were you there?[1]

Now, I'm all for KH's desire to share the gospel and uphold the authority of Scripture. And I can see where he's going—he's angling toward bringing out the verse in Job 38:4 that says, "Where were you when I laid the earth's foundation?" If all KH were trying to do was get MB to be open to the supernatural, Biblical worldview, it would be great!

However, I believe KH's question is counterproductive in several ways.

1. It's an insult to the entire scientific method, implying that since creation is unrepeatable, science (which is based on repeatable experiments) can have nothing to say about our origins.
2. It ignores the central thrust of the intent of Genesis 1, as we covered in chapter 10, which was to assert the superiority of the one true God over all the other gods.
3. It confuses the Biblical worldview with its own peculiar wedding of a specific theory of the Bible interpretation with a specific theory about Earth's origins—a theory that is assumed to be *exactly and without* question the only possible way Genesis 1 should be read.
4. It settles in MB's mind that KH is not the kind of person with whom it is possible to have a reasonable discussion.
5. It reinforces the stereotype in MB's mind that Christians are oblivious to what science is about.
6. It gives MB the impression that if he's ever to become a Christian, he will have to take over KH's understanding of Genesis 1 lock, stock, and barrel—thus abandoning science altogether.

In short, this approach makes the same kind of mistake the church made in the case of Galileo. It's ineffective evangelism.

By contrast, in Acts 15 the Messianic Jewish believers did not force the non-Jewish Gentile believers to adopt all the Jewish patterns and traditions. They did not confuse the Biblical worldview with a particular cultural expression of that worldview. It was enough that the Jewish and Gentile believers agreed that there was a supernatural Creator God in heaven, that He had spoken in the Scriptures clearly, that Jesus was the Messiah, that He paid for the sins of the world on the cross, that He rose again from the dead, that He is coming again—and that all believers in Jesus should accept one another (even despite differences about nonessentials) and try to live lives that commend the gospel to others.

We should be very careful about identifying the Biblical worldview with particular scientific, political, social, or cultural norms. When we cross over from the gospel and the Biblical worldview into these other areas, we need to exercise some humility.

CLOSE ENCOUNTERS OF THE CREATIVE KIND

Let's get creative in our encounters with people. How? By asking creative questions. I don't mean dumbbell or softball questions. Rather, incisive, cut-to-the-chase kinds of questions that help reveal hidden worldview assumptions and agendas. Here are five types of questions you could ask:

1. Questions that define key terms
2. Questions that clarify
3. Questions that classify
4. Questions that challenge
5. Questions that point out what is assumed

1. Questions That Define Key Terms

The story that opened chapter 1 is about a friend of mine in a freshman philosophy class. When the professor asked, "How many of you believe in God?" she was the only person who raised her hand. It was a setup! For the rest of the semester, the professor ragged on God and raged against Christians, blaming Christianity for nearly all the misery in the world. It was a wicked abuse of power by the professor, but unfortunately this kind of thing happens more often than you might think.

I told this story to a friend of mine who is a philosophy professor. He thought for a moment and gave this entertaining response: "How about answering the question with a question? She could have raised her hand, immediately and politely interrupting, 'Professor, since this is a philosophy class, could you please define for us *what you* mean by *God?*' "

Socrates used this method all the time. He'd ask really basic questions like, "What is justice?" (If he were alive today he'd probably be asking, "What is tolerance?") Then he'd follow up with other questions that would reveal people's hidden assumptions. This annoyed some people to no end. Lesson: Know when to quit.

But do you see how this kind of *defining-key-terms* question can shift the discussion? Now the focus would be *off* the professor's anti-Christian hobbyhorse and *on* the critically important, hidden worldview assumptions of the professor!

2. Questions That Clarify

If someone says, for example, that he doesn't believe in God, you might ask really simple open-ended clarifying questions like, "Why do you think that?" and "What do you mean?" Or you could get a bit more specific and ask, "Can you be sure there is no God?" Or to be just a tad less pointed, you could ask (using the third person), "How could anyone *know for sure* there is no God?"*

Similar questions could be raised whenever someone objects to the specific and particular message of the Bible. You could say, "If there is a God who created the universe, should it be an insurmountable problem for Him to reveal His character and will to us humans?" You'd be trying to get the person to explain to you why he or she believes God is so limited that He can't do such a simple thing.

---

*Don't fear if someone reverses the question back to you: "How can anyone know for sure there *is* a God?" You don't have to prove there's a God, but you can show evidence for the reasonableness of Christian faith, for Jesus as the most influential person in human history, and so on. The point of the question was to sow seeds of doubt in the person's absolute certainty that there's no God. To be able to know for sure that there's no God, you'd have to know everything in the universe exhaustively. Only then could you say, "I have experienced everything and I can tell you authoritatively that there is no God to experience"—an audacious claim indeed! On the other hand, to claim that there is a God who can be known, you don't have to know everything—just a few things, really.

Asking clarifying questions shows your interest in people and your respect for them as fellow human beings. It may be that someone will respond to your question with a personal story. If this happens, *pay close attention!* Remember, each person's story is important, both for knowing him or her personally and for understanding how to communicate the gospel into his or her worldview.

You can find a perfect example of this technique in the old TV detective show *Columbo*. (Rent a season on DVD if you've never seen it.) In every episode, Columbo would catch the bad guy or gal with dumb-as-a-fox clarifying questions. Sometimes he would intentionally say the wrong thing to see if the perpetrator of the crime would correct him.

3. Questions That Classify

If someone says something that reveals or hints at his or her worldview, don't just assume that he or she truly holds that worldview. The person may just be playing around, trying to get your goat or trying an idea on for size (this happens a lot with Designer Religion). Rather, be ready to follow through with *identifying* or *classifying* questions.

Once you've taken the time to accurately clarify where a person is coming from, you've earned the right to be heard. You can say, "Can I show you my worldview and how I see that it's different?" Once you get permission, you can start talking about the basics of the Biblical worldview. (You might even use the box diagrams.)

A while back I was in a three-way conversation with a friend of mine and a professor who teaches religion at a local community college. In his classes, the professor teaches religions and belief systems in terms of themselves, unaffected by the beliefs of other religions. He seeks to be totally nonjudgmental of any religion; he "becomes" whatever religion he is teaching about. In one sense, this is good; in the scholarly study of religion you want to try as best you can to understand religions from within, as they understand themselves. (Worldview helps you do this, by the way.) In another sense, though, it's trouble because it seems to promote a generic universal religion, and a generic universal religion is not at all what Jesus was about.

Anyway, this professor began talking about interpretations of dreams. He spoke of archetypes (common pictures and symbols that people experience in dreams) and how the archetypes "want to teach us things." He treated the archetypes as if they were personalities with independent minds, emotions, and wills—rather than just internal dream-symbols people experience. At one point I asked this clarifying question: "If the archetypes have a mind, emotions, and a will, as you say, aren't they gods, spirits, or demons?" I was trying to find out if he was in the Haunted or the Omnipresent Supergalactic Oneness worldview. He dismissed the question with, "I don't mean polytheism or anything"—yet went on telling stories about what archetypes do, exactly as a polytheist would. He even tried to fit Christian ideas and symbols into his worldview.

This professor denied he was a polytheist. Although we ran out of time to clarify further, I'm pretty sure he's operating from within the Haunted worldview. As we have seen, the Biblical and Haunted worldviews are incompatible. This professor thinks he's helping others by advocating a kind of universal religion and receiving life guidance from these archetypes.

Does knowing this help me pray for the guy? Yes! Does it help me know better how to share the gospel with this fellow? Hopefully, yes. If I were a student, would knowing this help me avoid being taken in by him? Certainly! Would it help me understand the big picture of what he's trying to teach all his classes? Absolutely!

4. Questions That Challenge

The best kinds of challenging questions aren't mean—rather, they help shift the discussion to reveal worldview assumptions behind the negative opinions or attacks on the Christian faith.

If someone is really in your face about your faith, sometimes a *challenging* question is in order. The best kinds of challenging questions aren't mean—rather, they help shift the discussion to reveal worldview assumptions behind the negative opinions or attacks on the Christian faith.

For example, one of the high school students to whom I have taught this worldview course has a former Black Panther as his history teacher. This teacher regularly casts the most negative light on anything European and Christian. Whites are racist and violent, white society is racist and violent, Christianity supported slavery and racism, missionaries are racists, evangelicals opposed the civil rights movement, and so on.

This former Black Panther teacher has a point. An honest look at history will show that there are lots of terrible examples of Christians not living up to the best and highest Christian teachings. However, later in the year this teacher complained about how the Black Panther movement was unfairly tarred and feathered by the media as being a violent group. He also said, "You can't say an entire group is violent just because a few were violent." At that point my friend piped up with this fair, *challenging question*: "If that's the case, then why do you judge Christian faith by the worst examples of those who call themselves Christians?"

Great question! It revealed the double standard that was being used. If you can flip things or turn the tables, you can help break people out of their stereotypical mind patterns and maybe point them to the gospel.

5. Questions That Point Out What Is Assumed

The key phrase for this question is: "That assumes (thus and so), doesn't it?" You can use it in personal conversations and also in public settings—such as at lectures, forums, and sessions with graduate student teacher assistants.

The five worldview mantra points that we covered in the third chapter give us rich resources for employing the "That assumes ... doesn't it?" question.

Worldview Mantra point #1: "Not everybody has a religion, but everybody has a worldview." All worldviews are "religious" in the sense that they want your assent and approval of their core agendas. You may hear people say things like, "Anyone who has a brain in his head will agree that (fill in the blank)." Or "People who (fill in the blank) are moral idiots." When people say stuff like this, it shows they regard disagreement with their position as an offense against the way things ought to be as well as a personal affront. If people start getting hot with you about not agreeing with their dogma (whatever it is), you can point out the intolerance and judgmentalism of their position. You could say, "That assumes that I have to agree with you on your key point or I am inferior to you, doesn't it?" Or "Before I respond, I'd like to know—is dissent permitted here?"

Worldview Mantra point #2: "A worldview begins with a set of assumptions that can only be taken 'by faith.'" If someone starts ragging on you about how Christianity is an irrational leap of faith, key in on how *that person is making leaps of faith with his or her own worldview.* If the person is a materialist, you could say something like this: "Well, that assumes that this physical world is all there is, doesn't it? And isn't that also a leap of faith?"

We'll skip **Worldview Mantra point #3,** which is "Worldview assumptions are rarely acknowledged openly, questioned, or challenged by those who hold them," because this whole section is an amplification of that idea.

Worldview Mantra point #4: "Every worldview forces some narrowing of the mind." Face it: One flash point for worldview conflict in our culture is homosexuality and homosexual marriage. If you dissent from the near unanimous approval in the media of homosexuality and homosexual marriage, you'll pay the price. If you say, even in the most gentle way, that the Bible teaches that homosexual practice is a sin, you're going to be in for all kinds of abuse—in the name of tolerance! If this happens, you have a choice: You can point out what they have just done to you in the name of tolerance. "That assumes, doesn't it, that bigotry and stereotyping are okay with you, right?" Or you can go deeper and point out the root of their objection: "That assumes that God cannot have any say about what's right and wrong in our sexual practices, doesn't it?"

Worldview Mantra point #5: "Every worldview has strict and inflexible rules, or Absolutes, that must never be broken." If someone starts complaining about how Christianity is based on social control through guilt, you want to find out why that person is rejecting the concept of guilt and with it the idea of right and wrong. Simply point out the person's own worldview rules: "That assumes that there's no such thing as right or wrong, doesn't it?" Or if you want to point out the slippery slope down which moral relativism leads, you can say, "In your view, is there anything at all that's universally right or wrong, for all people, times, and places?" Always remember as this discussion progresses that if the person continues to deny there are any universal morals, you can say, "That assumes that what the Nazis did was permissible, doesn't it?"

More and more, the moral relativist's response to that question is: "Well, in their own minds the Nazis were right. Not in my mind, but then, it's only my mind. I can't control the right or wrong of somebody else's conscience. I can only control my own." In this case, try to work with what the person has told you. Ask, "Well, why do *you* think what the Nazis did was wrong?" Try to find the basis for the little bit of moral judging that he or she is doing, even if it's just limited to his or her own conscience. See if you can ground that feeling to something outside the person's own personal experience, on something that's going on outside the person's own head.

LIGHTEN UP!

Sometimes the best thing for starting or maintaining a good conversation is to have some jokes ready or at least be able to laugh at yourself. Banter and kibitzing are good. Everything doesn't always have to be really heavy. God enjoys creative conversations; you ought to be able to enjoy them yourself, as well.

As an example of banter and fun, I give you the following story about J. P. Moreland, a professor at Biola University—a Christian university. Moreland enjoys lecturing at secular college campuses about Christian faith. One time, a heckler who advocated extreme relativism was mercilessly giving Moreland the business. After the question-and-answer session, Moreland found out where the student was staying and went to his dorm to see if he could talk to him. When he got to the room, the door was open but the student wasn't there. Moreland went in and disconnected the guy's stereo. Coming out of the room with the stereo, he started to look for the student. The guy suddenly appeared and said, "Hey! What are you doing! You can't do that!" To which Moreland quietly replied, "Why?" The guy said, "Because it's *wrong!*"[2]

EARNING THE RIGHT TO BE HEARD

> **The point of asking creative questions is to earn the right to be heard, to win an audience for the gospel— not to get the best of people.**

The point of asking creative questions is to earn the right to be heard, to win an audience for the gospel—not to get the best of people. You want to show it's not just Christians who take a leap of faith—*all* worldviews are the same in this regard, including atheism! It's not just Christian faith that narrows options—*all* worldviews force some narrowing of the mind—*otherwise they wouldn't be worldviews!* It's not just Christianity that has absolute standards, rules, and prohibitions—*all* worldviews have strict, inflexible rules, whether called Absolutes or not.

As confident, public representatives of Christian faith in a pluralistic culture, what we want to do is bring worldview assumptions out into the open so that they can be openly compared. As the Biblical worldview is presented side-by-side with the other worldviews, many people will find it amazingly attractive for what it says both about God's love and our God-given human dignity. Christians have nothing to be ashamed of. The Bible's message stacks up just as well as the other worldviews—and more so!

Imagine what would happen in colleges, universities, and workplaces if, instead of going down silently like lambs to the slaughter, an army of Christians could confidently, politely, and persistently pose worldview-savvy questions. What kind of impact would that have in the market-place of ideas?

A BRILLIANT ANSWER

So far, this chapter has been about creative questions. I'd like to finish with a creative answer to a tough interview question.

David French, president of the Foundation for Individual Rights in Education, was applying for a position to teach at Cornell Law School. The interviewer noticed French's evangelical background and asked, "How is it possible for you to effectively teach gay students?"

Think about that question for a second. Think of all the ways you could give the kind of answer that would never get you hired. So how would you answer it? David French said this: "I believe that all human beings are created in the image of God and should be treated with dignity and respect, regardless of whether I agree with their personal conduct or beliefs. I will treat all my students well, but I can't guarantee that they will treat *me* well when they learn that I'm a dreaded 'Christian conservative.'"

The interviewer, a woman, responded with a long silence, then said, "I never thought of things from that perspective."[3]

This is exactly what we want to see happen in the marketplace of ideas, whether we're asking creative questions or giving creative answers: to give people opportunities to encounter the Biblical worldview in ways they've never considered before.

16 | NASTY, TRICKSY HOBBITSES

Y ou may not be where I'm coming from, but I know that relativism isn't true for me.

–Alan Garfinkle, American physicist[1]

In *The Lord of the Rings* by J. R. R. Tolkien, the creature Gollum complains that the hobbits are nasty and tricksy–while at the same time using all his wiles to charm them into thinking he is helping them. Our culture has a lot of postmodern* Gollums running around. This chapter will focus on four of these Gollums and the nifty little games they play.

THE BUTLER IN THE HOUSE OF RELATIVISM

You have arrived at the House of Relativism. You walk up a leafy pathway to the big, imposing double door. You raise the giant iron knocker and let it fall. A mighty "thunk" echoes through the interior. Presently an impeccably dressed butler opens the door and greets you. "Good evening, sir. How may I help you?" You reply, "I understand that

---

*In art and literature criticism, "postmodern literature and art" is narrowly defined as beginning after World War II. In this book, postmodernism has roots all the way back to Kant.

this is a big house with lots of rooms, and I'm not sure where to start. Can you show me around?" The butler says, "Certainly, sir," and ushers you into a vaulted entryway. Three cavernous halls branch out before you—each hall festooned with ornate doors that lead off into numerous side rooms. On the archway to the hall on the left an inscription reads, Materialism: The Way of Rationality. *The inscription over the middle hall says,* Monism: The Way of Mysticism. *To the right, the archway sign reads,* Paganism: The Way of Power.

CONTEMPORARY WESTERN CULTURE: THE HOUSE OF RELATIVISM
POSTMODERNIST, PLURALISTIC, MULTICULTURAL

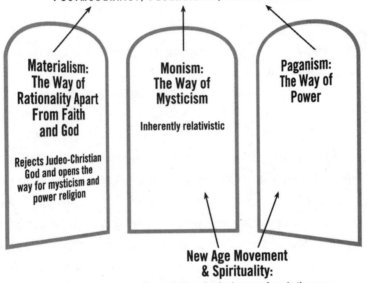

**Materialism:
The Way of
Rationality Apart
From Faith
and God**

Rejects Judeo-Christian
God and opens the
way for mysticism and
power religion

**Monism:
The Way of
Mysticism**

Inherently relativistic

**Paganism:
The Way of
Power**

**New Age Movement
& Spirituality:**
Syncretistic, eclectic; borrows from both rooms

You're curious about all three, but before you choose which room to explore, you ask the butler, "May I know your name—since I think I may be spending much time here?" The butler replies, "Certainly, sir. My name is Postmodernism." Suddenly he jumps back and pulls the rug out from under your feet! You land hard on your tailbone, hitting your head and badly spraining your wrist trying to break the fall. The butler, not lifting a finger to help, just smirks at you.

The House of Relativism is a tricky house. Its butler is particularly tricky.

I'm going to try to make this very simple. Postmodernism is basically an advanced form of relativism, a way of thinking we have already come across in the Haunted and WYSIWYG worldviews, and what we found in the "Spirituals 'R' Us" chapter.

Before there was postmodernism there were premodernism and modernism. Premodernism was the pre-scientific medieval synthesis that existed in Western culture before the Enlightenment. It accepted the supernatural realm but also mixed in pre-scientific and superstitious ideas.

Modernism was the beginning of the era of modern science and modern philosophy. It includes both the Glory-to-God and the Radical Enlightenment, since both Enlightenments accepted human rationality as a reliable guide to truth and science as a valid enterprise. (Remember that the Glory-to-God Enlightenment accepted the supernatural, but the Radical Enlightenment was highly suspicious of it.)

Our culture has begun to be (or is well on the way to becoming) postmodern. Postmodernism takes the main premises of the Radical Enlightenment—agnosticism and skepticism—and turns them against the Radical Enlightenment itself. Thus, postmodernism lives in ambiguity: It rejects certainty.

Postmodernism uses the crowbar of linguistic theory to pry the lid off our ability to know or convey any truth or knowledge at all. Since no one knows "the truth," no one can ever have a solid grounding to judge anyone else. This attitude erodes healthy skepticism and rational debate, opening the door to fuzzy anything-is-possible thinking and arguments based purely on shrill emotionalism. Personal experience is seen as the only path to truth, but it's only "your truth" as you experience it. In postmodernism, since there is no common truth, no common ground, no common cultural or historical heritage, all that's left is a struggle for power and control.

Yet here's an interesting thing: While that part of modernism based on the Radical Enlightenment slammed the door shut on the supernatural, postmodernism opens it up again. Any mystical or supernatural experience is welcome, provided it does not break the Prime Directive[2] of postmodernism: Thou shalt not interfere with relativism!

IF A MAN'S STANDING ALONE IN THE FOREST AND THERE'S NO WOMAN TO HEAR HIM, IS HE STILL WRONG?

This subsection's title refers to George Carlin's amusing take on the famous conundrum, "If a tree falls in the forest and there's no one there to hear it, does it make a sound?"

This question is not just an exercise in defining terms and clear thinking. It is the first shot across the bow against what many consider the naïve belief that the mind can obtain objective knowledge, or adequate knowledge, based on external reality.

One thing that took me a long time to figure out on questions like this was the importance of the use of the terms *subject* and *object*. In everyday language a subject is something you study, like geometry or American literature, and an object is a person, place, or thing.

In English grammar, the subject is the noun or noun clause of the sentence and the object is what the subject acts upon.

However, in epistemology—the study of how you know what you know—a "subject" is *the person making observations* about the world and the "object" is either *the thing being observed and studied* or *the mind's experience of the senses* as they (the senses) interact with the physical world.

"Subjective reality," then, is *the perceptions of the mind.* Subjective reality is distinguished sharply from "objective reality," or the things that exist in the world independent of the mind's perception of them.

There's one other aspect of subjectivity we need to consider: the psychological. When someone says, "That's just your subjective opinion," they may be telling you that your opinion is invalid because it is based upon unexamined emotions. So watch for how that phrase is used and be very careful how you use it yourself—it comes off as a huge put-down.

With that background on subject-object games, we can return to the tree-falling-in-the-forest-with-no-one-to-hear question. The assumption behind it is that "truth" (objective reality) is totally subjective (to individuals, to cultures, to the inner workings of the mind, to perception), so if there is no objective reality (or at least none than can be "known"), then there can be no "truth" or "Truths" with a capital T.

In other words, the system (the way the question is set up) is rigged to push toward outcomes that reject the Biblical worldview—as well as other vital documents in Western culture.

For example, notice what happens when we apply the above perspective to the shared assumptions of objective truth expressed in the Declaration of Independence:

> We hold these truths to be self-evident, that all men are created equal, that they are endowed by their Creator with certain unalienable rights, that among these are life, liberty and the pursuit of happiness. That to secure these rights, governments are instituted among men, deriving their just powers from the consent of the governed. ...[3]

Whatever these words meant to the framers and first readers of the document (and there is useful debate about how they were understood and ought to have been understood), to postmodernism everything about the document is anathema. Postmodernism rejects the assumptions it is based upon ("self-evident truths," which don't exist); it critiques "equality" as a total and utter sham (because of slavery); it considers the phrase "endowed by their Creator" as an illegitimate infringement of religion and God (who doesn't exist or whom we must keep out of politics) in politics; and it judges "unalienable rights" as a mere social construct* and another deceptive sham. In short, postmodernism says that *all* judgments are *inevitably* subjective. Therefore, we don't just say, "Hasta la vista, baby!" to God and the church—we kiss off any ideas of objective moral truths being legitimately applied to political systems.

So what's left? In postmodernism there can no longer be any appeal to "self-evident truths"; there is *nothing* on which people can or should morally agree (except the postmodernists' ideas of relativism and tolerance!). When there are no more self-evident truths, how can it be "wrong" to lie, cheat, and steal? In this view, rules are just social constructs used to oppress people anyway—how does any "authority" have the legitimacy to tell me what's good and bad?

---

*Social constructs are formed and propagated to legitimatize social control. A construct favors some groups and oppresses others. Social constructs have nothing do to with trying to discover and apply moral truth to social systems.

Can you see how if the premises of postmodernism are accepted widely, they could very well lead to more bias and less fairness in journalism; less civility in public debate; shriller voices that shun reason and rely on pure emotion; less objectivity and more fudging of results in science to obtain fame and grants; attack ads that are totally misleading and a win-at-any-cost mentality? If people have been taught in their philosophy, English, and history classes that there is "no truth, only truths," then do you think those ideas aren't going to work out in actions later in life? What's your take? Do you see any signs of these things happening in our culture?

HOUSE OF FLYING DAGGERS

In an earlier chapter, we saw that language was the guardian, facilitator, and transmitter of all branches of knowledge. We saw that the Medieval Synthesis and the Biblical worldview both acknowledge the power and the limitations of language. We learned that human language, for all its ambiguities and ways it can be abused, was seen as an adequate tool for conveying truthful ideas about nature, God, and humans. Because God created the universe through His spoken word, and since God has communicated through the written word of the Old Testament prophets, and since Christ is the

> **Behind all truth is the Word; behind all true communication are words based on the Word.**

unwritten Eternal and Living Word of God (John 1:1–3), behind all truth is the Word; behind all true communication are words based on the Word. Therefore, *communication through language is possible and meaningful.*

In fact, even lies (which are communicated through words) are based on the truth-carrying capacity of words. If words never expressed truth, lies would have no persuasive power.

Postmodernism has brought us to the place where language is a house of flying daggers. Contrary to everything we just saw above about the Biblical worldview, the Medieval Synthesis, and the Western intellectual tradition, postmodern linguistic theory tosses all that traditional stuff out the window.

In its place, the theory of deconstruction says that language is inherently deceptive; it's never to describe or promote truth but only to gain social control over others. This theory assumes from the get-go that there is no God, that God cannot and never has communicated, and that it is absurd to believe that God would ever speak a true word to humanity. Furthermore, this language theory denies any author the right to determine the meaning of what he or she has said. Instead, the receiver of a message determines the meaning. A favorite saying is: "Well, that's just your interpretation." Essentially, this theory says that words can mean anything.

Here's Jacques Derrida, one of the fathers of postmodernism, robbing the world of God and meaning: "The ether of religion will always have been hospitable to certain spectral virtuality." Let's translate this. Derrida calls religion nothing but ether—an imaginary, invisible substance the ancients thought filled the universe. For Derrida, the imaginary and false ideas of religion (including Christianity) project a ghostly fantasy that has no real basis.[4]

Let's acknowledge that people are not static; they can and do change their viewpoints. What they say in their twenties they may refute in their fifties. In this regard, Derrida, long known as an intellectual prankster, has lately been turning back to his religious roots. An Algerian Jew, he has been talking more and more of forgiveness.[5]

THE WEST IS MESSED

Postmodernism and deconstruction are kissing cousins. Like deconstructionists, postmodernists believe there are absolutely no absolutes (except the absolutes that they teach). Jean-Francois Lyotard said, "Simplifying to the extreme, I define postmodern as incredulity towards metanarratives."[6]

Let's translate again. (Isn't translating modern French linguists fun?) A narrative is any story, small or large. Metanarratives are grand overarching stories that are intended to give meaning to life, like the history of Western civilization, Chinese civilization, Islamic civilization, and redemption in Christianity. Even children's books and fairy tales can be deconstructed. For Lyotard and other postmodernists, these metanarratives, by definition, are nothing but tools of oppression by powerful classes over the less powerful.

Another example of a metanarrative might be the American story of the progress of equality, democracy, and human rights. Some postmodernists would say this nice story simply conceals our society's underlying, pervasive, and unchanging racism and the structures that support the status quo. Certainly the American story is mixed, but painting it as uniformly evil is where postmodernism often leads.

Postmodernism often charges that the Christian story of salvation is inextricably linked to colonialism—the rich classes' oppression of the poor and conquering of the world. Truth be told, lots of bad things have happened under the banners of Christianity and colonialism. But what many postmodern people don't seem to get is that colonialism and colonial attitudes that support theories of racial superiority are a total perversion of Christianity and Christian faith.

WHERE THE WILD THINGS ARE

If postmodernism turns everything in Christian faith so topsy-turvy, is there anything we as Christians can learn from it? As a matter of fact, there are plenty.

- Postmodernism teaches us to embrace the wildness of human experience. There are so many ways we can be surprised.
- Postmodernism checks Enlightenment arrogance and allows for the possibility of the supernatural.
- Postmodernism recognizes the importance of worldview.
- Postmodernism is a stance of humility: It says we don't know it all; nobody has a monopoly on the truth; perceptions are not the same as reality; and that we are all mired in subjectivity.

These are all true statements of the human condition. As Christians, we want to remind postmoderns that (if there is a God like the Bible says) there is no reason why God wouldn't be big enough, smart enough, and powerful enough to break through our mazes of subjectivity and actually get through to us. But that belief itself is a faith proposition. We believe it to be true, and it is. If we want to be convincing to others about our faith, we have to live as if it is true. We need to live authentically. This is what postmodern people are looking for, and this will always be the biggest challenge for all Christians—"to act justly and to love mercy and to walk humbly with your God" (Micah 6:8).

> **If we want to be convincing to others about our faith, we have to live as if it is true. We need to live authentically.**

A Christian wrinkle on postmodern humility would be to admit ignorance and say that only God knows truth "as it is." Which of us can say that we know the smallest truth "as it is" in its fullness and its glory? Think of all the glory of God packed into a blade of grass: life, photosynthesis, food, cells, chemical reactions, color, grasslands, forage, erosion prevention . . . and on and on. That little piece of creation is more than our minds can get around—and all of creation is shouting the glory of God in similar ways. What do we "know"? Not a lot.

The Radical Enlightenment slammed the door on God. Postmodernism opens the door again to the supernatural. This can be a two-edged sword, since a lot of people start moving into spiritualities and spiritual experiences that are far from the Biblical worldview and may actually lead them toward demonic spirits. How should we respond? First, the devil is clever and Christians are not immune to deception, even deception and harassment by demons, as seen in the book of Acts. Therefore we need to constantly do look-to-yourself-lest-you-too-be-tempted moves (Galatians 6:1–2). Second, we need to learn to tap into our position in Christ and our God-given authority in the spiritual realm to deal with these things. It's not in the scope of this book, but it is an important topic in Christian discipleship. Third, we want to have compassion for people who are trying to fill their cup with drinks that will never satisfy. We need to pray for them and love them, even if it takes them a long time to make a U-turn.

A last one (for now), and we've seen it before: Postmodernism gives us a chance to look critically at Christian rationalizations for oppression (slavery, anti-Semitism, unjust wars, treatment of women). Horrible things have happened in Biblical and Christian history. They should make us uncomfortable. And they should cause us to get honest and look at ourselves. God's people have not been perfect or anywhere close, whether in history or to this very day. We, who stand in line with our ancestors, are stained by sin. We all need God's mercy and forgiveness.

In sum, with the right spirit we can learn some profound lessons from postmodernism that will deepen our faith—that is, if we keep our wits about us and don't let postmodern worldviews trip us up.

17 | THE WHITE-HOT CORE

When it comes to Christian doctrine, Christians tend to be either hypercritical or completely clueless. If hypercritical, we can spot a false teacher at six hundred yards and drop him at three hundred. Only problem is, at that distance, it's easy to misjudge. Over time, so many Christians have been so quick on the trigger that we've gotten the reputation for being really good at shooting each other out of the saddle.

The other danger is not having the foggiest notion of what's going on. Unable to recognize a false teacher two feet away, much less at a distance, these Christians are easy pickin's for any kind of snake-oil salesman or two-bit charlatan who comes down the road.

THE UNBEARABLE LIGHTNESS OF A FALSE CHOICE

We can do better than feel forced to choose between these two options. What we desperately need is a way to draw reasonable boundaries around Christian faith and yet allow for good-faith differences. When you put things in a worldview perspective, you'll find that *Christians, of whatever stripe or flavor, have more in common with each other than with any other religion or philosophy.*

You might catch me up short and say, "Hey, wait a minute! Who are you to say that *your interpretation* of Christian faith is the one by which to judge others?" Excellent question!

The short answer is: What I'm talking about here is not just *my* private interpretation. It is a grand cross-cultural consensus worked out over twenty centuries on every continent and in every branch of Christian faith by people from all walks of life who have loved Jesus. A central assumption in this whole project has been the Biblical worldview. It might seem like I'm beating a dead horse to keep stressing this, but when you compare the Biblical worldview to the alternatives, there really are worlds of difference.

Our basic operating assumption in this chapter will be: *Any Christian interpretation of Christian faith must begin with the Biblical worldview—and no other.* In the first part we'll mine the mother lode of Christian unity, the white-hot Core of the gospel. In the second part, we'll see what happens when the Core is abandoned.

Sometimes Christians feel uncomfortable or threatened about differences they know exist in the family of believers because things can get so emotional so quickly. We might feel we don't have the knowledge, vocabulary, or skill to talk about these things calmly. The following diagram will hopefully begin to remedy that.

The beauty of the concentric circle diagram ("Targeting the Essentials") is that it enables us to put a visual and verbal finger on (1) what is absolutely essential for Christian faith, (2) what is important for major church branches but not necessarily essential, (3) what is important to minor church branches, (4) what is possible to have friendly disagreements over, and (5) what is a threat.

THE WHITE-HOT CORE

The white-hot Core of Christian faith* is actually quite simple, namely: (1) the necessary and essential truths of the gospel of salvation; and (2) a genuine experience of God as Trinity—Father, Son, and Holy

---

*In this book, when I refer to the essentials of Christian faith as the Core, Core will be capitalized.

TARGETING THE ESSENTIALS

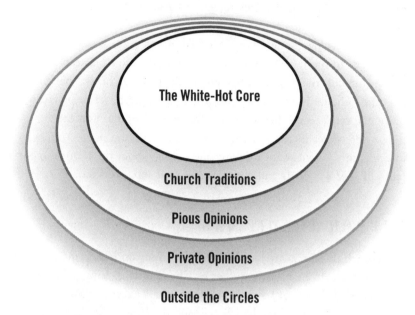

Spirit. Together these things fire up our souls with incredible love for God. We are so amazed at His grace and goodness to us in Christ that we want to live our whole lives to honor Him.

Please remember (this is key) that the Core of Christian faith assumes the Biblical worldview: God the Father as maker of heaven and earth; the Bible as authoritative and reliable in matters of faith and practice; God as active and communicative in history; Jesus Christ who died for our sins, rose from the dead, healed the sick and did miracles, sits at the right hand of the Father, and will come again to judge the quick and the dead; and the Holy Spirit as the one who causes us to be born again and who gives us the power to do what God wants us to do. These authoritative truths of Scripture require universal assent of all authentic Christian churches. They are summarized quite well in the Apostles' and Nicene Creeds.[1]

In short, without the Biblical worldview undergirding it, there can be no Core to Christian faith—and any sort of uniqueness to the Christian message evaporates.

The Core of Christian faith cannot be dusty, rational knowledge. Rather, *it is a life-transforming revelation of God the Father to our hearts of Christ, made real to us through the work of the Holy Spirit.*

Before moving to the other circles, I'd like to make something clear. I don't mean to imply that there's always a hard, fast line between the different circles in the diagrams. Sometimes the lines are fuzzy; sometimes it's hard to figure in which circle to peg a particular belief or practice. Since you can be sure there will be differences of opinion on these things, the circles merely provide some visual tools and non-inflammatory language for thinking and talking about the relative importance of specific beliefs and practices and their interpretations.

CHURCH TRADITIONS

Church traditions are long-standing positions on important questions over which the major branches of Christian faith have gathered. The largest divisions of Christian faith are: the Eastern Orthodox churches, the Roman Catholic Church, and the Protestant churches.*

Over time, the major branches of the church have hammered out their own thoughtful conclusions† to such questions as: What is the basis of church authority? (Scripture alone? Scripture plus tradition? Prophecy?) How should churches be organized institutionally? (A top-down hierarchy? Present-day apostolic and prophetic leadership? Consent-of-the-governed independent congregations?) What constitutes proper worship? ("High" or "low" liturgy? Are priests necessary?) What is the role of Mary the mother of Jesus in Christian devotion? (None? Some? Extensive?) How many sacraments are there? (Seven? Two? None?) What about the Lord's Supper? (How often should it be practiced?

---

*If you are Roman Catholic or Orthodox, you may have noticed that the way I've organized the circles frames the argument in favor of the Protestant perspective. Traditionally, Catholics and Orthodox believe their churches, teachings, and practices represent the Core. So even as I try to make the point that there is a *common something* that all Christians can agree on, the Catholics and Orthodox would consider what I'm calling the white-hot Core as insufficient—they would want to see church tradition in the Core.

†In the early church, bishops and theologians in councils and enclaves would discuss whether certain ways of talking about God were "permissible" or "impermissible." The key question was, Is it consistent with already revealed Core teachings? Issues were decided by vigorous discussions over time, gradual agreement, and finally by formal voting.

Does a miracle happen to the bread and wine? Should wine or grape juice be used?) What is the role of good works? (Necessary for salvation? A result of salvation? Some combination?) Are we saved by grace through faith in Christ alone? (What else is needed, if anything?) How should people be initiated into Christian faith? (Should infants or adults be baptized? How much water is necessary?) What does membership in the church mean? (How are the Holy Spirit's gifts distributed?) What are the roles of faith and reason? How should we understand God's sovereignty and human responsibility? (Weighted toward free will? Weighted toward predestination? Some middle ground?)

Church traditions have a lot to say about how we practice Christian community and how we reach out with Christ's love to the world. Church traditions require much theological study and time to change, and they are not changed lightly.

PIOUS OPINIONS

When it comes to the Core of Christian faith, the main things are the plain things and the plain things are the main things. But not everything in the Bible is main and plain.

Pious opinions, then, are good-faith interpretations of things in the Bible that are less clear, ambiguous, or silent. Unlike the Core, pious opinions are not slam dunks.

Devoutly and publicly held, pious opinions divide the church into hundreds of denominations and subdenominations.* Pious opinions provide the basis for determining the required beliefs and standards for church members. Each church has a perfect right to do this. It's okay to say, "This is where we stand. If you agree, come with us."

Each church brings its own understandings and unique gifts to the rest of the Body of Christ. Problems come when churches mistake their pious opinions for the Core. People may emphasize their church's unique understandings so much that they treat other believers like cold fish.

---

*Too often people trash-talk denominations. They say, "Jesus prayed for us to be one (John 17:21), so why can't we all be one?" My response is: (1) Jesus didn't say we must be one *institutionally*. We can be one *spiritually* if we hold fast to the Core; and (2) denominations are good—were it not for the many denominations, many cultural and social groups of people might never have heard the gospel.

Now, if people have any pride or appreciation for their church's history, traditions, missionaries, and martyrs—and they should!—it's not so easy to filter their church's strongly held beliefs from the Core. I believe Jesus wants us to do it anyway because of His prayer that *all* those who follow Him (whatever branch or subbranch of Christian faith) might be "one." (See John 17:9–23, especially verses 11, 21, and 23.)

Pious opinions can cover both beliefs and social relationships: How should we interpret the end times and the book of Revelation? Is drinking alcoholic beverages permissible? What are acceptable and unacceptable clothing or hairstyles? To what extent should we be separated from the world, or be involved in it? Should wives be submissive to their husbands, and if so, what does that mean?

Pious opinions can also cover broader issues, such as: How do faith and science relate to each other? What, if anything, does the Bible say about the Big Bang and evolution? What is the proper relationship between church and state? What is the Christian view of the best way to organize a government? How important are political and economic freedom? When is it justified for Christian citizens, or a country, to go to war? When is it justified for Christians to rise up and overthrow tyranny? Should Christians be involved in trade unions? Work on Sunday? Vote for a particular political party? These are all very important questions over which Christians will vigorously (and hopefully civilly) disagree—even though they agree on the Core!

PRIVATE OPINIONS

Private opinions are just that: opinions that originate within individuals. They may or may not be convincing to anyone else. Private opinions are idiosyncratic and may or may not spring from the desire to remain faithful to the Core of Christian faith, a particular church tradition, or others' pious opinions. They are much more subjective and speculative than pious opinions. Private opinions can be about innocuous things like: Do all dogs go to heaven?

Private opinions can also come from strong-willed, charismatic individuals who captivate whole churches, leading them into extreme and divisive doctrines. It isn't uncommon for these kinds of individuals to narrow salvation to one little group of people—their group! They just don't care what other Christians think.

OUTSIDE THE CIRCLES: ABANDONING THE CORE

I have really busted my chops trying to figure out what to call what lies outside the circles. My first thought was "heresy." And why not? Dictionaries give relatively neutral, noninflammatory definitions of *heresy* like "opinion or doctrine at variance with the orthodox or accepted doctrine, esp. of a church or religious system."[2]

But several recent incidents have given me pause.

#1: My eighteen-year-old daughter has a friend whose mother is part of a quasi-Christian group and whose father is Christian. When my daughter read an earlier manuscript version of this book, she said to me, "I don't want to give your book to my friend. Calling her a heretic would hurt our friendship and stifle open discussion about our faith." Now, I wasn't calling her friend a heretic (I don't know her friend personally; I don't even know what her beliefs are), but even so, my daughter had several valid points: (1) Using these words stifles open discussion; (2) These words carry *huge* amounts of emotional baggage; (3) You can't assume that people who are somehow associated with a belief system (like being children of parents) are committed to it; (4) No matter how careful you think you are in making a distinction between a belief system (a heresy) and the people who promote it (heretics), people hear you talking as if they are the same evil thing; (5) To call people who are just along for the ride and the leaders who take advantage of their followers heretics alike is inaccurate and unfair.

So I began to think of a name that would diffuse the situation and allow things to be explained in a calm, rational manner—without having people flip their mental switch off because I used the *H* word.

#2: This morning I saw a guy at the gym who said, "Haven't seen you for a while." I said, "Yeah, I've been working on finishing up this book." "Oh—is it fiction or nonfiction?" "Nonfiction. It's called *Blah, Blah, Blah: ...*" (He smiles.) "... *Making Sense of the World's Spiritual Chatter.*" (Furrowed brow; long pause, then,) "Well, they're all the same anyway, aren't they?" I said, "Well, that's one answer." (A smile of acknowledgment, then another long pause.) "Be sure to be nice. Do unto others what you'd have them do unto you. It's simple, really. It's so [expletive deleted] simple." Me: "Thanks. That's a good word." I sensed the Lord was using this fellow gym rat to reinforce some important things.

#3: I've struggled about the tone of this and the next chapter. It was too easy to slip into sarcasm or harsh language, pouring gas on the flames rather than speaking peace. I've come to realize more and more how in our postmodern, pluralistic culture, these ways of speaking/writing are not only big turn-offs, they're self-defeating in terms of communicating the gospel. So I've combed through these two chapters several times toning things down yet still trying to tell things as straight as I can (hopefully in love).

That Which Shall Not Be Named: The Dreaded H Word

With my evangelical background, until recently I had just assumed it would be okay to use the words *heresy* and *heretic*. They're good words in those circles. But for postmoderns, they sound positively medieval. Get the witch! Start the Inquisition! Break out the torture tongs! Prepare the stake! Gather the wood! Let's have a fire! These are the associations that go through many people's minds today. It's how they have been trained to respond.

They've also been trained to think that matters of doctrine are foolish and stupid controversies over opinions that can't be verified, since "there is no truth, only truths."

With these kinds of attitudes, it stands to reason that postmoderns grind their teeth when Christians talk about heresy or heretics. If they're more a barrier to communication than a help, why use them?

YOU HAD ME AT "VIRUS"

Here are some substitute names I've considered: "Beyond the Outer Limits," "Twisty, Turny Roads," "Nasty, Tricksies," "That Unnamed Dread," "The Dread Mocus," and "Oops!" I wanted to get away from straight-ahead grim terms that would make people say "grrrr," like "That Present Darkness," "Deceit," "Spiritual Darkness," or "The Spirit of the Antichrist."

I finally settled on "Virus Alert!"

A "Virus Alert!" is such a severe rupture from the Core of Christian truth that it can no longer be considered Christian. A Virus Alert! attacks the Core of Christian faith, but it always begins *within the circle of a "church" or of Christian faith.* It might give lip service to church tradition or pious or private opinions. But it always seeks to impose on the Core a worldview that is alien and hostile to the gospel.

The main tactic of Virus Alerts! is twisting God's Word so it means something far from what God intended—just like in the Garden (Genesis 3:1–8) and with Jesus in the wilderness (Matthew 4:1–11; Luke 4:1–13). Traditionally, two of the biggest twists have been (1) demoting the Lord Jesus Christ from God the Son to an angel, a prophet, or a great man; and (2) suggesting that salvation is earned rather than a gift given by grace through faith. "For it is by grace you have been saved, through faith—and this is not from yourselves, it is the gift of God— not by works, so that no one can boast" (Ephesians 2:8–9). More recently, a big twist has been to deny that God created the world and is separate from it.*

Contacting the CDC

When doctors come across any unfamiliar infection or disease, they check with the Centers for Disease Control and Prevention in Atlanta, Georgia. So what do you do if you suspect you're dealing with Virus Alert! teachings or practices in your church?

The first thing you need to *not* do is start screaming, "Heretic! Witch! Burn 'em now!"

Rather, put on humility. The book of 1 John boils it down to this: The false teachers bring fake teaching, fake living, and fake love. We are to hold to the true teaching about Christ, live consistently with gospel

---

*According to the Bible, God is both transcendent (over and above the world) and immanent (every-where present in it). One of the main heretical ideas today tries to deny the distance and difference between God and His creation by emphasizing only God's immanence. By the way, which worldview does this heresy represent?

values, and love our brothers and sisters in Christ from the heart.

So we first need to ask ourselves: How are we ourselves doing on these basic things? We all live with a thousand sins, foolishnesses, misperceptions, and prideful attitudes from the day we are born until the day we die.[3] Only when we have developed a decent level of self-awareness can we make good judgments. See Matthew 7:3–5 for the log-in-eye passage and John 8:7 to read about casting the first stone.

> **People can change over time if we give them some space and allow them to learn things the hard way if they have to.**

Second, regarding the people mixed up in Virus Alert! stuff, our job is not to decide who is "in" or "out" of God's kingdom. People can change over time if we give them some space and allow them to learn things the hard way if they have to. We have to leave some things up to God. The Bible says that everyone is created in the image of God, therefore everyone deserves some respect as a human being. Jesus took it further and calls us to love everyone. Even our enemies. This means that people mixed up with Virus Alert! stuff qualify as people who need respect and love.

Third, sometimes it will be easy to tell which teachings or practices are Virus Alerts! Others will be more difficult. On the tough ones our job is not to preemptively strike and decide these things on our own. Rather, we need to seek wise counsel.* Instead of just paying attention to believers living around us, we need to also listen to those who have been faithful through the ages. In short, we need to join . . .

THE GREAT CONVERSATION

The Great Conversation is the marvelous exchange of ideas and opinions of the best Christian examples through history. It is the mature reflectionsof the communion of saints regarding God's revelation of him-

---

*See Proverbs 11:14 (NASB): "In abundance of counselors there is victory."

self and His purposes for us. We have much to learn from those who have gone before us.

For many of us, placing ourselves within or under tradition makes us uncomfortable. It cuts against the grain of much of our culture that says, "Go, be autonomous. Ditch that musty, cobwebbed religion. Open your eyes. Be free. Create your own truth. Find your own reality. Be your own law."

When I say "placing ourselves within or under tradition," I mean respecting a tradition. Respecting a tradition doesn't mean that you have to be slavishly and legalistically devoted to following and obeying its every major and minor detail. Sometimes you need to cut loose from parts of it.

Our twenty-first century American culture generally doesn't put a lot of stock in the wisdom of the ages or value its own Western heritage. This attitude has bled through to the church; few believers care about or feel the need for the Great Conversation. Generation-to-generation continuity and inheritance of culture (Christian and secular) is considered a waste of time. All that counts is the here and now. It seems most would prefer to be spiritual Lone Rangers than to have any connections to the past.

A legitimate issue here is being your own person. Nobody wants to be a clone; everybody wants to be recognized for his or her own unique personhood. This is a good thing, part of the image of God implanted in us. Sometimes Christians need to take a stand against conformity: As the apostle Paul said, "Do not be conformed to this world, but be transformed by the renewing of your mind" (Romans 12:2 NASB).

PRESSING IN TOWARD THE CORE

Reading the Bible on our own, listening for God's voice, setting our affections on things above and not on earthly desires (Colossians 3:1–4), allowing Christ to form our character over time so that we might exhibit the fruit of the Spirit (Galatians 5:22–23), and watching for God's guidance on an individual level are all vital and good. But we also need the church! If we isolate ourselves from the best of Christian tradition, we open ourselves up to all kinds of deception and self-deception.

The Biblical worldview does not support the extreme go-it-alone attitude. It reverses our culture's priorities, giving greatest authority with the Core and lesser as we move outward into more human interpretations and speculation. Applying this to our circles diagram:

1. Trust God's self-revelation, the white-hot Core, implicitly;
2. Appreciate church traditions but realize that they are *interpretations* of the Core, not *the* Core (you don't have to buy into them hook, line, and sinker);
3. Entertain pious opinions, but take them with a grain, yea shakers, of salt; and
4. Be relatively indifferent and flexible toward private opinions, which are mainly based on human reason anyway.

As you move away from the Core there is more and more room for discussion, debate, and (dare I say it?) disagreement.

No matter how strongly we feel in these discussions, debates, and disagreements, we are all called to Christian humility, charity, and civility. A little humor wouldn't hurt, either. We're not God. None of us has a monopoly on the truth. We might be wrong on just a couple of things!

Our objective as faithful Christians should not be to excessively glorify human interpretations and systems, but to set our sights on the Core! Stick as close to Jesus as possible.

Anyway, as we try to figure these things out, by all means let's ask God's Holy Spirit for wisdom. But as we ask, we shouldn't assume that just because we've asked, we're entitled to think that we've got everything right. It's okay to be proud of our church's traditions, successes, missionaries, and martyrs, but we also need to be willing to honestly grapple with its horrible mistakes (and each tradition has its share of those). Whichever branch of Christianity or denomination we come from, our objective as faithful Christians should not be to excessively glorify human interpretations and systems, but to set our sights on the Core! Stick as close to Jesus as possible.

It's like target practice. You're at camp, and you've got your guns or your arrows all set. There's the target, looking kind of far away. Ready, aim, fire! You take your shots, then go up and see how you did. Maybe you didn't hit the bull's-eye all that often, but at least you were trying. With practice and some coaching, maybe you'll hit it a little more often.

Even if we miss the mark, the target is supremely important.* Just because nobody can hit the bull's-eye perfectly each time doesn't mean we just give up and imagine it's not there or that it's irrelevant. No! We try to sight better, control our breath, concentrate harder, and do everything else to get closer to the goal. *Jesus is definitely worth it.*

---

*One of the definitions of sin is to miss the mark (Romans 3:23). You're trying to do right, but you goof up.

18 | VIRUS ALERT!

hen your computer gives you the warning box *Spyware Alert!* you can't just pretend it's not there or that it's harmless. If you do, you could soon find yourself in a frustrating situation. For the sake of your data, your computer, and your peace of mind, you need to take effective action.

Same with Virus Alert! stuff. We bring untold damage to the church and to the gospel by taking the easy road and not standing up to a virulent worldview, especially when it's blatant and in your face. To that end, in this chapter we're going to query five religions–deism, Mormonism, Spongism, Islam, and Scientology–and see how they stack up to the Core.

DEISM: "OUT TO LUNCH—BACK IN TEN THOUSAND YEARS"

In early American history, deism was a major contributor to our cultural landscape.* Deism portrays God as the divine watchmaker—He creates the world, hangs it out in space, and leaves it to tick its way until the end of time. Someday there will be a judgment. Or not.

Deism objected to Christian specificity. Thomas Jefferson mockingly

---

*For a fascinating discussion on the contribution of deism to religious freedom in America, see the chapter "The Religion of the Republic" in Richard T. Hughes' book *How Christian Faith Can Sustain the Life of the Mind* (Grand Rapids, MI: Eerdmans, 2001).

compared the Trinity to a mythological three-headed dog that guarded the underworld and depended for its livelihood on death:

> The hocus-pocus phantasm of a god like another Cerberus, with one body and three heads, had its birth and growth in the blood of thousands and thousands of martyrs.[1]

For deists, no other revelation than nature was necessary. Thomas Paine concluded in his book *The Age of Reason* that everything anyone needed to know about God was available through nature and reason:

> The creation is the Bible of the Deist. He there reads, in the handwriting of the Creator himself, the certainty of his existence and the immutability of his power, and all other Bibles and Testaments are to him forgeries.[2]

I have often heard well-meaning Christians make the blanket statement that the Founding Fathers of the United States were Christians. The quotes above prove that's just not true. Some of the Founding Fathers were Christians, but some were obviously deists.

DEISM

The diagram shows that deism is only superficially similar to the Biblical worldview. The God of deism is remote and aloof from human affairs—out to lunch or on vacation, as it were. Miracles, revelation from God, prophesy, and Jesus as Savior are unnecessary. It is a pull-yourself-up-by-the-bootstraps religion. As Benjamin Franklin said, "God helps them that help themselves."[3] By the way, this phrase is *not* found in the Bible.

There are deists who know they are deists and say so, and there are deists who don't know they are deists and believe they are Christians. But it should be clear that deism denies some of the most fundamental truths about God—such as that He acts in concrete history,* that He has spoken in Scripture, that Christ is unique in all of history as the Son of God, and that God listens to and answers prayer.

The choice for all who call ourselves Christians is either to act as if God is the deistic God, unconcerned for us, or as if God is who He says he is. From a worldview perspective, if we take the first option, we are "practical atheists" and our God is like the "pirates who don't do anything" in *Jonah: A VeggieTales Movie*.

On the other hand, if we take the second option and believe God and His promises, and believe that He wants to act in our world and answer prayer, then there is no end to the depths of love we can receive and give to others.

MORMONISM: WHAT IF GOD WAS ONE OF US?

Forget about the dubious history of the *Book of Mormon*, the shift regarding barring blacks from the priesthood, or disputes about how particular Bible passages ought to be correctly translated. Let's cut to the chase regarding Mormonism's worldview.

For most of its history, the Church of Jesus Christ of Latter-day Saints (LDS) has promoted the idea that the God of this world was

---

Concrete history is actual human history, as opposed to legends and mythologies. The biggest example of God working in real human history in the Old Testament is the Exodus. The most dramatic example of God working in real human history in the New Testament is Christ taking on flesh and dwelling for thirty-some years among us.

once a man, and that faithful Mormons can progress toward becoming gods. This concept has been consistently taught by Mormonism's founders, Joseph Smith and Brigham Young; by past presidents and apostles in sermons, general conferences, and speeches; and in LDS-sponsored educational materials.

Lorenzo Snow, Mormonism's fifth prophet/president, claimed to get this couplet by direct revelation from God: *As man is, God once was; as God is, man may become.*[4] When Snow reported the couplet to Joseph Smith, Smith commended the revelation as "true gospel doctrine." Just a few months later (on April 6, 1844), Smith delivered his famous King Follett Discourse. A funeral oration, it was a bombshell of a sermon that reverberates to this day. Smith declared:

> God was once as we are now, and is an exalted Man, and sits enthroned in yonder heavens. That is the great secret. ... I am going to tell you how God came to be God. We have imagined and supposed that God was God from all eternity. I will refute that idea, and will take away and do away the veil, so that you may see.[5]

In this one sermon, Smith denied God's eternity; affirmed polytheism; claimed that all gods progress to becoming gods "by going from one small degree to another"; claimed that God the Father was once a man like us; and urged us to "climb a ladder" and ascend "step by step" until we become gods ourselves.

If that were not enough for the consternation and controversy gristmill, here's more. Brigham Young identified Adam as our Heavenly Father and Eve as our Heavenly Mother.[6] But then he went even further and said that God himself had a father and mother.[7] For Young, the God of *this world* had to learn to become God on some other planet by learning obedience to *his* father-and-mother god(s). With so many gods in the picture, it's hard to make this kind of Mormonism fit with any sort of belief in "one God." (Please refer to the Traditional Mormonism illustration.)

Then there's polygamy. Within early Mormonism, it isn't hard to see why some Mormon men who observed Joseph Smith's and Brigham Young's bountiful marriages (Smith had between thirty-three and forty-eight wives[8] and Young had fifty-six[9]) might have thought, "If it's good enough for Adam-God and our leaders, it's good enough for us" (hence "& Consorts" in the illustration). Brigham Young was actually pretty hard-nosed about it. He said, "The only men who become Gods, even the Sons of God, are those who enter into polygamy."[10]

To this day in parts of Utah, diehard Mormons clinging to the example of Smith and Young defy the law of the land and practice polygamy, hoping, perhaps, to capture some of that god-mythos.

TRADITIONAL MORMONISM

Adam, Eve (& Consorts?)

Heavenly Father & Mother (& Consorts?)

Heavenly Father & Mother (& Consorts?)

Heavenly Father & Mother (& Consorts?)

A Coming Change of Doctrine?

Official Mormon doctrine is not set in stone. It can change with revelation to the prophets and council of twelve apostles. This has been the case in the past in rulings on polygamy (1890, a condition for Utah's admission to the United States) and opening up the priesthood to blacks (which happened in 1978).

Over the past twenty to thirty years, high-ranking Mormons have been distancing themselves from some of the stranger teachings we have outlined above. For example, President Spencer W. Kimball renounced the Adam-God theory in 1976.[11] People involved in current Mormon-evangelical discussions report that highly-placed LDS teachers are backing off the God-was-once-a-man dogma and that some are denouncing mistakes in the writings of Brigham Young.

In addition, the LDS Church seems to be focusing more on Bible truths with which evangelicals can agree. For example, Robert L. Millet, a leader in the Mormon-evangelical dialogue from the Mormon side, recently said, "The central saving doctrine is that Jesus is the Christ, the Son of God, the Savior and Redeemer of humankind; that he lived, taught, healed, suffered and died for our sins; and that he rose from the dead the third day with a glorious, immortal, resurrected body."[12] And on November 14, 2004, Ravi Zacharias, the well-known Christian apologist/philosopher, spoke to a packed house at the Mormon Tabernacle. These are encouraging signs.

But momentous change doesn't come easy. Mormons naturally will want to defend their heroes. And there's the problem of, "Well, if our leaders were wrong on Adam-God, or God-was-once-a-man, what else are they wrong on?" So we can expect change—if it comes—to be gingerly slow and not shouted from the rooftops. If you're a Christian, this is a golden opportunity for conversations with your Mormon friends.

SPONGISM: SPONG-BOB AND THE "BARBARIAN IDEA"

John Shelby Spong is the retired Episcopal bishop of the diocese of Newark, author of many books, and cultured despiser of historic Christian faith. In 1998 he wrote a "Call to a New Reformation,"[13] in which he stated that the church needs a new reformation, one that goes much further than the one in the sixteenth century. He softens up his readers by pointing out that the first Reformation—which led to religious wars in Europe between Catholics and Protestants—didn't alter the basic Christian worldview at all:

> Neither side was debating such core teachings of Christianity as the doctrine of the Holy Trinity, Jesus as the incarnate son of God,

the reality of heaven and hell, the place of the cross in the plan of salvation or the role of such sacraments as Baptism and Communion. These rather were faith assertions held in common. . . . The time had not arrived in which Christians would be required to rethink the basic and identifying marks of Christianity itself.[14]

Actually, Spong is doing us a favor here: As the position he's attacking, he's outlined the Core of the Biblical worldview pretty well. (I'd quibble that baptism and Communion are church traditions, not the Core, but here that's a relatively minor point.) Spong then proposes that for post-modern people, the works of Copernicus, Newton, Darwin, and Freud have made belief in historic Christian faith impossible. Here are his twelve debating points, along with my responses in parentheses and italics:

1. Theism, as a way of defining God, is dead. *(Does this phrase "God is dead"—sound familiar?)* So most theological God-talk is today meaningless. A new way to speak of God must be found. *(Spong is rejecting monotheism! With what will he replace it? He has only two choices: Omnipresent Supergalactic Oneness or the WYSIWYG worldview. My best guess is that he's opting for the pantheism of Omnipresent Supergalactic Oneness, since he seems to want to talk about God a lot.)*

2. Since God can no longer be conceived in theistic terms, it becomes nonsensical to seek to understand Jesus as the incarnation of the theistic deity. So the Christology of the ages is bankrupt. *(Notice Spong's inflammatory language.)*

3. The biblical story of the perfect and finished creation from which human beings fell into sin is pre-Darwinian mythology and post-Darwinian nonsense. *(Spong's agenda here is to say that if you believe in evolution, you can no longer believe in the God of the Bible. Therefore, the stories in the Bible about the fall of man are pure fable; we are not fallen; and we don't have a sin problem. He's tying a particular view of science to his own worldview.)*

4. The virgin birth, understood as literal biology, makes Christ's divinity, as traditionally understood, impossible. *(Spong's worldview rejects all miracles; he's not going to make an exception for the virgin birth of Christ!)*

5. The miracle stories of the New Testament can no longer be interpreted in a post-Newtonian world as supernatural events performed by an incarnate deity. *(The strict, inflexible rules of Spong's worldview forbid miracles because miracles require a God who is supernatural.)*

6. The view of the cross as the sacrifice for the sins of the world is a barbarian idea based on primitive concepts of God and must be dismissed. *(Spong is saying that not only are you not a sinner, but there was no need for Jesus to die on the cross for you. The atonement is really distasteful to Spong. It offends his sense of propriety.)*

7. Resurrection is an action of God. Jesus was raised into the meaning of God. It therefore cannot be a physical resuscitation occurring inside human history. *(Spong rejects Paul the apostle: "If Christ has not been raised, our preaching is useless and so is your faith. . . . If Christ has not been raised, your faith is futile; you are still in your sins" [1 Corinthians 15:14, 17].)*

8. The story of the ascension assumed a three-tiered universe and is therefore not capable of being translated into the concepts of a post-Copernican space age. *(Of course not! Spong belittles the Bible's supernatural worldview. He assumes that nature is all there is, that nature is "God.")*

9. There is no external, objective, revealed standard writ in Scripture or on tablets of stone that will govern our ethical behavior for all time. *(Spong totally rejects the concept of authoritative Scripture. God is unable to speak because He is not supernatural.)*

10. Prayer cannot be a request made to a theistic deity to act in human history in a particular way. *(Why? Because Spong's "God" is not supernatural! You are God or part of God. You can meditate and chant Om. But please, no prayer!)*

11. The hope for life after death must be separated forever from the behavior control mentality of reward and punishment. The church must abandon, therefore, its reliance on guilt as a motivator of behavior. *(Spong both rejects heaven and hell and blows down a straw man, assuming the only possible motivations for traditional Christian faith are guilt and fear. He knows nothing about what it means to have a joyful relationship with God. But*

you can't have a "relationship" with an Impersonal Absolute.)

12. All human beings bear God's image and must be respected for what each person is. Therefore, no external description of one's being, whether based on race, ethnicity, gender, or sexual orientation, can properly be used as the basis for either rejection or discrimination. *(Of course we should not discriminate on the basis of race, ethnicity, or gender. But this is a deceptive argument. First, Spong uses the very Scripture he rejects [see #9] to make his point: "God created man in his own image, in the image of God he created him; male and female he created them" (Genesis 1:27). Second, for Spong we only "bear God's image" because we're all part of the big circle of life. Third, Spong makes nonjudgmentalism of homosexuality an essential part of his "Core." In so doing, Spong throws out the Biblical understandings of love, sex, marriage, and the relationship between Christ and the church.)*

It's tragic that a leader in a Christian church would say such things. I'm not trying to be mean here, but let's face it: Bishop Spong is a poster child for Virus Alert! religion. He took vows at his ordination to preach and defend the gospel, and now he's a New Age guru on a quest for Omnipresent Supergalactic Oneness.

Sadly, views like Spong's have prevailed in many mainline churches, seminaries, and denominational headquarters. Therefore, I must warn you: If you find yourself looking for a church, do not assume that every church with a Christian-sounding name is necessarily Christian. It may have all the trappings of a church—a venerable stone or brick building, a minister with a collar, Bibles in the pews, part of a well-known denomination—but have given itself over wholesale to a worldview that rejects the Core of biblical faith.*

ISLAM: ALL IN THE FAMILY?

Literally, *Islam* means submission to Allah. Islam claims to be the "mother of all true religion," the source of the guidance sent to the Old Testament prophets, to Jesus, and to Muhammad—and that these

---

*Read Galatians 1:6–10 for a particularly strongly worded warning in this regard.

Jewish-Christian-Muslim prophets are "all in the family."

This claim immediately brings to mind some pertinent worldview questions. (1) Who is closer to the Biblical worldview: Bishop Spong or Islam? (2) Are Allah "and the God of the Bible" the same creator God? and (3) With all the current unrest in the world, we want to know— What about Islam as a political religion?

Lastly, at the very end of the chapter we'll ask: (4) Is the Islamic worldview under the Biblical worldview category, or for Islam do we need to create a completely separate worldview category?

A COMPARISON OF BISHOP SPONG AND ISLAM

Bishop Spong	Islam
~~Theism~~	Theism
~~The Incarnation~~	~~The Incarnation~~
~~The Sinfulness of Humanity~~	~~The Sinfulness of Humanity~~
~~The Virgin Birth~~	The Virgin Birth
~~The Divinity of Christ~~	~~The Divinity of Christ~~
~~Miracles~~	~~Miracles~~
~~The Cross as Atonement~~	~~The Cross as Atonement~~
~~The Resurrection~~	~~The Resurrection~~
~~The Ascension~~	~~The Ascension~~
~~Authoritative Scripture~~	Authoritative Scripture
~~Prayer~~	Prayer
~~Heaven and Hell~~	Heaven and Hell
~~Traditional Heterosexuality~~	Traditional Heterosexuality

Spong v. Islam

Please look at the comparison chart of Bishop Spong and Islam. Bishop Spong rejects all thirteen Biblical worldview affirmations listed.* Islam only rejects seven. In terms of worldview, sad to say it, even

---

*I split Spong's single debating point #4 into two (the virgin birth and Christ's divinity), expanding the list from twelve to thirteen.

though Bishop Spong is a bishop in a Christian church, his worldview is so far from the Biblical worldview that Islam is closer.

We might conclude from this observation that the Islamic worldview and the Biblical worldview are really quite close to each other, like peas in a pod or birds of a feather. Ahhh. If only it were that simple.

Take "traditional heterosexuality." I struggled when I put Christian faith and Islam on the same side of this question since the Christian and Islamic understanding of relationships between men and women are so different. Jesus elevated women to equal dignity with men; Muhammad was very good to some women and very bad to others.*

Roaming through the Spong-Islam chart, the same kind of serious qualifications need to be made for "Heaven and Hell," "Prayer," "Authoritative Scripture," and "The Virgin Birth." In none of these cases is the Islamic viewpoint the same as the Biblical; it's just that Bishop Spong's refutation of the Biblical worldview in each case is so strong that it makes it look like Islam and the Christian faith agree on those things.

Are Allah and God the Same Creator God?

Take "Theism." Are the God of the Bible and the god of Islam (Allah) the same? The following answer is probably going to be very dissatisfying to you: Yes and no.

> **Between the God of the Bible and the god of Islam (Allah), you can never get away from a constant tension between similarities and differences.**

Between the God of the Bible and the god of Islam (Allah), you can never get away from a constant tension between similarities and differences.

---

*Muhammad referred derogatorily to women, calling them "lewdness and pudenda" (genitals) (see the Koran 24.31 and 4.15). Compare to Aluma Dankowitz's June 22, 2005, Inquiry and Analysis Series #227 article entitled "First Mixed Friday Prayers Led by a Woman: Muslim Reactions to a Historical Precedent," www.memri.org/bin/articles.cgi?Page=archives&Area=ia&ID=IA22705 (accessed June 22, 2005). See also Special Dispatch #890 of April 12, 2005, "Arab Feminists on Women's Rights: Cats and Dogs in the Developed World Have More Rights Than Women in the Arab and Muslim World" at http://memri.org/bin/articles.cgi?Page=archives&Area=sd&ID=SP89005. The Middle East Media Research Institute, http://memri.org/index.html, is a great resource for "bridging the language gap between the Middle East and the West."

On the side of emphasizing similarities: Muslim evangelists begin their appeal to Christians with the idea that we are worshiping the same God. Interestingly, Christian missionaries often also start with the same premise when evangelizing Muslims. Two reasons called forth in support of this idea are the "similar-names" and the "unknown High God" arguments.

The similar-names argument goes like this: The Hebrew and Aramaic language names for God *(El, Elohim,* and *Elah)* are closer to the Arabic *Allah* than, say, the English word *God,* which comes from the German *Gott,* a tribal god of trees and forests. Christians accept the name God because of the meanings we have infused into it, wiping out the old pagan idea.

The unknown High God argument follows: Most missionaries in the modern era have generally accepted whatever the local term for the High (or Creator) God is. Normally this High God is "unknown" or otherwise inaccessible. Therefore, the people have to deal with the local gods/ demons on a daily basis because they cannot connect with the High God. The gospel, of course, allows reconciliation and a relationship to finally take place with this High God. Experience has shown that the most effective missionary work starts with people who are in their (imperfect) understanding, and allows the Scriptures and the Holy Spirit to shine light and revelation on flawed concepts—like Allah—so they come to understand things in a more biblical way.

On the side of emphasizing differences: Here is the best short set of contrasts between the God of the Bible and Allah that I've found.[15]

1. Islam actively teaches that Allah is unknowable. Christians are called to know the Father and Jesus whom the Father sent (see John 17:3).
2. Allah is basically impersonal. In Islam, you're not supposed to think of Allah as a person, since he is totally beyond description. Muslims pray to Allah the god of Abraham, but they do not expect Allah to speak to them or reveal himself to them. On the other hand, while Christians accept that "we see through a glass, darkly" (see I Corinthians 13:12 KJV), a core Christian affirmation is that God is self-revealing and that God is not silent.
3. In Islam Allah is free to do whatever he wants, and his actions are

uninhibited by character or moral principles. Christians believe that God is a moral God, that God makes promises and keeps them, and that God even makes covenants with humans, voluntarily limiting His freedom to have a relationship with us!

4. Muslim theologians teach that passions or emotions in Allah would be demeaning to his greatness. Allah is unmoved, almost indifferent; he might have mercy and he might not. If so, it's good for you and it's Allah's will. If not, tough luck. Contrast this picture to the God of the Bible who grieves, rejoices, and loves passionately.

5. Muslims believe that Allah is absolutely unitary and can have no associates or partners (Koran 6.22–23). Christians do not believe Jesus is an "associate" or "partner" of God, but that He is God the eternal Son who became a man (see John 1:1–3, 14, 18).

On the seesaw of similarities and differences: In our culture, many people unthinkingly assume that all monotheisms are basically the same. But as we've seen in this short survey, despite the similarities, Islam's idea of God is very different from the Biblical worldview. Living with this tension of similarities and differences requires a lot of discernment and patience.

Wall of Separation Between Mosque and State?

When evaluating Islam, most Christians only look at the theological or doctrinal errors of Islam. But in doing this they miss a very important aspect of Islam. Traditionally, Islam is a political religion, not just religion as Westerners think of religion. We can talk about the theological and doctrinal differences between Islam and Christianity until the cows come home, but this aspect of Islam as a political religion doesn't get enough attention.

The long-term goal of Islam is not just individuals submitting to Allah on their own terms but for whole societies to become political Islamic states that enforce Islamic law.

Now we have to be honest: For about fifteen hundred years—since Constantine turned Christianity from a politically powerless and persecuted sect into the official religion of the Roman Empire—Western Christianity was practiced in many ways as a political religion. That incredibly strong church-state connection was not broken until the American Revolution. Then, for the first time in history there arose a secular state with complete freedom of religion.

Historically, Islamic law has had plenty of experience with warlords, kings, and despots, but hardly any with democracy. This may have something to do with the Islamic worldview: Islamic law comes from the Koran; it is essentially theocratic. It doesn't particularly cotton to the idea of a *secular* democracy in which law derives from the will of the people rather than from Allah.

Two keystones of Western democracies are the dignity of the individual and the suspicion of concentrating political power in one or a very few individuals. These ideas derive from experience and the Biblical worldview understanding of man: that although people are created in God's image (thus civil liberties and civil rights must be protected), they are sinful (thus cannot be trusted with absolute power, and thus our system of checks and balances). As a result of this biblical underpinning, Western law respects the conscience of the individual, allows religious freedom (including freedom to change religions, or to have none), enforces civil laws instead of imposing religious laws on everyone, has *separation* (not unity!) of church and state to prevent abuse of religious power, and provides equality under one law to all.

In contrast, traditional Islamic societies make the Koran the sourcebook (or a major sourcebook) for law; forbid Muslims from converting from Islam on pain of death (the "law of apostasy");[16] and discriminate against non-Muslims. Furthermore, traditional Islamic law has very different perspectives regarding women, civil rights, and a host of other "image of God in man" (worldview) issues.*

This makes the transition to democracy difficult. Traditional Muslim people are unfamiliar with democratic institutions and mindsets, and if they think things are moving in the direction of "the Great Satan," they resist. Muslim-majority nations that now have democracy—Turkey, Indonesia, Afghanistan, and Iraq—have in each case departed from traditional political Islam in order to adapt and adopt Western forms of law. That transition has not come without a price.

---

*If you want to learn more about Islam as a political religion, read anything by Bat Ye'or. A good place to start is her Web site: *www.dhimmitude.org/index.php* (accessed November 15, 2005).

SCIENTOLOGY: YOU, TOO, CAN BECOME AN OPERATING THETAN

Here's an answer to a frequently asked question from the Church of Scientology's official Web site:

Q: What does Scientology have to say about Christianity?

A: Scientologists hold the Bible as a holy work and have no argument with the Christian belief that Jesus Christ was the Savior of Mankind and the Son of God. We share Christ's goals for man's achievement of wisdom, good health and immortality. Christianity is among the faiths studied by Scientology ministerial students.[17]

Boy, that sounds pretty good. Let's sign up!

But wait, Tom Cruise, a committed Scientologist, says, "Buddhism is the grandfather of Scientology."[18]

Hmmm. So what are we looking at here? Is Scientology a "church" like a Protestant denomination? Is it a form of Buddhism? Or is it something else?

Until recently, Scientology's core beliefs and rituals had been a closely guarded and legally defended secret—as well as a highly profitable source of cash for the organization. It used to be that the only way you could learn the deep things of Scientology was to spend lots of money and devote years of your life to it. Now Scientology's secrets are spilled all over cyberspace.

So let's shine our worldview searchlight on two of Scientology's most tightly held secrets: the Xenu story and the MEST Universes.

A Galactic Space Opera

According to L. Ron Hubbard, the founder of Scientology, seventy-five million years ago Xenu, an evil ruler of many planets, had an over-population problem. There were far too many people on these planets. So with the help of psychiatrists and income tax inspectors, Xenu tricked the people, froze them in glycol and alcohol, and packed them into spaceships that looked just like DC-8 planes, only with jets instead of propellers. He sent them all to earth, gathered them around volcanoes, put hydrogen bombs in the volcanoes, and blew everything to smithereens. The souls of the people (called *thetans*) splintered and were whirled around in the nuclear winds.

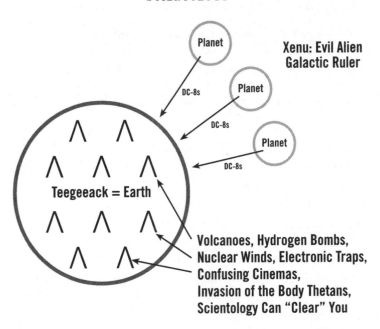

SCIENTOLOGY

Planet

Xenu: Evil Alien Galactic Ruler

DC-8s

Planet

DC-8s

Planet

DC-8s

Teegeeack = Earth

Volcanoes, Hydrogen Bombs, Nuclear Winds, Electronic Traps, Confusing Cinemas, Invasion of the Body Thetans, Scientology Can "Clear" You

Then Xenu gathered the fragmented thetans with "electronic ribbons" and forced them into cinemas where for a long time they had to watch confusing movies that said they were God, the devil, and Christ. After this, the poor thetans clumped together and invaded the bodies of the few humans who were left alive.[19]

So the great human problem is that we are possessed by thetans who make us do counterproductive things that we simply don't understand. Scientology promises a technological solution to our spiritual problem. It promises to dispossess us of our thetans so we can "think clearly" (or, be "clear"), which means something very specific, as we shall shortly see.

MEST Universes

Another top-secret Scientology story seems to have a whole different worldview behind it. A Dutch scholar of religion observes:

[C]rucial for any understanding of its notion of God is the idea of theta. This is the original ocean of being, and the origin of thetans. The latter are the creators of the universes of matter, energy, space and time (MEST). Thetans ultimately became entrapped in those MEST universes, and forgot that they were, in fact, the creators of them. Scientology reminds thetans of their divine origin and nature, potentially converting each of us again into an "operating thetan."[20]

Notice the differences between these two stories. The first explains why people need to go through exorcisms to free themselves from splintered thetans. The second shows that our main problem is ignorance and that Scientology gives us the revelatory experience that we are really divine thetans, the original creators of the space-time universe. An interesting twist, wouldn't you say, on Omnipresent Supergalactic Oneness's "I am God" theme?

Hubbard's Fantasia

Scientology is a neo-Gnostic system of a series of ever higher, more expensive, and more secret initiation levels. The goal is attaining supernatural powers. The Xenu story comes from the OT-3 course: "Operating Thetan, Level 3."

Hubbard's definition of Operating Thetan is an individual (Hubbard's term is *thetan exterior*) "who can have but doesn't have to have a body in order to control or operate thought, life, matter, energy, space and time."[21] Being able to cause effects at a distance and control others' thoughts is precisely the objective in occult and black magic.

The Xenu and MEST stories sound like pretty good science-fiction stories, don't they? Oh, did I mention that before L. Ron Hubbard founded the religion of Scientology, he was a science-fiction writer?

That operating thetan stuff is pretty out there, isn't it? And did I mention that Hubbard was heavily immersed in Aleister Crowley's occult system, that he had a spirit guide called "The Empress," and that he practiced black magic?*

---

*A phone conversation with Dr. Michael McClymond, professor of the Steber Chair of Theological Studies at Saint Louis University, revealed that according to Hubbard, a devout follower of Crowley, Scientology was born on the day Crowley died.

So why did Tom Cruise say that Buddhism is the grandfather of Scientology? I'm not sure. The Xenu story definitely isn't Buddhist. Mythical stories aside, it looks like both seek ultimate truth within one's own self-consciousness. Scientology goes far beyond the Buddhism of Siddhartha Gautama in that it is so centered on ego's desire to control and use spiritual power. (Time to reread Isaiah 14:12–14.)

Well, now that you've read this, you don't have to run out and join Scientology to learn its secrets; you just saved yourself several years of your life and a cool twenty to fifty thousand bucks. Was the price of this book worth that knowledge?

COME ON BABY, NOW . . . WORK IT ON OUT

In the previous chapter we defined Virus Alerts! as imposing alien and hostile worldviews on the Core of Christian faith, subverting the gospel *from within the church*. By this definition, Buddhism, Hinduism, Native American religions, and Australian aboriginal religions are not heretical—they are just different religions. Using this definition and our knowledge of worldviews as analytical tools, let's think through a few questions regarding the religions we've just studied.

1. To which worldview would you assign the Church of Scientology?

My response: Scientology calls itself a "church," but it actually has three non-Biblical worldview hooks: the WYSIWYG hook (technology; electronic gadgets; the "science" of mental health); the Quasi-Biblical/Haunted hook (a wild science-fiction mythology; thetans as evil spirits needing exorcism; emphasis on magic); and the Omnipresent Supergalactic Oneness hook (akin to Buddhism with its ignorance-is-the-problem and enlightenment themes, also the "Operating Thetan" idea fits with "the-Divine-is-you" perspective).

Best guess: Designer Religion. (It's nice to have the catch-all Designer Religion category when you need it!)

2. Is Scientology a Virus Alert!?

My response: Tricky. Scientology isn't really Christian and doesn't try to be, and yet it poses as a religion above all religions, a universal answer. In this way Scientology is subverting from within because it must seek to pass itself off as compatible with Christian faith.

On all the important Biblical worldview basics, Scientology inverts values, elevating various spirits and its version of the Divine Self over God the Creator. Its black magic side takes Christian ideas and twists them. In public it pitches itself as a "church," its teachers "ministers," and its teaching as compatible with the Bible and Jesus. Get inside Scientology, though, and the contempt for Christian faith is profound. Bottom line: As a counterfeit church, Scientology is not Christian ever.

3. What about deism, then? Is it Virus Alert!?

My response: Deism wants to keep the idea of a generic God but throw out miracles and God's self-revelation in the Bible. So yeah, it's Virus Alert!

4. What about Mormonism?

My response: Clearly traditional Mormonism is Virus Alert! Mormonism claims to be Christian but wavers between outright polytheism and you-are-godism.

I have a hunch that many Mormons might actually believe in Christ. They may just have some strange ideas mixed in with their theology. We need to remember we're not saved by the purity of our doctrine but by grace through faith (Ephesians 2:8–9).

5. What about John Spong?

My response: Virus Alert! obviously. Even though this bishop uses Christian language, he reinterprets Christianity through the grid of pantheistic Omnipresent Supergalactic Oneness worldview.

6. And finally, what about Islam? Is Islam a Virus Alert!? Or do I need to go back to the drawing board with my worldview thinking and create a seventh worldview category entirely for Islam?

It could go either way. I'll argue both sides and try to choose the best argument.

Response A—Islam is a Quasi-Biblical worldview, not a totally separate worldview.

Here's my thinking: The relationship between Christianity and Judaism is complex but not hard to understand. Christianity claims to be the fulfillment of promises God made to the Jewish people. It doesn't reject anything God revealed through the Jewish history or prophets, but rather affirms them (see Matthew 5:17). Since Judaism and Christianity share the same Biblical worldview (minus the belief in Jesus as Messiah and thus the Trinity), Judaism cannot be considered as a Virus Alert!*

However, Islam's stance toward Judaism and Christianity is in some fundamental ways profoundly rejectionist. Islam depends on Judaism for its idea of one God but rejects the Jews as God's chosen people.

Conclusion: Claiming to support the idea of God revealing himself through prophets and Scripture, Islam subverts the Biblical worldview from within.

Response B—Islam is an entirely separate worldview and deserves a seventh worldview category.

If you have eyes, look around the world. Islamic civilizations, for all their variations, are very different from what we experience in Western civilizations (whether we're looking at more-or-less Christian or post-Christian manifestations). Yes, there's been cultural borrowing between Western and Islamic civilizations. Yes, there are some common values. But if we think about how strikingly different Islam is as a total civilizational package, it's hard not to ascribe that difference to worldview.

Now that I've argued both sides of the question, how to decide? I have to admit, I've struggled with this one. But my bottom line is this: I believe Islam is a Virus Alert! It's a religion based originally on a Judeo-Christian framework. Very early in its development it diverged from the Biblical worldview, and now in many of the most important things it is far from it.

The six-worldview scheme holds. Whew! That was close.

---

*Jews who lived before Jesus and believed in God's promises were saved by God's grace through the gift of faith, just as Jews and Gentiles after Jesus who believe in God's promises are saved by God's grace through the gift of faith (Ephesians 2:8, 9). The apostle Paul said his earnest hope and prayer for Israel is that they will embrace their Messiah (Romans 10:1–4).

19 | TRINITY, SCHMINITY?

The one true God has always existed as God the Father, God the Son and God the Holy Spirit.*
—Father Peter Gillquist, archpriest in the Antiochian Orthodox Christian Archdiocese of North America

The Athanasian Creed (sixth century A.D.):
We worship one God in trinity and the Trinity in unity, neither confusing the persons nor dividing the divine being. For the Father is one person, the Son is another, and the Spirit is still another. . . . And yet there are not three eternal beings, but one who is eternal. . . .[1]

Institute of Islamic Information and Education pamphlet:
Let's put this together in a different form:

one person, God the Father
+ one person, God the Son
+ one person, God the Holy Ghost
= one person, God the What?

Is this English or is this gibberish?[2]

*A statement that succinctly summarizes the early church's teaching on the Trinity.

It's unfortunate, but the title of the movie *Chariots of Fire* was never adequately explained. You had to be British and an Anglican Christian to know that the phrase came from a well-known hymn that says "bring me my chariot of fire" so that I can help "build Jerusalem here." You can enjoy the movie without knowing that, but knowing it is very satisfying indeed.

The Trinity is like that. Hidden in plain sight. Underappreciated. Mysterious yet beautiful. Abundantly supported in Scripture yet scarcely taught and almost unknown in many Christian churches. If only people knew about the Trinity, it would make their experience of Christian faith so much more fruitful.

Ignorance and rejection of the Trinity is not new. From the third to the eighth centuries, the Arian controversy attacked the Trinity by teaching that Jesus was an exalted but created being.* In the seventh century, Muhammad and the Koran denied the Trinity by claiming that Christians worship three gods: God the Father, Mary the Mother, and Christ the Son.[3] In the seventeenth and eighteenth centuries, deists rattled the cages of traditional Trinitarian churches by trashing many distinctive Christian doctrines as nonessential. From the nineteenth century to the present the Unitarian and Universalist† churches have demoted the Trinity to merely one out of many mythological ways religions talk about God.

Most recently, revisionist Christians,‡ radical feminist theologians,§ and gender activists** have sought to re-envision Christianity, de-emphasizing or completely eliminating Trinitarian language from prayer

---

*Arius believed Jesus was a created being, not God. The modern equivalent of Arianism is the Jehovah's Witnesses movement and their Watchtower Society.

†Unitarians say that God is one (unitary) and is known by many names. Universalists reject hell and say everyone is saved. These two movements began in the nineteenth century and merged in 1961.

‡Revisionist Christians reject the Core of Christian faith. They want to rewrite, re-interpret, and re-imagine Christian faith using worldviews alien and hostile to the Biblical worldview.

§Some feminist theologians are evangelicals who respect God's authoritative Word and do an excellent job of interpreting Scripture. When I refer to radical feminist theologians, I am talking about those who want to replace "patriarchal religion" with pantheistic and neopagan worldviews. They want Christianity to be more "inclusive" of the goddess, but their brand of "inclusiveness" excludes God's own self-revelation as Father.

**Gender activists reject heterosexuality as normative. They seek to interpret the Scriptures through highly partisan homosexual, bisexual, and transsexual agendas.

books, hymn books, and Bible translations. Three recent examples: God addressed as "Nurturing Mother," "Holy Mother God," and "Loving Lady, have mercy; Mother Jesus, have mercy; Loving Lady, have mercy."[4]

We need to wake up and realize that worldview agendas lurk behind such language; it's not just fun and games. When mother-goddesses or sensuous gods and their consorts abound, the likely agenda is the Haunted worldview.[5] If the primary metaphor is the womb, the likely agenda is Omnipresent Supergalactic Oneness, since the womb, the baby, and the mother are one living being, at least for a while. In short, there's a lot going on in churches today that is an explicit repudiation of God's self-revelation, a U-turn from Christian faith into paganism and an abandonment of the Biblical worldview. It's like watching a slow-motion replay of Israel's train wreck in the Old Testament.

Someone advocating for these changes might say, "Well, God is beyond gender. Besides, we need to change with the times." Both of those things may be partially true, but let's mind the worldview store and not abandon the Core. Here are a few things to remember on this issue.

First, our most solid source of information about God is the Bible, and in the Bible God reveals himself primarily in male metaphors. Second, these male metaphors are integral to the whole biblical story: God is seen as the King, Father, and the Husband of Israel; Jesus is the Bridegroom and the church is His Bride. Third, Jesus referred to God as His Father and himself as God's Son. We simply can't blow these things off.

Even so, an important principle of biblical interpretation recognizes that God accommodates himself to our limited human understandings so our finite minds can grasp Him better. Hence, someone who holds to the Biblical worldview should have no trouble with the idea that God's essence is too infinite to be confined simply to maleness. In support of this we find that the metaphors for God in the Bible are not completely one-sided in this matter. In a very important and formative passage, men *and* women are created "in God's image," therefore God has given us permission to reflect on God as beyond mere maleness and femaleness (Genesis 1:26–27). Although feminine metaphors for God are relatively infrequent, God is not embarrassed to liken himself to a nursing mother (Isaiah 49:15).

The move to deny the Trinity is not just found in non-Christian religions and revisionist mainline churches. In the twentieth century, the Oneness ("Jesus Only") Pentecostals, reviving a Virus Alert! from the second and third centuries of the church,* say that God is Jesus and Jesus is God, taking away the relationship Jesus (as both the eternal and incarnate Son) has always had with God (the eternal Father). Other churches that might still consider themselves Trinitarian have such a sad lack of teaching about the Trinity that parishioners may be forgiven if they can't even tell the difference between the deistic or Islamic idea of God and God's self-revelation in the Bible.

My objective here is not about getting people to agree intellectually to what might be considered strange and esoteric beliefs. Instead, I believe the Trinity reveals the heart of God and the heart of what Christian worship and practice is all about. In fact, the Trinity is the basis for everything that is unique, good, and wonderful about the Christian life. Without the Trinity, we might as well convert to some other worldview or make up our own religion.

AN OBSCURE, DIFFICULT, AND USELESS IDEA?

A lot of people in churches think the Trinity is an obscure, difficult, and useless idea, an add-on totally irrelevant to practical Christian faith. They may point out that the word *Trinity* never appears in the Bible, therefore it can be dismissed. In effect they say, "Trinity, schminity."

A big reason for this attitude may come from how the Trinity is taught. I don't know about you, but when I was taught the Trinity, it was all about analogies and diagrams. For example, we learned the Trinity is like the three sides of one triangle, or the light, heat, and particles we get from the sun, or the three states of H_2O (gas, liquid, ice). We got all tripped up trying to explain rationalistically how God could be three distinct persons yet one divine essence.

---

*If you have to know, the teaching is Sibellianism, also known as modalism or modal monarchianism.

In this book I'm not going to repeat that approach because I know that even if I were the smartest guy in the world, I wouldn't be able to explain the nature of the Trinity to you. Nobody could. Non-omniscient beings that we are, we'll never have comprehensive

> **Non-omniscient beings that we are, we'll never have comprehensive and exhaustive knowledge of the Trinity. We'll never be able to fully understand God as He understands himself.**

and exhaustive knowledge of the Trinity. We'll never be able to fully understand God as He understands himself.

Lest we be too hasty in writing off appreciation of the Trinity, I'd like to ask a question: What is the best stuff about the Christian faith—to you personally? What keeps you coming back to Jesus? What have you found are your own benefits of being a Christian? List your top three.

1.

2.

3.

How'd you do? Find it hard to put into words? Sometimes we aren't able to name or even express what keeps us coming back to Jesus. But even though we're not able to comprehend all the ins and outs of these things, the Bible clearly says we can actually experience the Trinity. And a basic understanding of the Biblical worldview reveals that *all the best stuff about Christian faith is directly related to and dependent upon God as Trinity.* To put it another way: *If there were no Trinity, nothing worthwhile would remain of Christian faith.*

SURVEY SAYS!

Okay, this isn't a scientific survey. Nevertheless, I asked several groups of high school kids the same question I asked above—What's the best stuff about Christian faith to you personally?

Here's what they answered:

- Love
- Forgiveness
- Friendship and intimacy with God
- Friendship and fellowship with other Christians
- Salvation
- No more fear
- Joy, peace, and hope
- Prayer
- Hope of heaven, being with God forever
- Healing
- Life transformation
- Meaning and purposefulness to life
- Direction of the Holy Spirit
- Experiencing God through experiencing nature

There's no way we can cover all the items above in the rest of this chapter. We'll only have time and space to explore a small corner of this ocean of truth. But as I attempt to show you a few things now, please remember that I'm not trying to convince you rationally of a doctrine. Rather, using what we have learned about worldviews, I'll just try to help you *experience* why the Trinity is so important.

The Trinity in Creation

The Bible teaches Trinitarian monotheism. God clearly tells Israel that he is one when he says, "Hear, O Israel: The Lord our God, the Lord is one. Love the Lord your God with all your heart and with all your soul and with all your strength" (Deuteronomy 6:4–5). Yet even when the Old Testament is making its strongest pitches for worshiping the one true God, it leaves the door open for later revelation about Who that God is.

Accordingly, the Bible in its entirety teaches that the Trinity created the universe—and you. "In the beginning God created the heavens and the earth" (speaking of God the Father; see Genesis 1:1). "In the beginning was the Word, and the Word was with God, and the Word was God.... Through him [the Word] all things were made.... The Word became flesh and made his dwelling among us" (speaking of God the Son; see John 1:1, 3, 14). "And the Spirit of God was hovering over the waters [of creation]" (speaking of God the Spirit; see Genesis 1:2). It's a mistake to think of Creation as something only God the Father did, with the Son and the Spirit tagging along later.

The Trinity and Salvation

Again, I'm only scratching the surface here. But one of the things the New Testament clearly teaches is that all three members of the Trinity are intimately involved in bringing us salvation. I'll cite just one incomplete sentence of Scripture to support this point. First Peter 1:2 says, "[You] who have been chosen according to the foreknowledge of God the Father, through the sanctifying work of the Spirit, for obedience to Jesus Christ and sprinkling by his blood ..." According to this verse, the Father plans for our salvation, Jesus Christ purchases it, and the Holy Spirit effects it. It's not just a God-the-Father thing or a Jesus thing, or a Holy Spirit thing. It's a one-God-all-members-of-the-Trinity thing.

The Trinity and Intimacy With God as Father

More than anyone who ever lived, Jesus as God the Son had intimacy with God the Father. And yet He invited us into a similar experience with God as our Father. Again, I'm only going to take one verse, but there are lots of good ones. Galatians 4:6–7 says, "Because you are sons, God sent the Spirit of his Son into our hearts, the Spirit who calls out, 'Abba, Father.' So you are no longer a slave, but a son; and since you are a son, God has made you also an heir."

When we compare this verse with the Jewish tradition (which was Jesus', the disciples', and the apostle Paul's tradition), we may remember that saying or writing the divine name was, and is to this day, strongly discouraged, even in English (hence the convention in some Jewish circles of spelling God as "G-d"). Addressing G-d as Father is rare and, in the main, considered inappropriate familiarity with G-d. Yet Jesus addressed God as "my Father" and "Abba," which is kind of like saying "Papa" or "Daddy." Jesus actually invited us into the same kind of intimate fellowship He had with His heavenly Father.

Compare this intimacy to Islam. Muslims deny that Allah is "Father" because that would imply that Allah has a literal son. From the perspective of Islam, Jesus could only have had an ordinary person's relationship with Allah. In the Islamic mindset, calling God "Father" is even more inappropriate than it would be in Judaism.

What about the Impersonal Absolute of non-theistic religions (the Omnipresent Supergalactic worldview)? These religions propose an impersonal energy or force that is everywhere and in us. The whole idea of an intimate personal relationship is out of the question, since by definition you can't have "relationship" without persons sharing with each other and being in each other's presence.

In the Biblical worldview, calling God "Abba" as our Father is an inestimable privilege. We have no natural right to be considered children of God (John 1:12). Neither is it something that could ever be earned. It is a gift given by God the Father, God the Son, and God the Holy Spirit—totally apart from our merits or demerits.

The Trinity and Love

The hallmark of Christian faith is love. But where does love come from? Please meditate on the following Scripture (again, this is only a sampling of the full teaching). As you read, note the references to all three members of the Trinity in this passage.

> Therefore, since we have been justified through faith, we have peace with God through our Lord Jesus Christ, through whom we have gained access by faith into this grace in which we now stand. And we rejoice in the hope of the glory of God. Not only so, but we also rejoice in our sufferings, because we know that suffering produces perseverance; perseverance, character; and character, hope. And hope does not disappoint us, because God has poured out his love into our hearts by the Holy Spirit, whom he has given us. (Romans 5:1–5)

People often think the reason God created humans was that He was lonely and needed companionship. However, the Scriptures teach that love began *within* God and has always been in God—a perfect fellowship and union between God the Father, God the Son, and God the Holy Spirit. Think about this: Which view brings more glory to God: that God was perfect in communion and love within himself before creating humans, or that God was needy and lonely before He created humans? Which view is closer to "creating God in our image"?

Even though we are sinful humans, God invites us to experience the eternal love that has always existed within the Trinity. When we become Christians we actually *experience* that eternal love! Isn't that incredible!

The eternal love within the Trinity beats mono-monotheism cold. Mono-monotheism (absolute monotheism without the Trinity, like in Unitarianism, Jehovah's Witnesses, Islam, and deism) looks at God as a supernatural monad and relationally deprived. There is no communication within the God of mono-monotheism, no fellowship, and no love because there are no persons. And without love within this monadic God, there can be little hope of communion, fellowship, or love to share with humans. No wonder the God of mono-montheism is inaccessible, aloof, and remote compared to the Trinity.

In an earlier chapter we discovered how the only worldview in which it makes sense to say "God loves you" is the Biblical worldview. Here we find out *why* that is true!

TAKE OFF YOUR SHOES—THIS IS HOLY GROUND!

The Trinity is the underappreciated crown jewel of Christian theology. We are called to give glory to and worship God *as He has revealed himself.* In our increasingly pluralistic world, it is vital that Christians learn to think and speak comfortably about the Trinity. How can we do so? Here are three ideas:

The Forrest Gump Factor

Forrest Gump had to take a lot of guff in his life, but he wasn't ashamed of his beliefs. Even more so, the Trinity is nothing to be ashamed of. The Trinity is an incredibly beautiful synthesis of biblical revelation. In Ephesians 5:32, Paul says, "[Marriage] is a profound mystery—but I am talking about Christ and the Church." The truth of the Trinity is just as important and profound a mystery. We must not take the Trinity for granted!

> **The Trinity is an incredibly beautiful synthesis of biblical revelation. We must not take the Trinity for granted!**

If it's true that *all the best stuff of Christian faith is completely dependent on the Trinity,* right now would be a good time to put this book down, enter God's throne room, and praise Him and thank Him profusely for who He is, for revealing himself to us through Christ, for inviting us to call Him "Abba," and for being present to us through the Holy Spirit.

Pride Goeth Before the Fall

Among rock climbers, "Pride goeth before ... a fall" is an insider's joke, a cautionary word, and a Bible verse (Proverbs 16:18 KJV) all rolled into one.

When it comes to climbing the rock of the Trinity, we need to respect the rock. We are trying to put our limited hands, feet, and brains on something that is beautiful and rugged beyond description. We will never apprehend the mystery of God's essential nature; that will always be veiled from us. But God is not just an inanimate object; He is a person who has revealed himself to us through his energies,* His mighty

---

*God's energies are everything that God does.

works,* and preeminently through His Son as illuminated to us through the Holy Spirit.

We must also allow God to reveal himself as He sees fit. God is beyond male and female. For His own reasons, *God has revealed himself to us primarily as God the Father, God the Son, and God the Holy Spirit.*†

The passages we have just studied show the sublime workings of the Trinity in our lives. We should be careful how we speak about these things. Some language is permissible but some is very misleading. For example, it's okay to say, "Jesus is God." But we should avoid saying things like "God is Jesus" or "Jesus is the Holy Spirit." These statements confuse the beauty of unity and diversity within God as revealed in Scripture. Using confusing language about the Trinity prevents us (and those we teach) from appreciating how unity and diversity can exist together.

All mono-monotheistic ideas of God arrogantly impose a uniformity on God that just isn't there. The results are crushing. The Unitarian God is vague and cannot communicate. The Muslim god is non-personal and non-emotional. The monistic and pantheistic Impersonal Absolute cannot love anyone. All these views flatten God's full revelation of himself.

The Shield of St. Patrick

Many of the people who regularly go to churches and sit in the pews are in reality Binitarians rather than Trinitarians—they believe in Jesus and God the Father, but they have very little idea about the Holy Spirit.

This has far-reaching consequences. The Holy Spirit is the giver of life and the giver of gifts in the church. If people know nothing about the Holy Spirit, how can they grow spiritually? The Holy Spirit is also the river of spiritual power for God's people. "You shall receive power

---

*God's mighty works are the great and powerful things He does in history to bring deliverance and salvation to His people.

†Genesis 1:27 says God "created man in his own image ... male and female he created them." This indicates that there is something about both maleness and femaleness in God. There are also a few passages where the biblical imagery of God is feminine, such as when He says, "As one whom his mother comforts, so I will comfort you" (Isaiah 66:13 NASB).

when the Holy Spirit has come upon you; and you shall be my witnesses both in Jerusalem, and in all Judea and Samaria, and even to the remotest part of the earth" (Acts 1:8 NASB). If we know nothing about the Holy Spirit, how can we receive his power to be Christ's witnesses in the world?

There is also a real spiritual danger: If people in our churches tend to default to bi-theistic, Unitarian, monistic, and mono-monotheistic views of God, they are ripe pickin's for false teachers in the church, for syncretistic New Age movements, and for Muslim evangelists.

So let's get together with other believers and really *worship* God as He has revealed himself, with our whole hearts, opening ourselves up to God the Father, God the Son, *and* God the Holy Sprit.

Long ago St. Patrick taught his disciples this prayer:

I bind unto my self today
The strong name of the Trinity;
By invocation of the same,
The Three in One, the One in Three.[6]

Peter Gillquist said, as quoted at the beginning of this chapter, "The one true God has always existed as God the Father, God the Son, and God the Holy Spirit." I like this quote because it preserves the unity of God, as in "Hear, O Israel: The Lord our God, the Lord is one" (Deuteronomy 6:4), and it embraces the advanced revelation of God in the New Testament. It accomplishes this in simple, clear biblical language. Unashamed, worshipful humility. A fine combination.

20 | TWO TREES

This chapter is a warning against spiritual and intellectual pride.

The danger in examining worldviews, trying to figure them out, and seeking to categorize them is that we can take our eyes off the prize. As humans, we tend to think that reason alone is sufficient to delve into the mystery of life; we want to believe that we can figure things out on our own. We can too easily succumb to the temptation of thinking of God as an abstract philosophical concept to be explained—rather than a loving Father to be experienced!

Thinking this way doesn't just happen to non-Christians. It also happens to Christians. When it does, it leads to dead, lifeless religion,* not to mention an arrogant lack of humility.

Where I live, scrubby, barren hills overlook the city. On one of these hills were once planted thirteen big blue gum eucalyptus trees. Now only two are left. They are a landmark visible for miles and miles around. Although these two trees carry no edible fruit in real life, they still serve as inspiration for the following cautionary tale.

---

*I define religion as man's best attempts to reach "God," truth, and meaning. Christianity is God's best attempt to reach us. Therefore, I have always felt uncomfortable calling Christian faith a religion, with all the rules and regulations that religions entail. Rather, Christian faith is a living relationship with Jesus Christ—the same Jesus Christ who walked on Earth two thousand years ago, who died for our sins, who is with God the Father in heaven right now, and who is available to us right now through the Person of the Holy Spirit.

A TALE OF TWO TREES

Scene: A barren hill with two trees at its top. Hanging from each tree's branches is wonderful-looking fruit, ripe for the picking. One tree represents Knowledge and Experience. The other tree represents a Love relationship with God.

Up this hill comes a man, who there is met by another man. A dialogue ensues . . .

QUESTIONER: What do you seek?

SEEKER: Meaning in my life.

Q: Here are two trees: Do you want to eat the fruit of Knowledge or the fruit of Life with God?

S: Not so fast. I don't know if I can accept your premise of eating only one or the other. Can't I have both?

Q: Yes, but you have to pick God first if you want meaning in your life.

S: Hmm. How about I just try a little tiny piece from that tree there?

Q: Which one?

S: Well . . . Knowledge.

Q: Why would you want to do that?

S: Because I want to know.

Q: Know what?

S: You know . . . stuff!

Q: Stuff?

S: Yeah, lots of stuff.

Q: It'd be nice to be like God, to know lots of stuff, huh?

S: Yes.

Q: But you don't want to first choose Life with God?

S: Well, sure. Everybody wants that.

Q: Really?

S: Yeah.

Q: So what's your choice?

S: Darn. Tough choice!

Q: Take your time. I'm not in any big hurry.

S: Okay. (thinks)

Q: Well?

S: I've got all these questions banging around in my head.

Q: God loves you.

S: I want to know how things work. I want to know how to play the piano really well. I want to know how the stock market works.

Q: *God loves you.*

S: *I need to know how to win friends and influence people. I need to have a good explanation for good and evil.*

Q: *Do you think a relationship with God might have anything to do with it?*

S: *I need to know if we're free or determined . . . Huh?*

Q: *You have a choice before you just now.*

S: *Yeah. I know. But it's such a hard choice.*

Q: *Do you think you might have already made it?*

S: *No, no. I just want to keep my options open. Y'know, there's so much I'd really like to know. . . .*

PAY YOUR MONEY AND TAKE YOUR CHOICE

In life, there are some choices you just can't avoid and that are going to cost you either way. And just like the seeker in the story, there is one choice right before each of us. This choice has taunted us ever since there have been humans.

> **In life, there are some choices you just can't avoid and that are going to cost you either way.**

The book of Genesis talks about this choice. The message in this book of beginnings is that God created us and has good intentions for us—of blessing, of perfect shalom,* of meaning and purpose—but that we have turned away from God, opting instead for anything and everything except a close relationship with Him.

Although God provided many trees in the Garden of Eden, the spotlight of the story is on two: the Tree of Life—of a beautiful love relationship with God; and the Tree of the Knowledge of Good and Evil—of experience and human-based wisdom. God had said to Adam, "You are free to eat from any tree in the garden" (Genesis 2:16). This clearly included the Tree of Life. There was just one little problem. God said, "You must not eat from the tree of the knowledge of good and evil, for

---

Shalom is the Hebrew word usually translated into English as "peace." But it means a lot more than just absence of war or contentment. Shalom means harmony in all relationships and with the land. It means fulfillment, joy, and meaning for people in their own selves, in their social relationships, and in their relationship with God. Essentially, shalom means the presence of God and the blessing of God in fullness.

when you eat of it you will surely die" (Genesis 2:17).

Given acres of trees to eat from, Adam and Eve's attentions got riveted on the second tree. And the serpent, crafty charmer that he is, used guile and appealed to their vanity—"Eat [this fruit] ... and you will *be like God*" (italics added). Given our natural inclinations of wanting to be our own "gods," how can you argue with that logic? It seemed to Adam and Eve, and it seems to us, that God's ways, desires, objectives, and rules grind us the wrong way. A relationship with God seems to us to muck up all our great plans. We want to be free from God. And when we break from Him, that break creates a gigantic hole in our soul that *must* be filled.

That hole can't be filled by any created thing—including carnal knowledge, experiential knowledge, knowledge of science and technology, knowledge of the arts, or wisdom. None of these things will fill the hole left by the absence of God.

THE GREATEST STORY EVER TOLD

Genesis sets the stage for the main theme of Scripture, which is, basically, that *we need God!* Left to our own devices, we choose our own way rather than a love relationship with God. The story of the Bible tells how God has repeatedly stepped into history and shown us the way back to Him. God's most vivid invasion of history was when the only begotten God—the Word of God, the Son—became a man and dwelt among us (John 1:1–3, 14). In His passionate love for us, He gave himself on the cross as a sacrifice for all human pride and rebellion against God that had ever been or will ever be committed.

Many of the best-loved Scriptures contain the tension of the ancient choice between the two trees.

Jesus said, "Seek first [God's] kingdom and his righteousness, and all these things will be given to you as well" (Matthew 6:33). Jesus says our first affections need to be wrapped up in God, His purposes, and His character. *Then,* the promise is that "all these things" will be granted. What are "all these things"? In the immediate context, "all these things" refers to what is needed for survival: food, drink, clothing, and shelter.* By extension, I think it is fair to extend the promise to include shalom and whatever knowledge, wisdom, and experience God deems that we need from him.

This precise perspective is also found in Proverbs 3:5–6: "Trust in the Lord with all your heart and lean not on your own understanding; in all your ways acknowledge him, and he will make your paths straight." The passage is saying, Do not trust in your own (human-based) wisdom and understanding—do not eat of the second tree! Instead, pursue God! Put your trust in his goodness, faithfulness, and mercy. Let your relationship with God be the priority in your life. *Then*, the promise goes, He will "direct thy paths" (KJV). He will "make your paths straight." Both of these expressions are another way of saying that God will give you "all these things."

Psalm 1:1–6 echoes this truth:

> Blessed is the man who does not walk in the counsel of the wicked or stand in the way of sinners or sit in the seat of mockers. But his delight is in the law of the Lord, and on his law he meditates day and night. He is like a tree planted by streams of water, which yields its fruit in season and whose leaf does not wither. Whatever he does prospers. Not so the wicked! They are like chaff that the wind blows away. Therefore the wicked will not stand in the judgment, nor sinners in the assembly of the righteous. For the Lord watches over the way of the righteous, but the way of the wicked will perish.

Jeremiah 17:5–8 says the same thing:

> This is what the Lord says: "Cursed is the one who trusts in man, who depends on flesh for his strength and whose heart turns away from the Lord. He will be like a bush in the wastelands; he will

---

*I don't have an answer for the fact that not all Christians have what they need to survive. It is often the Christians who seek God the most passionately who are the ones who have the least. They're the ones struggling to survive in prison, or in a famine, or in a thousand and one other places where the hardships of life bring people to a place where they "seek God first." Human systems, wars, and sin must have something to do with it, but that doesn't make it any less painful. In some cases, "all these things" might be the strength to hang on to God and hope when all human hope has failed. Surely this is a justice issue close to the heart of God.

not see prosperity when it comes. He will dwell in the parched places of the desert, in a salt land where no one lives. "But blessed is the man who trusts in the Lord, whose confidence is in him. He will be like a tree planted by the water that sends out its roots by the stream. It does not fear when heat comes; its leaves are always green. It has no worries in a year of drought and never fails to bear fruit."

Jeremiah 9:23–24 puts it this way:

This is what the Lord says: "Let not the wise man boast of his wisdom or the strong man boast of his strength or the rich man boast of his riches, but let him who boasts boast about this: that he understands and knows me, that I am the Lord, who exercises kindness, justice and righteousness on earth, for in these I delight," declares the Lord.

It should be clear by now that examples like these above could easily be multiplied. The point is, where is your heart? As Jesus says, "For where your treasure is, there your heart will be also" (Matthew 6:21; Luke 12:34).

WILD HORSES COULDN'T DRAG ME AWAY

You might be getting excited about going to college. You might be in college and wishing you were done. You might be out of college and wishing you were back in. You might be sick of school and planning a year abroad. You might be starting out on some alternate plan.

Whichever direction you go, you'll soon be filling your head with all kinds of knowledge. It's unavoidable. So do the passages above mean that a life of the mind, or otherwise broadening your experiences, is inherently dangerous or detrimental to your spiritual health?

Some Christians think so. There is a strong sentiment among some that expanding your knowledge base is pretty useless at best for your spiritual life, precisely because of the tensions we have been exploring here.

In truth, the degree of danger depends on your priorities. To put it another way, it depends on your affections. What, or Who, is going to be your first love?*

Are you going to say to the Lord, with all the passion and plaintive longing of that song, "Wild horses couldn't drag me away from you"? Are you going to put your relationship with the Lord first, to experience Him as He wants you to experience Him in your life—or just coast

> **Are you going to put your relationship with the Lord first, to experience Him as He wants you to experience Him in your life—or just coast along on your past Sunday school experience?**

along on your past Sunday school experience? Are you going to seek fellowship with God's people and become part of what God is doing on campus—or are you going to withdraw and become a loner? Are you going to continually open yourself up to the incredible love and power of the Holy Spirit—or be afraid of God getting too much of you? When you fail again (for the umpteenth time), are you going to hang tough with Jesus and get up? Or are you going to give up?†

Are you going to put studies, activities, and fun times before the things you need to do to keep your first affections on Jesus?

Community college. Job. University. A year of travel abroad. College. A year of service. Career. No matter what, the two trees remain before you. And they will remain there the rest of your life. The question is, How will you respond to the amazing love God has shown for you in Christ? "We love because he first loved us," says I John 4:19. Are you going to love God back or not?

---

*Jesus' complaint against the church of Ephesus in Revelation 2:4 is that they had left their first love. Usually first love is considered to be the love you feel for God right after you are converted. It could also mean the affection that is first in your life.

†There are different names for this process. Some call it discipleship. Older Christian traditions call it spiritual formation. Eugene Peterson calls it *A Long Obedience in the Same Direction* (Madison, WI: InterVarsity Press, first edition 1980). The point is that growing into maturity in Christ does not come naturally or instantly, since our affections are so disordered by sin.

21 | WORLDVIEW LIMBO

Some people exist in worldview limbo. They may be working out of a certain worldview, but they have doubts and they're looking other places, unable to trust completely any of the worldviews or religions out there.

Some people are slowly transitioning from one worldview to another. They think like a Buddhist, but they want relief from themselves, maybe longing for a personal relationship of love with a God they can't or don't believe exists.

Or there are Christians who want to be good Christians but can't bring themselves to agree with all the Christian doctrine, or they experience doubt. Every worldview has followers who experience doubt.

–Karis Kazuko Taylor

Sooner or later, we all go through it. Worldview limbo. And since everyone goes through it, doesn't it make sense to provide some resources for reflection?

This book might not be the absolute final answer, but at least it's trying to deal with the issue in a compassionate way. To those of you who feel like you're in worldview limbo, let me say to you—God loves you. He can handle your doubts, miseries, and questions. He couldn't love you more than He already does. Hang in there.

The limbo situation leads me directly to the following story: At the request of a youth pastor friend of mine, I was presenting this material to a high school youth group. Word got to one of the parents about what we were doing. This parent came to the youth pastor and asked, "Why study other religions and worldviews in *Sunday school*?"

A fair question. Let me address it in two ways.

First, with all the emphasis on multiculturalism and diversity in public schools, we have to realize that the other religions and worldviews already have the jump on us. And of course, since no one can teach these things from a neutral perspective, Christian faith is often placed in the most negative light possible. Young people are already learning about the wonderfulnesses (is that a word?) of other religions from the perspective of worldviews alien and hostile to the Biblical worldview.

A really anti-Christian perspective in public schools is somewhat muted because of the separation of church and state and because local schools and school boards are usually more responsive to local people than state and federal layers of bureaucracy are.

But in college, students will get these anti-biblical worldviews in spades. So it's especially important that young people be able to recognize spades and that they know how to call a spade a spade when necessary.

Second, effective Bible teaching needs to make a connection to real life. Unfortunately, while we do a lot of good things in church youth groups, it's as if we are teaching about Christian faith in a complete, insulated bubble, hardly ever giving students significant help in thinking through how Christian faith relates to the other worldviews. Instead, before heading off for college, wouldn't it be better *at least once* for students to hear about worldviews from a solid biblical perspective that is friendly to Christian faith and that will help them communicate their faith in Jesus better?

CONCLUDING METAPHORS

To construct a building, first you survey the land and dig deep foundation trenches. Then you arrange and tie steel rebar in the trenches.

Then you pour concrete and wait for it to cure. Once it cures, you back-fill the foundation, and from that point on nobody sees all that work you've done. On this hidden foundation the building is attached and erected, but most people never think about the foundation or question it. Yet it is absolutely essential for the integrity of the building.

Worldview is like that.

A spider spins its web from one anchoring point to another. The anchoring points could be a wall, a branch, a brick—just about anything, really. But as the web is woven, it achieves greater and greater stability and strength. It can catch insects much larger than the spider; withstand gale force winds; get ripped and still function because the other anchors and webbing remain connected.

Worldview is also like that.

I realize that there are different ways Christians have proceeded to con-struct their own cathedrals of under-standing. But this book has been about laying the foundation and spinning a web for the Biblical world-view. This book will not take you to the finish line; it'll just help you get into the race. It's a rough begin-ning, not a book about finishing touches.

Do not conform any longer to the pattern of this world, but be transformed by the renewing of your mind.

And ultimately, the cornerstone of the church is God's self-revelation in Christ (I Corinthians 3:11; Ephesians 2:20). May we all be spurred on by the words of the apostle Paul:

> Therefore, I urge you, brothers, in view of God's mercy, to offer your bodies as living sacrifices, holy and pleasing to God—this is your spiritual act of worship. Do not conform any longer to the pattern of this world, but be transformed by the renewing of your mind. Then you will be able to test and approve what God's will is— his good, pleasing and perfect will. (Romans 12:1–2)

ENDNOTES

Chapter 1

1. Maddie Venezuela, personal communication, spring 2000.
2. Alison Lucic, personal communication, July 2001.
3. Micah White, "Spirituality on America's Liberal Campuses: A call for dialogue," *Free Inquiry* magazine, fall 2001.
4. "Twentysomethings Struggle to Find Their Place in Christian Churches," *The Barna Group,* September 24, 2003, quoted at *www.barna.org/Flex Page.aspx?Page=BarnaUpdate&BarnaUpdateID=149,* (accessed March 11, 2005).
5. See "America's One-Party State," *The Economist,* December 2, 2004, quoted at *www.economist.com/world/na/PrinterFriendly.cfm?Story_ID =3446265.* See also the Web site *www.studentsforacademicfreedom.org.*
6. David French, "Conformity on Campus," *The American Enterprise Online,* quoted at *www.theamericanenterprise.org/issues/articleID.18528/article _detail.asp,* (accessed May 16, 2005).
7. Andrea Billups, "Tufts Reinstates Christian Group Spurning Gay as Leader," *The Washington Times,* May 17, 2000, quoted at *www.thefire .org/index.php/article/4167.html* (accessed January 30, 2006).
8. A summary of Martin Kramer's *Ivory Towers on Sand* (Washington, D.C.: The Washington Institute for Near East Policy, 2001).
9. Stefan Beck, "'God Fearing' Dartmouth," *National Review Online,* September 27, 2005, quoted at *http://nationalreview.com/comment/ beck200509270812.asp* and William F. Buckley Jr., "Church/State at Dartmouth," *National Review Online,* September 27, 2005, quoted at *http://nationalreview.com/buckley/wfb200509271452.asp.*
10. Donald Alexander Downs, *Restoring Free Speech and Liberty on Campus* (New York: Cambridge University Press, 2005).
11. "Cal Poly in Court for Violating First Amendment," *Foundation for Indi-*

vidual Rights in Education, September 25, 2003, quoted at *www.thefire*
.org/index.php/article/25.html%20and%20"Brainwashing%20101.

12. See George Weigel's *The Cube and the Cathedral: Europe, America, and
Politics Without God* (New York: Basic Books, 2005). Weigel argues that
Europe's elites are Christophobic.

13. George M. Marsden, *The Soul of the American University: From Protestant establishment to established unbelief* (New York: Oxford University
Press, 1994).

Chapter 2

1. George Barna's research is important on this point; see *www.barna.org.*

Chapter 3

1. *www.monotremata.com/dead/archive/interviews/tinsel_interview.html*
(accessed March 31, 2003).

Chapter 4

1. Carl Sagan, *Cosmos* (New York: Random House, 1980).

2. Stan and Jan Berenstain, *The Bears' Nature Guide* (New York: Random
House, 1975), 10–11.

3. Disc 1. *The Lion King,* special ed. DVD, directed by Roger Allers and
Rob Minkoff (1994; Burbank, CA: Buena Vista Home Video, 2003).

Chapter 5

1. "Candidate Speeches," *Napoleon Dynamite,* DVD, directed by Jared Hess
(Beverly Hills, CA: Twentieth Century Fox, 2004).

Chapter 9

1. *Barbershop,* DVD, directed by Tim Story (Santa Monica, CA: MGM
Home Entertainment, 2002).

2. Quoted at *http://en.thinkexist.com/quotation/preach_the_gospel_at_all
_times_and_when_necessary/219332.html* (accessed August 5, 2005).

3. Quoted at *www.leaderu.com/ftissues/ft9704/articles/williams.html*
(accessed August 5, 2005).

Chapter 10

1. Sir James George Frazer, *The Golden Bough* (New York: Macmillan Publishing Company, 1922).

Chapter 11

1. Friedrich Nietzsche, "The Parable of the Madman," quoted at *www.fordham.edu/halsall/mod/nietzsche-madman.html*. Originally published in *The Gay Science* (New York: Vintage, 1974), 181–182.

Chapter 12

1. Auguste Comte, *Auguste Comte and Positivism: The essential writings*, ed. Gertrud Lenzer (New York: Harper, 1975), 71–86, quoted in *www.historyguide.org/intellect/comte_cpp.html*.
2. Charles W. Hendel, ed., *An Inquiry Concerning Human Understanding* (Upper Saddle River, NJ: Prentice Hall, 1748), quoted in *www.fordham.edu/halsall/mod/hume-miracles.html*.
3. The Catechism of the Catholic Church (6: PL 4, 519), quoted in *www.vatican.va/archive/ccc_css/archive/catechism/p1s1c3a2.htm*.
4. Epicurus, "Letter to Menoeceus," n.d., quoted in *www.philosophyofreligion.info/problemofevil.html*.
5. Robert A. Heinlein, *Time Enough for Love* (New York: Putnam, 1973).
6. Thomas Paine, *The Age of Reason*, rev. ed. (Buffalo, NY: Prometheus Books, 1984), quoted in *www.atheistalliance.org/library/morris-founding_fathers.html*.
7. Napoleon Bonaparte to Gaspard Gourmond at St. Helena, January 28, 1817, quoted in *www.skepticfiles.org/moretext/mystmet1.htm*.
8. Dr. Michael McClymond, professor of the Steber Chair of Theological Studies at Saint Louis University, personal phone conversation, August 2, 2005.
9. William James, *The Varieties of Religious Experience: A Study in Human Nature* (London, New York: Routledge, 2002), quoted in *www.pbs.org/wgbh/masterpiece/americancollection/american/genius/william_quote.html*.
10. Margaret Jacob, "Soul Searching Science," review of *Looking for Spinoza: Joy, Sorrow and the Feeling Brain*, by Antonio Damasio, *Los Angeles Times*, April 27, 2003, R8–9.
11. Peter Singer, *Animal Liberation: A New Ethic for Our Treatment of Animals*, 2nd edition (New York: Random House, 1975), quoted in *www.animalrights.net/quotes.html*; italics added.
12. Charles Darwin, *The Descent of Man*, facsimile of 1st ed. (1871; repr., Princeton, N.J.: Princeton University Press, 1981).
13. James A. Haught, *2000 Years of Disbelief: Famous People With the Cour-*

age to Doubt (New York: Prometheus Books, 1996), quoted in *www.positiveatheism.org/hist/quotes/*.

14. Italics added. The italicized words were removed in 1997 at the request of Alvin Plantinga, John A. O'Brien Professor of Philosophy at Notre Dame University, and Huston Smith, Thomas J. Watson Professor of Religion at Syracuse University. Quoted in *www.ncseweb.org/resources/articles/ 8954_nabt_statement_on_evolution_ev_5_21_1998.asp*.

15. St. Augustine of Hippo, *Confessions* (n.p., 1679), quoted in *www.ccel .org/pager.cgi?file=a/augustine/confessions/confessions-bod.html&up=a/ augustine/confessions/confessions.html&from=4*.

16. See *Pensees*, section vii, no. 425, quoted at *www.ccel.org/ccel/pascal/ pensees.viii.html*: "What is it, then, that this desire and this inability proclaim to us, but that there was once in man a true happiness of which there now remain to him only the mark and empty trace, which he in vain tries to fill from all his surroundings, seeking from things absent the help he does not obtain in things present? But these are all inadequate, because the infinite abyss can only be filled by an infinite and immutable object, that is to say, only by God Himself" (accessed February 26, 2006).

Chapter 13

1. Scaria Thuruthiyil, "Reincarnation in Hinduism," para. 2, *www.spiritual-wholeness.org/faqs/reincgen/hindrein.htm* (accessed April 19, 2005).

2. *Chandogya Upanishad* VI.8.4ff.

3. *Atma-Bodha Upanishad* 3.1.4, quoted in *http://nisargadatta.net/ advaita.html* (accessed November 15, 2005). An alternative translation using the first person may be found at *www.celextel.org/ebooks/ upanishads/atma_bodha_upanishad.htm*.

4. *Katha Upanishad*, part 2.

5. *I Ching*, section 34. Wing-Tsit Chan, *A Source Book in Chinese Philosophy* (Princeton, NJ: Princeton University Press, 1963), quoted at *http:// members.aol.com/heraklit1/laotzu.htm* (acessed March 13, 2006).

6. Ibid., section 5.

7. Ibid., section 21.

8. Quoted at *Full Moon Paradise*, *http://groups.msn.com/FullMoon Paradise/dalailamaquotes.msnw* (accessed July 7, 2005).

9. DT Suzuki, *An Introduction to Zen Buddhism*, ed., Christmas Humphreys (London: Rider, 1969), quoted at *www.homeoint.org/morrell/articles/ pm_homan.htm*.

10. Ralph Waldo Emerson, "The Transcendentalist," in *Nature; Addresses and Lectures* (Boston: Houghton Mifflin, 1903).

11. Ralph Waldo Emerson, "Self Reliance," in *Essays: First Series* (Boston: Houghton Mifflin, 1968), quoted in *www.emersoncentral.com/selfreliance.htm* (accessed April 23, 2004).

12. Henry David Thoreau, *Walden* (1854), ch. 2, para. 16, *http://eserver.org/thoreau/walden00.html* (accessed April 23, 2004).

13. *Little Women*, DVD, directed by Gillian Armstrong (1994; Culver City, CA: Columbia TriStar Home Video, 2000).

14. Helen Dukas and Banesh Hoffman, eds. *Albert Einstein: The Human Side* (Princeton, NJ: Princeton University Press, 1954), quoted at *www.positiveatheism.org/hist/quotes/qframe.htm* (accessed April 25, 2004).

15. Albert Einstein, "Religion and Science," *New York Times Magazine*, November 9, 1930, quoted at *www.positiveatheism.org/hist/quotes/qframe.htm* (accessed April 25, 2004).

16. Albert Einstein, following his wife's advice in responding to Rabbi Herbert Goldstein of the International Synagogue in New York, who had sent Einstein a cablegram bluntly demanding, "Do you believe in God?" Quoted at *www.positiveatheism.org/hist/quotes/qframe.htm* (accessed April 25, 2004).

17. Joseph Campbell, *The Hero With a Thousand Faces* (New York: Pantheon Books, 1949), quoted at *www.jcf.org/about_jc.php* (accessed April 24, 2004).

18. Dr. Peter Jones, "The Da Vinci Code: Part 2," *Christian Witness to a Pagan Planet*, *www.spirit-wars.com/v25/english/NewsArchive/News10.htm* (accessed May 18, 2004).

Chapter 14

1. Psychic ad, *Ventura County Reporter*, February 5, 2004.

2. Horoscope reading, *Ventura County Reporter*, February 5, 2004.

3. The Dalai Lama, quoted at *http://groups.msn.com/FullMoonParadise/dalailamaquotes.msnw* (accessed July 29, 2005).

Chapter 15

1. *Answers in Genesis*, *www.answersingenesis.org/home/area/feedback/negative10-16-2000.aps* (accessed June 10, 2004; site now discontinued).

2. Personal conversation with Dr. Michael McClymond, professor of the

Steber Chair of Theological Studies at Saint Louis University, August 8, 2005.

3. "David French's Brilliant Answer," *Opinion Journal,* May 17, 2005, *www.opinionjournal.com/best/?id=110006701.*

Chapter 16

1. Alan Garfinkle, *Reason, Truth, and History* (Cambridge: Cambridge University Press, 1981), quoted at *www.positiveatheism.org/hist/quotes/quote-g1.htm* (accessed March 29, 2004).

2. See *Star Trek*'s Prime Directive at *www.70disco.com/startrek/prime-dir.htm.* There's also an interesting article on postmodernism and *Star Trek*'s Prime Directive by Dino Felluga, "Applications of Postmodernism," *Introductory Guide to Critical Theory,* November 28, 2003, *www.cla.purdue.edu/academic/engl/theory/postmodernism/applications/postmodapplicTnStarTrek1.html* (accessed June 1, 2004).

3. Declaration of Independence, preamble 2.1–2.2, quoted at *http://early america.com/earlyamerica/freedom/doi/text.html* (accessed June 9, 2004).

4. Jacques Derrida, *Foi et savoir—Les deux sources de la 'religion' aux limites de la simple raison* (Paris: Seuil, 1996), 35–36, quoted at *www.hydra.umn.edu/derrida/foi2.html* (accessed March 29, 2004).

5. Personal conversation with Dr. Michael McClymond, professor of the Steber Chair of Theological Studies at Saint Louis University, August 2, 2005.

6. Jean-Francois Lyotard, *The Postmodern Condition* (Minneapolis: University of Minnesota Press, 1984), quoted at *www.scholars.nus.edu.sg/literature/theories/Lyotard.html* (accessed March 29, 2004).

Chapter 17

1. You can find these at "Presbyterian Creeds & Confessions," *www.creeds.net/reformed/creeds.htm* (accessed May 26, 2004).

2. *Random House Dictionary of the English Language* (New York: Random House, 1966).

3. Aaron Smith, "Emergent Dialogue: Emphatic points in the evolving church," *St. Bartholomew's Church,* June 2005, *www.stbs.net/Branches/The%20Branch%20June%202005.pdf* (accessed August 5, 2005).

Chapter 18

1. Letter to James Smith, December 8, 1822, quoted at *www.positiveatheism.org/hist/quotes* (accessed August 9, 2005).

2. Thomas Paine, *The Age of Reason,* rev. ed. (Buffalo, NY: Prometheus Books, 1984), quoted in *www.worldpolicy.org/globalrights/religion/paine-ageofreason.html* (accessed on May 25, 2004).

3. *Poor Richard's Almanac* (1736), quoted in *http://usinfo.state.gov/usa/infousa/facts/loa/bf1736.htm* (accessed May 25, 2004).

4. Bill McKeever, "Does Lorenzo Snow's famous couplet no longer have a functioning place in LDS theology?" *Mormon Research Ministry,* quoted at *www.mrm.org/multimedia/text/lorenzo-snow-couplet.html* (accessed February 23, 2006).

5. *The Mormon Literature Sampler,* quoted at *http://mldb.byu.edu/follett.htm* (accessed February 24, 2006). The sermon is found in an important Mormon resource, *Journal of Discourses,* 6, no. I, I–II.

6. "LDS Mormon Prophet Hinckley Interviews," *Rethinking Mormonism,* quoted at *www.i4m.com/think/leaders/Hinckley_dontknow.htm* (accessed February 26, 2006).

7. *The Mormon Challenge,* quoted at *http://mormonchallenge.com/ref_quotes.htm* (accessed February 24, 2006).

8. Todd Compton, *In Sacred Loneliness: The Plural Wives of Joseph Smith* (Signature Books, 1997). Found at *www.irr.org/mit/sacredlon.html* (accessed on May 25, 2004).

9. *Utah State History,* quoted at *http://historytogo.utah.gov/bywives.html* (accessed on May 26, 2004).

10. *The Journal of Discourses: General Conference Sermons, 1854–1886, Brigham Young, John Taylor, Wilford Woodruff, Lorenzo Snow & Joseph F. Smith,* August 19, 1866. Quoted at *http://journalofdiscourses.org/Vol_11/refJDvol11–41.html* (accessed February 27, 2006).

11. "We warn you against the dissemination of doctrines which are not according to the scriptures and which are alleged to have been taught by some of the General Authorities of past generations. Such, for instance, is the Adam-God theory. We denounce that theory and hope that everyone will be cautioned against this and other kinds of false doctrine." From the General Conference Report, October 1976, 115 (Greg Johnson, personal communication,, February 23, 2006).

12. Robert Millet, address given to Brigham Young University Religious Education Faculty, "What Is Our Doctrine?" September 12, 2003. Quoted at *http://home.uchicago.edu/spackman* (accessed February 23, 2006).

13. The Diocese of Newark Online, *www.dioceseofnewark.org/jsspong/reform.html* (accessed May 26, 2004).

14. Ibid.
15. Adapted from Ron Kernahan's "30 Days Muslim Prayer Focus 2003" bulletin of October 24, 2003, Day 1, *www.30-days.net.*
16. "The Punishment of the Apostate According to Islamic Law" by Abul Ala Mawdudi, translated and annotated by Syed Silas Husain and Ernest Hahn in 1994, quoted at *http://answering-Islam.org/Hahn/Mawdudi/index .htm* (accessed March 6, 2002).
17. *www.scientology-detroit.org/ans3.htm* (accessed August 8, 2005).
18. "Cruise Draws Religious Inspiration for Latest Movie Role," *ABC News Online,* January 11, 2004, *www.abc.net.au/news/newsitems/s1023568.htm* (accessed January 30, 2006).
19. See the Operation Clambake Web site, *www.xenu.net,* operated by Andreas Heldal-Lund (accessed February 26, 2006).
20. Dorthe Refslund Christensen, "Rethinking Scientology: Cognition and Representation in Religion, Therapy and Soteriology." PhD diss., Aarhus University (Denmark), 1999, quoted at *www.cesnur.org/2001/buffy _march01.htm* (accessed August 4, 2005).
21. Jon Atack, "Hubbard and the Occult," an essay based on his book *A Piece of Blue Sky* (New Jersey: Lyle Stuart Books, 1990), quoted at *www.factnet.org/Scientology/lrhoccult.htm* (accessed August 9, 2005).

Chapter 19

1. Quoted at *www.elca.org/communication/creeds/athanasian.html* (accessed May 27, 2004).
2. Aisha Brown, "Who Invented the Trinity?" *Islamic Web,* www.islamicweb .com/begin/trinity.htm (accessed May 26, 2004).
3. *The Qur'an* 5.116. And behold! Allah will say: "O Jesus the son of Mary! Didst thou say unto men, 'worship me and my mother as gods in derogation of Allah'?" He will say: "Glory to Thee! Never could I say what I had no right (to say). Had I said such a thing, thou wouldst indeed have known it. Thou knowest what is in my heart, Thou I know not what is in Thine. For Thou knowest in full all that is hidden."
4. "Eucharist Using Female Nouns and Pronouns," *Women's Ministries,* www.episcopalchurch.org/documents/WM_Eucharist.doc (accessed November 15, 2005).
5. Ted Olson, "Episcopal Church Officially Promotes Idol Worship," *Christianity Today,* October 27, 2004, *http://christianitytoday.com/ct/2004/ 143/21.0.html.* "Beyond the Episcopal Church's Pagan Eucharist," *Christi-*

anity Today, October 27, 2004, *http://christianitytoday.com/ct/2004/ 143/31.0.html* (both accessed November 15, 2005).

6. "St. Patrick's Breastplate," trans. Cecil Alexander, 1889, quoted at *www.cyberhymnal.org/htm/s/t/stpatric.htm* (accessed February 26, 2006).